First World War
and Army of Occupation
War Diary
France, Belgium and Germany

50 DIVISION
149 Infantry Brigade
Northumberland Fusiliers
1/5th Battalion (Territorial)
18 April 1915 - 31 July 1918

WO95/2828/2

The Naval & Military Press Ltd
www.nmarchive.com
Published in association with The National Archives

Published by

The Naval & Military Press Ltd

Unit 10 Ridgewood Industrial Park,

Uckfield, East Sussex,

TN22 5QE England

Tel: +44 (0) 1825 749494

www.naval-military-press.com

www.nmarchive.com

This diary has been reprinted in facsimile from the original. Any imperfections are inevitably reproduced and the quality may fall short of modern type and cartographic standards.

© **Crown Copyright**
Images reproduced by permission of The National Archives, London, England, 2015.

Contents

Document type	Place/Title	Date From	Date To
Heading	WO95/2828-2		
Heading	50th Division 149th Infy Bde 5th Bn Northumberland Fusrs Apr 1915-Jly 1918		
Heading	149th Inf. Bde. 50th Div. 5th Battn. The Northumberland Fusiliers April (18/30.4.15) 1915		
War Diary	Blyth	18/04/1915	18/04/1915
War Diary	Southampton	19/04/1915	19/04/1915
War Diary	Boulogne	20/04/1915	20/04/1915
War Diary	Cassel	21/04/1915	21/04/1915
War Diary	Winnezeele	22/04/1915	22/04/1915
War Diary	Poperinghe	23/04/1915	23/04/1915
War Diary	Ypres	24/04/1915	24/04/1915
War Diary	Wieltze	25/04/1915	25/04/1915
War Diary	St. Julien	26/04/1915	26/04/1915
War Diary	Wieltze	27/04/1915	28/04/1915
War Diary	Zillebeke	29/04/1915	30/04/1915
Heading	149th Inf. Bde. 50th Div. 5th Battn. The Northumberland Fusiliers May 1915		
War Diary	Zillebeke	01/05/1915	02/05/1915
War Diary	Poperinghe	03/05/1915	03/05/1915
War Diary	Watou	04/05/1915	09/05/1915
War Diary	Brandhoek	10/05/1915	12/05/1915
War Diary	Ypres	13/05/1915	15/05/1915
War Diary	Vlamertinghe	16/05/1915	21/05/1915
War Diary	Ypres	21/05/1915	21/05/1915
War Diary	Vlamertinghe	22/05/1915	22/05/1915
War Diary	Ypres	22/05/1915	22/05/1915
War Diary	La Brique	22/05/1915	23/05/1915
War Diary	Ypres	23/05/1915	23/05/1915
War Diary	Near La Brique	24/05/1915	31/05/1915
Heading	149th Inf. Bde. 50th Div. 5th Battn. The Northumberland Fusiliers June 1915		
War Diary	Near La Brique	01/06/1915	01/06/1915
War Diary	Vlamertinghe	01/06/1915	04/06/1915
War Diary	Busse Boom	05/06/1915	10/06/1915
War Diary	Sanctuary Wood	11/06/1915	18/06/1915
War Diary	Ypres	19/06/1915	20/06/1915
War Diary	Dranoutre	21/06/1915	21/06/1915
War Diary	Neuve Eglise	22/06/1915	30/06/1915
Heading	149th Bde. 50th 1Div.1/5th Northumberland Fusiliers. July 1915		
War Diary		01/07/1915	02/07/1915
War Diary	Neuve Eglise	03/07/1915	16/07/1915
War Diary	Armentieres	17/07/1915	31/07/1915
Heading	149th Bde 50th Div. 1/5th Northumberland Fusiliers August 1915		
War Diary		01/08/1915	05/08/1915
War Diary	Armentieres	08/08/1915	31/08/1915
Heading	149th Bde. 50th Div. 1/5th Northumberland Fusiliers September 1915		

War Diary	Armentieres	01/09/1915	30/09/1915
Heading	149th Inf. Bde. 50th Division. 1/5th Northumberland Fusiliers October 1915		
War Diary		01/10/1915	02/10/1915
War Diary	Armentieres	03/10/1915	25/10/1915
War Diary	La Creche	26/10/1915	26/10/1915
War Diary	St Razelle	27/10/1915	31/10/1915
Heading	149th Bde. 50th Div. 1/5th Northumberland Fusiliers November 1915		
Heading	War Diary Of 5th Bn Northumberland Fusiliers From November 1st 1915 (Volume 3)		
War Diary	St Razeele	01/11/1915	30/11/1915
Heading	149th Bde. 50th Div. 1/5th Northumberland Fusiliers December 1915		
War Diary	Strazeele	01/12/1915	17/12/1915
War Diary	Ypres	18/12/1915	31/12/1915
Heading	War Diary Of 5th Bn. Northumberland Fusiliers From January 1st 1916 To January 31st 1916 (Volume V)		
War Diary	Ypres	01/01/1916	31/01/1916
Heading	War Diary Of 5th Bn. Northumberland Fusiliers From February 1st 1916 To February 29th 1916 (Volume VI)		
War Diary	Ypres	01/02/1916	29/02/1916
Heading	War Diary Of 5th Bn Northumberland Fusiliers From 1st March 1916 To 31st March 1916 (Volume VII)		
War Diary	Ypres	01/03/1916	14/03/1916
War Diary	Poperinghe	15/03/1916	18/03/1916
War Diary	Dickebusch Huts	19/03/1916	21/03/1916
War Diary	Ypres	22/03/1916	31/03/1916
Heading	War Diary Of 5th Bn. Northumberland Fusiliers From 1st April 1916 To 30th April 1916 (Volume VIII)		
War Diary	In The Field	01/04/1916	01/04/1916
War Diary	Locre	02/04/1916	30/04/1916
Heading	War Diary Of 5th Bn. Northumberland Fusiliers From 1st May 1916 To 31st May 1916 (Volume 9)		
War Diary	Locre	01/05/1916	04/05/1916
War Diary	Bailleul	23/05/1916	23/05/1916
War Diary	Locre	24/05/1916	31/05/1916
Heading	War Diary Of 5th Bn. Northumberland Fusiliers From 1st June 1916 To 30th June 1916 (Volume)		
War Diary	Locre	01/06/1916	30/06/1916
Heading	War Diary Of 5th Bn. Northumberland Fusiliers From 1st July To 31st July 1916 (Volume)		
War Diary	Locre	01/07/1916	22/07/1916
War Diary	Dranoutre	23/07/1916	31/07/1916
Heading	War Diary Of 1/5th Bn. Northumberland Fusiliers From 1st August To 31st August 1916 Volume		
War Diary	Dranoutre	01/08/1916	07/08/1916
War Diary	Strazelle	08/08/1916	12/08/1916
War Diary	Fienvillers	12/08/1916	14/08/1916
War Diary	Naours	15/08/1916	15/08/1916
War Diary	Pierregot	16/08/1916	16/08/1916
War Diary	Henencourt	17/08/1916	17/08/1916
War Diary	Henencourt Wood	17/08/1916	31/08/1916
Heading	149th Infantry Brigade 50th. Division 5th Northumberland Fusiliers 149th Infantry Brigade September 1916		

Heading	War Diary Of 5th Bn. Northld Fusiliers From 1st Sep. To 30th Sep. 16 (Volume 13)		
War Diary	Henencourt Sheet 57d (V.26b)	01/09/1916	08/09/1916
War Diary	Contalmaison Sheet 57 D (X.22.b)	09/09/1916	09/09/1916
War Diary	N' Martinpuich Sheet 57c (5.3 Central)	09/09/1916	10/09/1916
War Diary	(S.2.b.d)	10/09/1916	11/09/1916
War Diary	Martinpuich Sheet 57c	11/09/1916	11/09/1916
War Diary	(S.3.d.)	11/09/1916	11/09/1916
War Diary	(S.3.b)	11/09/1916	12/09/1916
War Diary	Martinpuich Sheet 57c	12/09/1916	14/09/1916
War Diary	S.8.d.	14/09/1916	14/09/1916
War Diary	Martinpuich	15/09/1916	15/09/1916
War Diary	S.4.a.c.	15/09/1916	16/09/1916
War Diary	Martinpuich Sheet 57.c.	16/09/1916	16/09/1916
War Diary	(S.8.d.)	16/09/1916	20/09/1916
War Diary	Martinpuich Sheet 57.c	20/09/1916	21/09/1916
War Diary	(M33a To M.35d.)	21/09/1916	22/09/1916
War Diary	Martinpuich Sheet 57c	22/09/1916	22/09/1916
War Diary	M.33a To M.35.a	22/09/1916	23/09/1916
War Diary	Martinpuich	24/09/1916	24/09/1916
War Diary	Contalmaison Sheet 57.c	24/09/1916	28/09/1916
War Diary	Martinpuich Sheet 57c (S.3.d.)	29/09/1916	30/09/1916
Heading	War Diary Of 5th Bn. Northumbld Fusiliers 1st Oct To 31st Oct 1916 (Volume 14)		
War Diary	Eaucourt L'Abbaye (Sheet 57c.S.W)	01/10/1916	03/10/1916
War Diary	Contalmaison (Sheet 57 D.S.E) Albert Sheet 57 D.S.E Sheet 62 D.N.E	04/10/1916	04/10/1916
War Diary	Millencourt Sheet 57D.S.E Sheet 62 D.N.E	05/10/1916	06/10/1916
War Diary	Millencourt	07/10/1916	07/10/1916
War Diary	Albert Sheet 57D.S.E Sheet 62D.N.E	08/10/1916	08/10/1916
War Diary	Albert	09/10/1916	11/10/1916
War Diary	Millencourt Sheet 57D.S.E Sheet 62D.N.E	12/10/1916	14/10/1916
War Diary	Millencourt	15/10/1916	15/10/1916
War Diary	Millencourt Sheet 57 D.S.E Sheet 62 D.N.E	15/10/1916	15/10/1916
War Diary	Millencourt	16/10/1916	22/10/1916
War Diary	Albert	23/10/1916	23/10/1916
War Diary	Bazentin-Le-Grand (Sheet 57c.S.W.)	24/10/1916	24/10/1916
War Diary	Bazentin-Le-Grand	25/10/1916	30/10/1916
War Diary	Bazentin-Le-Grand (Sheet 57c.S.W)	30/10/1916	31/10/1916
Heading	War Diary Of 5th Bn Northumberland Fusiliers From 1st Novr To 30th Novr 1916 (Volume 15)		
War Diary	Flers (Sheet 57 C.S.W)	01/11/1916	03/11/1916
War Diary	High Wood (Sheet 57 C.S.W) S.10.a	04/11/1916	06/11/1916
War Diary	Martinpuich (Sheet 57c.S.W)	07/11/1916	09/11/1916
War Diary	High Wood	10/11/1916	11/11/1916
War Diary	Flers	12/11/1916	13/11/1916
War Diary	Butte De Warlencourt	14/11/1916	14/11/1916
War Diary	Butte De Warlencourt (Sheet 57 C.S.W)	14/11/1916	15/11/1916
War Diary	Flers	15/11/1916	18/11/1916
War Diary	Bazentin-Le-Grand	18/11/1916	18/11/1916
War Diary	Albert	19/11/1916	23/11/1916
War Diary	Albert (Sheet 57 D.S.E)	24/11/1916	30/11/1916
Miscellaneous	Genl Lieut the 1st Objective.		
Miscellaneous	Operation Order No. 35 A		
Operation(al) Order(s)	Operation Order No. 133	04/11/1916	04/11/1916
Operation(al) Order(s)	Operation Order No. 134	06/11/1916	06/11/1916

Operation(al) Order(s)	Operation Order No. 135	11/11/1916	11/11/1916
Heading	War Diary Of 5th Bn Northumberland Fusiliers From 1st Decr 1916 To 31st Dec. 1916 (Volume 16)		
War Diary	Albert	01/12/1916	01/12/1916
War Diary	Bresle	01/12/1916	01/12/1916
War Diary	Bresle (Sheet 62 D.N.E)	02/12/1916	06/12/1916
War Diary	Bresle (Sheet 62 D)	07/12/1916	27/12/1916
War Diary	Becourt (Sheet 57 D.S.E)	28/12/1916	28/12/1916
War Diary	High Wood (Sheet 57 C.S.W)	29/12/1916	29/12/1916
War Diary	Flers (Sheet 57 C.S.W.)	30/12/1916	30/12/1916
War Diary	Flers	31/12/1916	31/12/1916
Heading	War Diary Of 5th Bn Northumberland Fusiliers From 1st Jany 1917 To 31st Jany 1917 Volume 17		
War Diary	Flers Sheet 57 C.S.W	01/01/1917	03/01/1917
War Diary	Flers	03/01/1917	07/01/1917
War Diary	Bazentin-Le-Petit (Sheet 57 C.S.W)	08/01/1917	14/01/1917
War Diary	Flers (Sheet 57 C.S.W)	15/01/1917	23/01/1917
War Diary	Bazentin-Le-Petit Sheet 57 C.S.W	24/01/1917	25/01/1917
War Diary	Albert	26/01/1917	29/01/1917
War Diary	Dernancourt (Sheet 62c NE)	29/01/1917	31/01/1917
Heading	War Diary Of 5th Bn Northumbld Fusiliers From 1st Feby To 28th Feby 1917 (Volume 17)		
War Diary	Dernancourt (Sheet 62d)	01/02/1917	07/02/1917
War Diary	Mericourt Sur-Somme (Sheet 62D)	08/02/1917	09/02/1917
War Diary	Bois Lapin (Sheet 62D)	10/02/1917	11/02/1917
War Diary	Belloy (Sheet 62c)	12/02/1917	19/02/1917
War Diary	Fay (Sheet 62c)	20/02/1917	25/02/1917
War Diary	Proyart (Sheet 62D)	26/02/1917	28/02/1917
Heading	War Diary Of 5th Bn Northumberland Fusiliers From 1st March 1917 To 31st March 1917 (Volume 18)		
War Diary	Proyart	01/03/1917	09/03/1917
War Diary	Warfusee Abancourt	10/03/1917	29/03/1917
War Diary	Camon	30/03/1917	30/03/1917
War Diary	Bertangles	31/03/1917	31/03/1917
Heading	War Diary Of 5th Bn Northumberland Fusiliers From 1st April To 30th April 1917 (Volume 19)		
War Diary	Bertangles Sheet 51.c.	01/04/1917	07/04/1917
War Diary	Sheet 51.C.	08/04/1917	10/04/1917
War Diary	Sheet 51.B.	11/04/1917	21/04/1917
War Diary	Arras	22/04/1917	24/04/1917
War Diary	Sheet 51. B	25/04/1917	27/04/1917
War Diary	Mondicourt Sheet 57D	28/04/1917	29/04/1917
Heading	War Diary Of 5th Bn Northumberland Fusiliers From 1st May 1917 To 31st May 1917 (Volume 20)		
War Diary	Mondicourt Sheet 57d	01/05/1917	01/05/1917
War Diary	Souastre	02/05/1917	02/05/1917
War Diary	Mercatel Sheet 51.B	03/05/1917	03/05/1917
War Diary	Souastre Sheet 57D	04/05/1917	04/05/1917
War Diary	Mondicourt	05/05/1917	10/05/1917
War Diary	Mondicourt Sheet 57D	11/05/1917	17/05/1917
War Diary	Souastre	18/05/1917	18/05/1917
War Diary	Ayette	19/05/1917	20/05/1917
War Diary	Sensee Valley Sheet 51. B	21/05/1917	23/05/1917
War Diary	Croisilles Sheet 51. B.	23/05/1917	26/05/1917
War Diary	Croisilles	27/05/1917	27/05/1917
War Diary	Moyenneville Sheet 51. B.	27/05/1917	27/05/1917

War Diary	Monchy-Au-Bois Sheet 57.D.	28/05/1917	31/05/1917
Heading	War Diary Of 5th Bn Northumberland Fusiliers From 1st June 17 To 30th June 17 (Volume 21)		
War Diary	Monchy-Au-Bois Sheet 52D.N.E	01/06/1917	17/06/1917
War Diary	Boyelles Sheet 51 B.N.W.	18/06/1917	23/06/1917
War Diary	Cherisy	24/06/1917	27/06/1917
War Diary	Heninel Sheet 51.B.N.W.	28/06/1917	28/06/1917
War Diary	Henin	29/06/1917	30/06/1917
Map	Map		
Heading	War Diary Of 5th Bn Northumbld Fusiliers (T.F) From 1st July 1917 To 31st July 1917 (Volume 22)		
War Diary	Henin	01/07/1917	01/07/1917
War Diary	Heninel	02/07/1917	10/07/1917
War Diary	Neuville Vitasse	18/07/1917	18/07/1917
War Diary	Wancourt	19/07/1917	22/07/1917
War Diary	Cherisy	23/07/1917	28/07/1917
War Diary	Neuville Vitasse	31/07/1917	31/07/1917
Map	Map		
Heading	War Diary Of 5th Bn Northumbld Fusiliers From 1st Aug To 31st Aug 1917 (Volume 23)		
War Diary		01/08/1917	31/08/1917
Map	Map		
Heading	War Diary Of 5th Bn Northumberld Fusiliers From 1st Septr To 30th Septr 1917 Volume 24		
War Diary	Mercatel (Sheet 51 B.S.W)	01/09/1917	04/09/1917
War Diary	Wancourt	05/09/1917	08/09/1917
War Diary	Guemappe	09/09/1917	12/09/1917
War Diary	Sheet 51 B.S.W	13/09/1917	13/09/1917
War Diary	Neuville Vitasse	14/09/1917	16/09/1917
War Diary	Guemappe	17/09/1917	20/09/1917
War Diary	Sheet 51 B.S.W Mercatel	21/09/1917	28/09/1917
War Diary	Heninel	29/09/1917	30/09/1917
Map	Map		
Heading	War Diary Of 5th Bn Northumberland Fusiliers From 1st Octr To 31st Octr 1917 Volume 25		
War Diary	Cherisy (Sheet 51 B)	01/10/1917	05/10/1917
War Diary	Courcelles Le-Comte	06/10/1917	18/10/1917
War Diary	Arneke	19/10/1917	19/10/1917
War Diary	Proven (Sheet 27)	20/10/1917	22/10/1917
War Diary	Boesinghe (Sheet 28)	23/10/1917	23/10/1917
War Diary	Schaap Balie (Sheet 20)	24/10/1917	26/10/1917
War Diary	Boesinghe (Sheet 28)	27/10/1917	27/10/1917
War Diary	Elverdinghe (Sheet 28)	28/10/1917	29/10/1917
War Diary	Proven (Sheet 19)	30/10/1917	31/10/1917
Map	Map		
Miscellaneous	Message Pad		
Heading	War Diary Of 5th Bn Northumbld Fusiliers From 1st Nov To 30th Nov 1917 (Volume 26)		
War Diary	Suez Camp (proven) X 298 Sheet 19	01/11/1917	10/11/1917
War Diary	A 12 C Sheet 28	11/11/1917	13/11/1917
War Diary	Le Bas R.2a Sheet 27A	14/11/1917	30/11/1917
Heading	War Diary Of 5th Bn Northumbld Fusiliers From 1st Dec 1917 To 30th Dec 1917 Volume 27		
War Diary	Le Marais Sheet 27A	01/12/1917	03/12/1917
War Diary	Tournehem Sheet 27 A	03/12/1917	12/12/1917
War Diary	Paschendaele Sheet 28	13/12/1917	23/12/1917

War Diary	Brandhoek (Sheet 28)	24/12/1917	24/12/1917
War Diary	Potijze (Sheet 28)	25/12/1917	31/12/1917
Heading	War Diary Of 5th Bn Northumbld Fusiliers From 1st Jany To 31st Jany 1918 Volume 28		
War Diary	Potijze	01/01/1918	02/01/1918
War Diary	Poperinghe	03/01/1918	17/01/1918
War Diary	Watou	17/01/1918	18/01/1918
War Diary	Longuenesse	19/01/1918	26/01/1918
War Diary	Ypres	27/01/1918	27/01/1918
War Diary	Passchendaele	28/01/1918	31/01/1918
Miscellaneous	5th Batt. Northumberland Fusiliers		
Heading	War Diary Of 5th Bn Northld Fusiliers From 1st Feby To 28th Feb 1918 (Volume XXIX)		
War Diary	Paschendaele (D.17 Sheet 28 NE	01/02/1918	02/02/1918
War Diary	Potijze (1.8.6.9.9.86.28)W	03/02/1918	03/02/1918
War Diary	Brandhoek (Sheet 28)	04/02/1918	06/02/1918
War Diary	Ypres (Sheet 28)	07/02/1918	09/02/1918
War Diary	Seine (D.168.3.5.86.28)NE	10/02/1918	11/02/1918
War Diary	D.23a Sh 28.N.E	12/02/1918	15/02/1918
War Diary	Seine (D160.3.5 Sh. 28) NE	16/02/1918	16/02/1918
War Diary	Whitby Camp (1.8.6.9.9.57.28)	17/02/1918	20/02/1918
War Diary	Seine (D.16d.3.5 Sh. 28) NE	21/02/1918	22/02/1918
War Diary	St Jean (1.3.a.5.0)N.W. Sheet 28 N.W.	23/02/1918	23/02/1918
War Diary	Boisdinghem (Sheet 27A S.E)	24/02/1918	28/02/1918
Map	Map		
Heading	149th Brigade 50th Division 5th Battalion Northumberland Fusiliers March 1918		
Heading	War Diary Of 5th Bn Northumberland Fusiliers From 1st Mch To 31st Mch 1918 (Volume 30)		
War Diary	Boisdinghem Sheet 27A S.E	01/03/1918	09/03/1918
War Diary	Villers-Aux-Erables Sheet 66E NE	10/03/1918	22/03/1918
War Diary	Coulaincourt Sheet 62 C.S.E	23/03/1918	23/03/1918
War Diary	St. Christ Sheet 62 C S.W	24/03/1918	24/03/1918
Miscellaneous	Message Form		
War Diary	St. Christ Sheet 62C.S.W	24/03/1918	24/03/1918
War Diary	Assevillers Sheet 62C.S.W	25/03/1918	28/03/1918
War Diary	Merville-Au-Bois 66E.S.E	29/03/1918	31/03/1918
Miscellaneous	Cover For Documents. Nature Of Enclosures.		
Heading	149th Brigade 50th Division 1/5th Battalion Northumberland Fusiliers April 1918		
Heading	War Diary Of 5th Battalion Northumberland Fusiliers From 1st Apr-30th Apr 1918 Volume 31		
Map	Map		
War Diary	Domart (Amiens Sh.17)	01/04/1918	01/04/1918
War Diary	Longeau	01/04/1918	01/04/1918
War Diary	Saleux	02/04/1918	02/04/1918
War Diary	Vironcheux	03/04/1918	03/04/1918
War Diary	Gonnehem (Sheet 36A)	04/04/1918	07/04/1918
War Diary	Le Sart (Sheet 36A)	08/04/1918	09/04/1918
War Diary	Estaires (Sheet 36A Sheet 36)	09/04/1918	11/04/1918
War Diary	Neuf Berquin (Sheet 36A)	11/04/1918	12/04/1918
War Diary	La Couronne (Sh 36A)	12/04/1918	12/04/1918
War Diary	La Motte (Sheet 36A)	13/04/1918	17/04/1918
War Diary	Rebecq (Sheet 36A)	18/04/1918	26/04/1918
War Diary	Map Soissons (Sheet 22)	27/04/1918	30/04/1918
Miscellaneous	Supplementary		

War Diary	Merville (Sheet 36A)	11/04/1918	12/04/1918
Miscellaneous	Batt. Northumberland Fusiliers		
Map	Map		
Heading	War Diary Of 5th Bn Northumberland Fusiliers From 1st May To 31st May 1918 Vol 32		
War Diary	Coulonges (Soissons-22)	01/05/1918	05/05/1918
War Diary	Meurival (Soissons-22)	06/05/1918	07/05/1918
War Diary	Centre D'Evreux (Nr Pontavert)	08/05/1918	18/05/1918
War Diary	Ville-Au-Bois (Soissons-22)	19/05/1918	25/05/1918
War Diary	Concevreux (Soissons-22)	26/05/1918	27/05/1918
War Diary	Nr Chaudardes	27/05/1918	27/05/1918
War Diary	Concevreux	27/05/1918	27/05/1918
War Diary	Ventelay	27/05/1918	27/05/1918
War Diary	Lemoncet Fme	28/05/1918	28/05/1918
War Diary	Vandeuil	28/05/1918	28/05/1918
War Diary	Baslieux	29/05/1918	30/05/1918
War Diary	Romigny	30/05/1918	30/05/1918
War Diary	B. De Bonval	31/05/1918	31/05/1918
Map	Map		
Miscellaneous	5th Batt. Northumberland Fusiliers	31/05/1918	31/05/1918
Heading	War Diary Of 5th Bn Northumberland Fusiliers From 1st June To 30th June 1918 (Vol. 33)		
War Diary	Congy (Marne)	01/06/1918	01/06/1918
War Diary	Vert-La-Gravelle	02/06/1918	04/06/1918
War Diary	Nanteuil (Soissons Sh-22)	05/06/1918	06/06/1918
War Diary	Nappes	06/06/1918	06/06/1918
War Diary	Mont De Bligny (Soissons Sh. 22)	07/06/1918	12/06/1918
War Diary	M-De Bligny	12/06/1918	12/06/1918
War Diary	B. du Courton	12/06/1918	13/06/1918
War Diary	Germaine (Soissons Sh 22)	13/06/1918	19/06/1918
War Diary	Broyes (Marne)	20/06/1918	30/06/1918
Miscellaneous	Supplementary Diary		
War Diary	B. de Bonval (Soissons)	01/06/1918	01/06/1918
War Diary	Boujacourt	01/06/1918	01/06/1918
War Diary	Nappes	01/06/1918	01/06/1918
War Diary	Bde Courton	02/06/1918	02/06/1918
War Diary	Nappes	03/06/1918	08/06/1918
Heading	War Diary Of 5th Bn Northumbld Fusiliers From 1st July To 31st July 1918		
War Diary	Connantre (Marne)	01/07/1918	03/07/1918
War Diary	Citernes (Abbeville)	04/07/1918	12/07/1918
War Diary	Huppy (Abbeville)	13/07/1918	18/07/1918
War Diary	Rouxmesnil (Dieppe)	19/07/1918	31/07/1918
Miscellaneous	Report Of Address By Major General H.C. Jackson, D.S.O. Commanding 50th (Northumbrian) Division To 149th Infantry Brigade	11/07/1918	11/07/1918
Map	Map		
Miscellaneous	Message Pad		

WO95/2828(12)

WO95/282(2)

50TH DIVISION
149TH INFY BDE

5TH BN NORTHUMBERLAND FUSRS
APR 1915-JLY 1918

To 39 DIV 118 BDE

149th Inf.Bde.
50th Div.

Battn. disembarked
Boulogne from
England 20.4.15.

5th BATTN. THE NORTHUMBERLAND FUSILIERS.

A P R I L

(18/30.4.15)

1 9 1 5

Army Form C. 2118

WAR DIARY or INTELLIGENCE SUMMARY

(Erase heading not required.)

Instructions regarding War Diaries and Intelligence Summaries are contained in F. S. Regs., Part II. and the Staff Manual respectively. Title Pages will be prepared in manuscript.

Place	Date	Hour	Summary of Events and Information	Remarks and references to Appendices
BLYTH.	18.4.15	6.45 pm	Transport & Machine Gun Section under Captain W.J. Graham left here to embark at SOUTHAMPTON on S.S. "Archimedes."	
SOUTHAMPTON	19.4.15		About embarked aboard S.S. Archimedes for HAVRE.	
BOULOGNE	20.&.15 10.30 pm		Remainder of Battalion 27 Officers 915. O.R. left BLYTH & arrived 8.30 & 9.30 a.m. en route for FOLKESTONE. Embarked at FOLKESTONE aboard S.S. Victoria at 8.45 pm. Disembarked at BOULOGNE 10.30 pm. Proceeded to St Martin's Camp about 3 miles S.E. from Landing Stage.	
CASSEL	21.4.15		Left St Martin's Camp (BOULOGNE) at 2.30 pm and marched to PONT-DE-BRIQUES. Entrained there at 5 pm. Arrived at CASSEL station 10 pm. Billeted in a barn in BAVINCHOVE village adjoining CASSEL station. (Joined Transport etc. in barn at PONT-DE-BRIQUES	
WINNEZEELE	22.4.15		Left BAVINCHOVE at 10.0 am & marched via CASSEL and STEENVOORDE to FILLERS 1½ miles S.E. from WINNEZEELE. Battalion Billeted in various farms & barns.	
POPERINGHE	23.4.15		Marched off at 9.30 am and proceeded to WINNEZEELE. Halted there until 6 TH PM N.F. until 1.0 pm. Marched via WATOU to POPERINGHE and thence to a field 1½ miles S.E. of the town. Arrived there at 8 pm & bivouacked for the night.	
YPRES.	24.4.15		Remained in bivouac until 7.0 pm when marched off via VLAMERTINGHE to YPRES, coming under a heavy shell fire while passing through the town, which is much dilapidated. 5 men were wounded by shrapnel. Lay in a field just beyond YPRES for 2 hours under heavy shell fire.	
WIELTZE.	25.4.15		Moved off at 2.0 am and marched to dug outs roads ½ mile S.E. from WIELTZE. Were compelled by heavy shell fire to halt & dig dessent dugouts 400 yds S. of WIELTZE. Remainder of day spent in the dug-outs. 22 men were wounded during the day.	

WAR DIARY

Army Form C. 2118

Place	Date	Hour	Summary of Events and Information	Remarks and references to Appendices
ST. JULIEN	26/4/15		About 10 a.m. reported that the enemy were breaking through our line. Battalion moved out to verify this and "I could not make a counter attack. Arrived at position 11·40 a.m. and ascertained that report was not correct. Sent in message to Bde Major to that effect. Received answer to retire or if impossible to entrench. Sent message "Battalion was being heavily shelled, would entrench. Retired at dark to Bivouac. The Brigade had made an attack on ST. JULIEN during the afternoon. Specified up to a point but not being supported had to retire. Very heavy losses. Brigadier Sim Riddell killed. Captain Nash ("D" Coy) and Lieut. Bainbridge (attached R.E. Signal Coy) were also killed in this action. Casualties. Officers 2. O. Ranks Killed 9. Wounded 68. Missing 31.	
WIELTZE.	27/4/15		Battalion remained in dug-outs all day & under a heavy shell fire. Complimented on previous days work by H.O.C. Canadian Division.	
WIELTZE	28/4/15		Battalion remained in dug outs until 11 p.m. under shell fire & then moved up East about ½ mile & proceeded to dig trenches. A party of men was also detailed to collect bodies of men of the Brigade killed in action on 26th.	
ZILLEBEKE	29/4/15		Finished digging at 4·0 a.m. and occupied trenches, shelled heavily during the day. Ammunition boxes at adjoining refilling point being ignited & the ammunition exploded. Captain North & 10 men wounded by shrapnel. Retired from trenches at 6pm. moved about 3 miles S. to an old line of trenches (previously occupied by British) near ZILLEBEKE.	

Army Form C. 21

WAR DIARY
—or—
INTELLIGENCE SUMMARY
(Erase heading not required.)

Instructions regarding War Diaries and Intelligence Summaries are contained in F. S. Regs., Part II. and the Staff Manual respectively. Title Pages will be prepared in manuscript.

Place	Date	Hour	Summary of Events and Information	Remarks referring to Appendices
ZILLEBEKE	30.4.15		Lay in trenches all day, shells bursting frequently round about an adjoining farm. Paraded at dusk with entrenching tools & marched north to the neighbourhood of ST. JULIEN. On crossing a field, Captain & Adjutant Lovsar-Symons being slightly wounded. Started digging trenches at 10.30 p.m.	

149th Inf.Bde.
50th Div.

5th BATTN. THE NORTHUMBERLAND FUSILIERS.

M A Y

1 9 1 5

WAR DIARY

INTELLIGENCE SUMMARY.

5/Northumberland Fusiliers.

May 1915

Place	Date	Hour	Summary of Events and Information	Remarks and references to Appendices
LILLEBEKE	1.5.15		Finished digging at 2.0 a.m. These trenches were for use in case of a retirement by our forces. Returned to our trenches near ZILLEBEKE without mishap. Shelled during the day. Shelled heavily. At night returned to the scene of previous night's work and carried the line of trenches about 800 yds further to the north.	
ZILLEBEKE	2.5.15		Returned to our trenches about 3.30 a.m. Were shelled heavily all day by shrapnel. Asphyxiating shells and took a number of men. [7 men were killed] 7 wounded due to a shell bursting in the trench while they were sleeping by shrapnel. At 11.45 p.m. the Battalion moved off under heavy shell fire (1 man being killed & 4 wounded) & marched along the Railway south of YPRES.	
POPERINGHE	3.5.15		Marched by a route to the South of YPRES and VLAMERTINGHE arriving there about 3.30 a.m. & were billeted in the College Episcopal by 7.30 p.m. paraded with the remainder of the Brigade and marched to WATOU, arriving about midnight. The Battalion found billets about 1½ miles west of WATOU just past the French frontier.	
WATOU	4.5.15		The whole Brigade paraded at 10 a.m. in a field near DROGLANDT and were addressed by Field Marshal Sir J. F. French. After the address the troops dismissed & visited for the remainder of the day at their respective billets.	
WATOU	5.5.15 to 9.5.15		Battalion in billets during this period. Occupied during days in drill & short route marches. Extra signallers also being given instruction. On Sunday 9.5.15 stood by all day awaiting orders to move.	

Army Form C. 2118

WAR DIARY or INTELLIGENCE SUMMARY

(Erase heading not required.)

Instructions regarding War Diaries and Intelligence Summaries are contained in F.S. Regs., Part II. and the Staff Manual respectively. Title Pages will be prepared in manuscript.

Place	Date	Hour	Summary of Events and Information	Remarks and references to Appendices
BRANDHOEK	10.5.15		Reveille 4.30.a.m. Battalion paraded at 6.45 and assembled at the Flags in the DROOGLANDT–WATOU road. [At 8am Battalion was moved off in motor 'buses, 25 men per 'bus, to 1/2 mile east of POPERINGHE. (Transport & Machineguns came along in rear). Marched to a wood at BRANDHOEK about 2 miles E.N.E. from POPERINGHE and joined the remainder of the Northumbrian Bgde. Made ourselves comfortable in the wood. The 5th Border Regiment, having been attached to the Northbd. Brigade came up later in the day.	
BRANDHOEK	11.5.15		Battalion spent 2 days in bivouac in wood at BRANDHOEK in glorious weather.	
YPRES	12.5.15 13.5.15		Battalion paraded at 10.0am & marched with rest of Brigade to a field about 1 mile S.W. from YPRES. Constructed dugouts & bivouacs, but were flooded out by heavy rain. At 5pm moved off to some huts about 1/2 mile west of YPRES. [Huts however were not exactly water-tight].	
YPRES	14.5.15		Stay spent in hutments. At 8pm 200 men paraded and proceeded N.E. over YSER CANAL to dig & repair reserve trenches.	
YPRES	15.5.15		A few shells burst near huts early in the morning, too far away however, to do any damage. Battalion paraded about 5-0pm & marched back to VLAMERTINGHE where they bivouaced in the park adjoining a large chateau. The Hdqrs of the 4th Division, the Northumberland Brigade from this date is known as the 149th Brigade and the Northumbrian Division as the 50th Division. 200 men paraded at night to dig trenches near the firing line.	
VLAMERTINGHE	16.5.15		Lift Chateau (Residence of Vicomte du Parc) at 2pm and moved to some dug-outs between VLAMERTINGHE and BRIELEN. 200 men again paraded to dig & repair trenches. 1 man was wounded.	

WAR DIARY
INTELLIGENCE SUMMARY
(Erase heading not required.)

Army Form C. 2118

Instructions regarding War Diaries and Intelligence Summaries are contained in F.S. Regs., Part II. and the Staff Manual respectively. Title Pages will be prepared in manuscript.

Place	Date	Hour	Summary of Events and Information	Remarks and references to Appendices
VLAMERTINGHE	18.5.15		Rained heavily early in the day. Cleared up later & companies were taken short route marches for exercise.	
VLAMERTINGHE	19.5.15		The weather to-day having improved somewhat, the men were occupied in route marching under their Company Commanders. The Battalion having become attached to the 4th Division (along with 4th, 6th and 7th Battalions N.F.) was ordered to be held in Divisional Reserve. [Brigadier General S.P. Fielding D.S.O. to-day proceeded on 4 days leave and the command of the 149th Brigade devolved on Col A.H. Foles C.M.G. D.S.O. who left the Battalion for Hospital Farm (Ridges 149 & 150a) The Battalion now being in Divisional Reserve (4th Div.) was ordered to be attached to the 12th Brigade (4th Div.) for instruction in trench work and companies were detailed to the several units of this Brigade as follows:- "A" Coy, Headquarters, 1 Machine Gun, & M.S. Officer to the 2nd Bn "Monmouth Rgt." (a Territorial Battalion) "B" Coy to the 1st Bn "King's Own" (Royal North) Lancaster Rgt. "C" Coy, Signallers, Medical Officer & R.A.M.C. to the 2nd Bn "The Essex Regt." "D" Coy, 1 Machine Gun to the 2nd Bn. (18th) Royal Irish Regt. The Battalion with the exception of "A" Coy paraded at 9.0am & the Companies joined the Battalions to which they had become attached, at their respective billets. "B" Coy joining the "King's Own" at a Bivouac, south of Road A.23.d.2.2 (Sheet 28) "C" Coy joining "Essex Regt" in Bivouac at their Headquarters A.21.a.9.9 (Sheet 28) "D" Coy joining "Royal Irish" at billets in A.16.c. central (Sheet 28) "A" Coy left their bivouac at 11.30am, & joined the "Monmouths" in billets at VLAMERTINGHE B.2.a.6.1 (Sheet 28) This town was heavily shelled during the night 20-21. But no casualties occurred & little damage was done.	
VLAMERTINGHE	20.5.15			

Army Form C. 2118

WAR DIARY
— or —
INTELLIGENCE SUMMARY
(Erase heading not required.)

Instructions regarding War Diaries and Intelligence Summaries are contained in F.S. Regs., Part II. and the Staff Manual respectively. Title Pages will be prepared in manuscript.

Place	Date	Hour	Summary of Events and Information	Remarks and references to Appendices
VLAMERTINGHE	21.5.15		The men of the Companies were separated by Sections & attached to the various platoons of the units with which they were stationed. The Monmouths (with "A" Coy attached) and the Essex (with 2 "B" Coy attached) were engaged during the day in the ordinary routine parades. About noon the Kings Own (B Coy attached) and the Royal Irish (D Coy attached) moved from their respective billets to the woods adjoining the Chateau near VLAMERTINGHE (H.2.5.3.)(Sheet 28) & bivouaced there. The Kings Own moved off at 7.0 pm across country to over the YSER CANAL to the 1st Line trenches, 200 yds NE of IRISH FARM (C27.a.2.5)(9x28) the entrance to the trenches was barred but anyhow as they were taken over about 11 pm. The Royal Irish left the wood at 8.0 pm & moved up over the YSER CANAL taking up their quarters in a line of dug-outs situated on the East bank of the CANAL between Nos 3 & 4 PONTOON BRIDGES. (2.1.8 (2.5.21) (Sheet 28).	Map referred to 1/40,000 YPRES Sheet 28
YPRES			Owing to the O.C. of the 2nd Monmouths being invalided home, "A" Coy & H.Q.s were ordered to be attached to the 5th South Lancs [Rifles] (a Territorial Battalion) and joined this Battalion in the Chateau woods at VLAMERTINGHE about 11.45 am. The Essex left their bivouacs & moved to these woods about the same time. The Kings Own and Royal Irish spent a fairly May in their respective positions, which they took up the previous night, except for considerable activity on the part of the enemy's snipers against the Kings Own trenches. At 10 pm the Essex & J. Lanc moved up over the YSER CANAL, the 2 Lancs going into dug-outs on the East Bank, south of those occupied by the Royal Irish.	
VLAMERTINGHE	22.5.15			
YPRES				

WAR DIARY
INTELLIGENCE SUMMARY

Place	Date	Hour	Summary of Events and Information	Remarks and references to Appendices
LA BRIQUE	22-5-15		The Force continued their march & moved up to the 1st line trenches about 2000 yds N.E. from LA BRIQUE and stretching from a farm known as "TURKS FARM" past a ruined Estaminet on the cross roads to a farm known as CANADIAN FARM. To the left of "TURKS FARM" the trenches were held by the French. About midnight a severe thunderstorm broke and the trenches occupied by the Essex and King's Own (who each had one company in support about 300 yds from the firing line) were partially filled with water. On the CANAL bank the dugouts were also flooded and two or three men were injured by lightning. The Royal Irish who had left their dug outs about 10pm. were up a line of trenches on the right of the King's Own shortly after midnight 22nd & 23rd. Three companies going into the firing line & the remainder in support. Casualties during the day were as follows:— "B" Coy (attached King's Own) 1 man killed, 1 man wounded.	
LA BRIQUE	23-5-15		Shortly after midnight 22nd 23rd. Those portions of the firing line held by the Essex & Royal Irish Regts were subjected to a heavy bombardment, portions of the parapet being blown in. During the forenoon the Essex trenches were again shelled with shrapnel and high explosive shells, but little damage was done. The CANAL BANK was also shelled and several men of the Essex Lines were wounded and 1 man killed. The Remainder of the day was fairly quiet.	
YPRES.			No casualties were reported in the Battalion.	

WAR DIARY
INTELLIGENCE SUMMARY

Army Form C. 2118

Place	Date	Hour	Summary of Events and Information	Remarks and references to Appendices
Nr LA BRIQUE.	24.5.15		At 2.30 a.m. the Germans commenced an attack with asphyxiating gas, the wind being favourable for its use against our trenches. This gas was accompanied by Infantry, shrapnel & high explosive shell fire, with the result that portions of the trenches were practically demolished. The Essex who were on the left of the line held by the 12th Brigade endeavoured to disperse the gas by rapid fire but with little effect, although no doubt it saved many men from becoming asphyxiated had they lain low in the trenches. Shortly the bombardment started, the company of the Essex who had lain in support, advanced to the front line, losing several men during this advance, and two companies of the St James, who had been held in reserve on the CANAL BANK were ordered to move up into the 2nd line. The King's Own succeeded in holding their line, although suffering heavily from the gas and accompanying shell fire. Unfortunately however, suffered severely from the gas fumes, large numbers of men being overcome before they could take steps to extricate them. Under cover of the gas, the Germans delivered an infantry attack against the Dublin Fusiliers and Royal Irish on the right of the King's Own. The Dublins were forced to retire, with the result that the trenches occupied by the Royal Irish were swept, added large numbers of men being killed and wounded. The Irish were now compelled to evacuate their trenches, leaving many men behind suffering from gas poisoning, these men being either killed or taken prisoners by the enemy who swarmed into the trenches. From the trenches abandoned by the Royal Irish, the enemy directed their attack against the King's Own, who however repulsed it not however without losing several officers & men. [C.S.M. Allen & 2107 Pte Scott shewed conspicuous bravery whilst defending a barricade in the King's Own trenches. C.S.M. Allen gallantly defending the barricade with a revolver, when he was mortally wounded & Pte Scott with a hand grenade.	

1875 Wt. W593/826 1,000,000 4/15 J.B.C. & A. A.D.S.S./Forms/C. 2118.

Army Form C. 2118

WAR DIARY
INTELLIGENCE SUMMARY
(Erase heading not required.)

Instructions regarding War Diaries and Intelligence Summaries are contained in F.S. Regs., Part II. and the Staff Manual respectively. Title Pages will be prepared in manuscript.

Place	Date	Hour	Summary of Events and Information	Remarks and references to Appendices
Nr. LA BRIQUE	24.5.15		The German attack was also attempted against the line held by the Essex, but only by small numbers of the enemy, who were easily driven back. The two companies of the South Lancs. who had moved up to the Brigade Dugout, had meanwhile advanced to the support line, the other two companies which had been lying in reserve on the CANAL BANK advanced to the support line at 11.6 a.m. in rear of the King's Own and Essex. Heavy artillery fire was maintained by both sides till 5 p.m. At 8.0 p.m. the Lanc. Fusiliers & the Warwicks attempted a counter attack which was directed against our trenches abandoned in the morning the King's Own and the Essex meanwhile receiving orders to stand fast. On the failure of this attack the King's Own and the Essex received orders to retire the King's Own returning to the CANAL BANK at 11.0 p.m. their retirement being covered by the Essex, who towards midnight themselves moved back to a rest line & dug themselves in 600 yds in front of IRISH FARM, one company returning to IRISH FARM. The survivors of the Royal Irish, who had lain in some reserve trenches during the day also retired to IRISH FARM. The whole retirement was well carried out and without loss.	

WAR DIARY
or
INTELLIGENCE SUMMARY

(Erase heading not required.)

Army Form C. 2118

Place	Date	Hour	Summary of Events and Information	Remarks and references to Appendices
LA BRIQUE	24.5.15		The following casualties in the 5th & 13th Northumberland Fusiliers occurred to-day	

"A" Coy attached 5th D. Lanc[?] Rifles.

Officers: Nil.
O. Ranks: Killed - 3. Wounded - 18. Missing 12.

"B" Coy attached "King's Own"

Officers: Capt Lawson & H. Killed in Action
2/Lieut Richmond 6th "   "   "
O. Ranks: Killed - 5. Wounded - 31. Missing - 13. Suffering from Gas poisoning - 8.

"C" Coy attached Essex Regiment.

Officers: Nil.
O. Ranks: Killed - 5. Wounded - 15. Missing - 13

Numbers of men reported missing are probably in hospital suffering from gas poisoning.

WAR DIARY
INTELLIGENCE SUMMARY

Place	Date	Hour	Summary of Events and Information	Remarks and references to Appendices
Mar. LA BRIQUE	24.5.15		"D" Coy attacked Royal Irish.	
			2/Lieut R.K. Killed in action	
			Capt. Jones P.D. To hospital (Gas/poisoning)	
			2/Lieut Saunders S. " " "	
			2/Lieut Bevan E.S. " " "	
			2/Lieut Winfield F. Missing	
			Lieut Hill M.C. "	
			Lieut Patterson E.A. "	
			O. Ranks: Killed - 5. Wounded - 11. Missing - 123. To hospital suffering from Gas poisoning 10. There has also been a number of men died in hospital from gas poisoning who were previously reported missing. The Machine Gun Section attached to the Royal Irish lost their gun. Casualties in the section were as follows. Killed - nil. Wounded - 2. Missing - 9.	

Army Form C. 2118

WAR DIARY
INTELLIGENCE SUMMARY
(Erase heading not required.)

Place	Date	Hour	Summary of Events and Information	Remarks and references to Appendices
Near LA BRIQUE	23.5.15		The Germans during the day shelled the new front line trenches and IRISH FARM (which had been used as a dressing station until the preceding day). The village of LA BRIQUE to the rear of IRISH FARM being also shelled by gas shells and shrapnel. At 9.30 p.m. the "King's Own" moved up to the new front line trenches near CROSS ROADS FARM and CANADIAN FARM, having been situated in dug-outs on the CANAL BANK during the day, whilst the S. Lancs. occupied the 2nd line trenches to the E. of those occupied by the Essex near IRISH FARM. The Royal Irish retired to LA BRIQUE after dusk and later to the CANAL BANK. The following casualties occurred in the 5th Bn Northumberland Fusiliers during the day:— "A" Coy attached S. Lancs. Nil. "B" Coy " King's Own — 4 — "C" Coy " Essex Officers - Nil. O.Ranks: Wounded - 2. Missing - 1. "D" Coy " Royal Irish Nil. Brigadier-General B. P. Fielding D.S.O. (commanding 149th Bde) returned today from leave & relieved Col A.J. Foster C.M.G. D.S.O. who had acted as Brigadier since May 19th.	

WAR DIARY
or
INTELLIGENCE SUMMARY
(Erase heading not required.)

Army Form C. 2118

Place	Date	Hour	Summary of Events and Information	Remarks and references to Appendices
LA BRIQUE	26.5.15		Shelling continued at intervals during the day, but few casualties occurred. At dusk the South Lancs and Kings Own were engaged in repairing their trenches, whilst the Essex sent a strong working party forward to demolish the old firing line trenches which they had occupied on the 24th. These trenches were twelled from a turned extrement to a point near CANADIAN FARM. where the enemy had established a sap leading into our trenches. The Royal Irish also sent up a working party to repair trenches and the entanglements in front of them. The following casualties occurred in the 5th Bn. Northumberland Fusiliers to-day:- "A" Coy attached 5th S. Lancs Rifles. Officers:- Nil. O.Ranks. wounded - 2. "B" Coy attached Kings Own. Officers:- Nil. O.Ranks. wounded - 1. "C" Coy attached Essex Regt. Officers:- Nil. O.Ranks. wounded - 1. "D" Coy attached Royal Irish. Officers:- Nil. O.Ranks - Nil.	

WAR DIARY
or
INTELLIGENCE SUMMARY

(Erase heading not required.)

Army Form C. 2118

Instructions regarding War Diaries and Intelligence Summaries are contained in F. S. Regs., Part II. and the Staff Manual respectively. Title Pages will be prepared in manuscript.

Place	Date	Hour	Summary of Events and Information	Remarks and references to Appendices
Near LA BRIQUE	27.5.15		The trenches and IRISH FARM were shelled heavily at intervals with shrapnel and "coal boxes", several men being blown out of a dug-out near IRISH FARM. The shelling ceased at about 6 p.m. except for a number of shells passing over and dropping into YPRES. The South Lancs being ordered to occupy the 1st line trenches near CROSS ROADS FARM, relieved the "King's Own" there at 10 p.m., the King's Own retiring to the 2nd line. The company of the Essex Regt. which had been in reserve near IRISH FARM, and a party from the Royal Fus. formed working parties at night digging & repairing trenches. Only 1 casualty occurred in the 5th Bn. Northumberland Fusiliers during the day, 1 man of "E" Coy being wounded.	
"	28.5.15		The day was fairly quiet, the weather continuing fine & warm. After dark, the Company of the Essex which had been in reserve near IRISH FARM now moved further back to the bank of the YSER CANAL. The rest of the 12th Brigade did not make any move, being engaged in digging & repairing trenches and working on the barbed wire. No casualties occurred to-day amongst the personnel of the 5th Bn Northumberland Fusiliers.	

Army Form C. 2118

WAR DIARY
or
INTELLIGENCE SUMMARY
(Erase heading not required.)

Instructions regarding War Diaries and Intelligence Summaries are contained in F. S. Regs., Part II. and the Staff Manual respectively. Title Pages will be prepared in manuscript.

Place	Date	Hour	Summary of Events and Information	Remarks and references to Appendices
LA BRIQUE	Nov 29.6.15		A quiet day. At night another company of the Essex came back into reserve on the CANAL BANK, being relieved by a company of the 5th South Lancs.	
		7.30 pm	The French attacked the German trenches on the left of TURI'S FARM, and were reported to have captured 2 forts, 1 machine gun and a number of prisoners. Our trenches during this attack were heavily bombarded by the enemy, which delayed working parties from the R.E., Essex and Royal Irish. The enemy attempted to sap up to FORWARD COTTAGE (in front of the South Lancs trenches) and we got our artillery laid on to it if the South Lancs trenches and the 5th Bn Northumberland Fusiliers on this day were as follows:—	

"A" Coy attached 5th South Lancs
  Officers — Nil. O. Ranks wounded — 3.
"B" Coy attached King's Own — Nil
"C" Coy attached York Regt.
  Officers — Nil. O. Ranks killed — 1.
"D" Coy attached Royal Irish — Nil.

WAR DIARY or INTELLIGENCE SUMMARY

Army Form C. 2118

Place	Date	Hour	Summary of Events and Information	Remarks and references to Appendices
Near LA BRIQUE	30.5.15		Fairly quiet during the day except for sniping. At 9.p.m. the Germans attempted a counter attack against the trench on the left. This attack evidently failed. After dark, a company of the Essex came up from the CANAL BANK and relieved a company of the Essex in the firing line, this latter company retired back to the dug-outs, along the YSER CANAL. Strong working parties were sent out at night to improve the barbed wire entanglements, parties also for this purpose coming up from the men of the Royal Irish and Essex in reserve on the CANAL BANK. No casualties occurred today amongst the personnel of the 5th 13th Northd Fusiliers.	
Near LA BRIQUE	31.5.15		Shortly after midnight 30th–31st, Major Liebes and Lieut York (Capt 5th N.F.) crawled up to the vicinity of the sap, which the Germans were working up towards the North Lancs trenches and at 1.30 a.m. a strong bombing party was sent up to annoy the enemy working at the sap. At 2.30 a.m. the French made another attack, and the enemy immediately commenced shelling the British 1st line. Trenches thinking we might attack. The shelling moderated about 4.30 a.m. but continued at intervals during the day. At night strong working parties were engaged in digging additional trenches and improving the old ones, also in putting down crops (Reys) in front of the barbed wire which was a source	

Army Form C. 2118

WAR DIARY
or
INTELLIGENCE SUMMARY

(Erase heading not required.)

Instructions regarding War Diaries and Intelligence Summaries are contained in F. S. Regs., Part II. and the Staff Manual respectively. Title Pages will be prepared in manuscript.

Place	Date	Hour	Summary of Events and Information	Remarks and references to Appendices
Nr. LA BRIQUE	3/5/15		A bombing party was also sent out to annoy the enemy who still continued sapping towards the trenches occupied by the S. Lancs. No casualties occurred today amongst the personnel of the 5th & 13th Northumberland Fusiliers.	

149th Inf.Bde.
50th Div.

8th BATTN. THE NORTHUMBERLAND FUSILIERS.

J U N E

1 9 1 5

WAR DIARY
or
INTELLIGENCE SUMMARY.
(Erase heading not required.)

Army Form C. 2118.

5/Northumberland Fusiliers.

June 1915

Place	Date	Hour	Summary of Events and Information	Remarks and references to Appendices
near LA BRIQUE	1-6-15		Shortly after midnight the Warwicks relieved those of the Essex who still held the front line trenches, the Essex retiring to the CANAL BANK where they lay of the Battalion lay in bivouac. The weather continued fine & a fairly quiet day was spent except for occasional shell fire, our guns scattering a pretty warm fire on the saps leading up to our trenches. At 9.30 pm the King's Own was relieved from the second line, which they had held for some days & moved back to north of VLAMERTINGHE where "B" coy 5th N.F. passed them. Meanwhile the Essex had also left the CANAL BANK and moved back to their own billets, "C" coy 5th N.F. leaving them & proceeding to a wood 1½ miles north east of VLAMERTINGHE where they bivouaced, being later joined by "B" coy and "D" coy who had left the Royal Irish after moving back from the CANAL BANK. The South Lancs were relieved at 10 pm by the Seaforths, and moved back to the vicinity of VLAMERTINGHE, "A" coy 5 N.F. leaving them and joining the rest of the Battalion in their bivouac about 1.30 am 2nd June.	
VLAMERTINGHE			No casualties occurred in the 5th & 13th Northumberland Fusiliers to day.	

WAR DIARY or INTELLIGENCE SUMMARY

Army Form C. 2118

Place	Date	Hour	Summary of Events and Information	Remarks and references to Appendices
VLAMERTINGHE	2·6·15 to 4·6·15		Battalion in Bivouac in the wood to which they moved on being relieved from the trenches. The usual routine parades were carried out, and men were instructed in signalling and telephone work, also extra machine gunners received training. A number of men also received instruction in Bomb-throwing under Lieutenant Bomb-throwing being a very necessary part of an infantry-man's training. In the morning the Battalion received orders to move and at 12.30 pm 4/6/15 the wood and marched with the rest of the Brigade (who had also been bivouaced there) to the vicinity of BUSSEBOOM where the Battalion bivouaced in a field (B22C Sheet 28) adjoining a farm. The transport which during the time the Battalion had been in the trenches was stationed at BRANDHOEK now joined the Battalion.	
BUSSEBOOM	5·6·15 6·6·15 to 9·6·15		The Battalion during this period was situated in bivouac and engaged in the ordinary routine. Physical drill, route marching and instructional classes for signallers, machine gunners etc being carried out. Hot baths were also supplied for the men at POPERINGHE about 1½ miles distant from the bivouac. The Bomb throwers also received additional instruction. A thunderstorm broke on Tuesday 8th, but the rain did not cause much inconvenience although the heavy rain which came down 8th - 9th caused a number of the men to remove their quarters to a barn. On Tuesday Evening (8th June) several of our officers reconnoitred the roads near the YSER CANAL north of YPRES in view of a possible move.	

Place	Date	Hour	Summary of Events and Information	Remarks and references to Appendices
BUSSE BOOM.	June 10	1915	Re-embarked with parades during the morning — at 4.30 p.m. we suddenly received orders that we were to go into the trenches that night in the neighbourhood of Hooge — Bicycles and the Company Commanders had to proceed at once by bus to look over the trenches we were going to take over while it was light. The remainder of the Battalion paraded and left on motor-buses about 7 p.m. — We disembarked just south of YPRES on the main road and marched into the town — where we were met by guides from the 1st SOUTH LANCASHIRE REGT. who we were relieving — We left the town by the ST ELOI Gap, crossed the Railway & went across country to SANCTUARY WOOD — our guides led us alright, but it came on to rain, was pitch dark, and what with the number of troops on the road and transport, we had numerous halts to let the rear catch up and it was very late by the time we got to MAPLE COPSE — Here after some difficulty and a long wait we found the Company officers who took their companies straight off through the wood to the various trenches. It was a nasty job going up through the wood, there were a lot of bullets coming over striking the trees & ricochetting in all directions — I man was killed & several wounded — We took over the trenches about 1 & 2 a.m. and the	

WAR DIARY
or
INTELLIGENCE SUMMARY.
(Erase heading not required.)

Army Form C. 2118.

Instructions regarding War Diaries and Intelligence Summaries are contained in F. S. Regs., Part II. and the Staff Manual respectively. Title pages will be prepared in manuscript.

Place	Date	Hour	Summary of Events and Information	Remarks and references to Appendices
SANCTUARY WOOD	1915 June 11th		1/L SOUTH LANCS. are just able to get away before daylight — A & B coys are in the front line & C & D in support. Trenches about 200 yds behind are in the wood. We found the trenches pretty fast on the whole, though rather swampy in parts. B coy are within 150 yds of the enemy trench opposite. A coy the German trench are out of view, over the ridge some 500 yds away.	
	12th		The day was pretty quiet except for sniping, which was generally pretty active — 1 man was wounded. Quiet except for sniping — The Germans do not appear to shell the wood much, though it has apparently been shelled a good deal in the past — The sniping becomes very bad at night — the German trenches are on slightly higher ground than ours and they shoot right down into the wood — one man was wounded on the ration dump and another near the dug-out in MAPLE COPSE on this night.	
	13th		A fairly quiet day, a few shells on our right but no damage done — The wire on the whole on our front is very scanty. No strengthening parties were sent out so soon as it was dark enough — 2 men were wounded on this job.	

WAR DIARY or INTELLIGENCE SUMMARY

Army Form C. 2118.

Place	Date	Hour	Summary of Events and Information	Remarks and references to Appendices
SANCTUARY WOOD	14th June 15		A fairly quiet day — no shells though they have been sending over rifle grenades over B Coy — the enemy have been seen and heard working in what appears to be a sap, opposite the right of B Coy — so when it was dark Capt GRAHAM took out a patrol to try and discover if this was so — He reports that the enemy had an advanced trench in this spot, but that they were not sapping towards us — No enemy working parties were heard on this night — one man was accidentally wounded by falling on a bayonet. Nothing to report during the day — but the enemy were rather more active at night — sniping a great deal and cheering the horses — our transport was only able to get up to the dumps after considerable delay and it was luckier than some, as the 7th Bn. had wagons and several horses blown to bits — one man was wounded.	
	16th		We received orders in the afternoon that the 16th Brigade were going to attack on the North of HOOGE the following morning — we were to co-operate by keeping up rifle & machine gun fire. After a fairly heavy bombardment & lasting about ¾ of an hour, the 3rd Division	10CM

WAR DIARY or INTELLIGENCE SUMMARY

Army Form C. 2118.

Place	Date	Hour	Summary of Events and Information	Remarks and references to Appendices
SANCTUARY WOOD	1915 JUNE 17th		attacked about 4 a.m. on our left — We could see them advancing over the German first line trench — after that everything was obscured by the smoke — HOOGE itself on our left got shelled with some pretty big stuff, but we escaped — nor did they shell our trenches — we subsequently heard that the 3rd Division took all three German lines, but were subsequently driven out of them by shell fire & only succeeded in keeping the first — that evening when things were quiet again C coy relieved A in the front line.	
	18th		2 men were wounded during the day & a stretcher bearer was killed while he was taking one of the wounded men through the wood to the Aid-Post. A quiet day. Casualties 2 men wounded. In the morning the enemy sent a number of rifle grenades into the trench held by B company — 1 man was killed and 4 wounded by one unlucky shot, which landed right on a group — Capt GRAHAM & Lt. ELLIS both received slight scratches, but remained on duty.	

Army Form C. 2118

WAR DIARY
or
INTELLIGENCE SUMMARY
(Erase heading not required.)

Instructions regarding War Diaries and Intelligence Summaries are contained in F. S. Regs., Part II. and the Staff Manual respectively. Title Pages will be prepared in manuscript.

Place	Date 1915	Hour	Summary of Events and Information	Remarks and references to Appendices
YPRES	19.6.15		We were relieved from our trenches in SANCTUARY WOOD early in the evening of the 19th by the 5th LOYAL NORTH LANCASHIRE REGT:– this relief was carried out by daylight. The Battalion assembled in MAPLE COPSE (just south of the wood) and waited till dark – we then marched back across country by companies and crossed the canal south of YPRES by bridge No. 14. and thence by road through KRUISSTRAAT to a bivouac in G.18.d. – by bridge No. 14. and thence by road through KRUISSTRAAT to a bivouac in G.18.d. – the night was quiet and fine and we had no casualties. As soon as we got in (about 2.0 am.) we got orders that the Brigade was to march to DRANOUTRE the next day	
	20.6.15		The Brigade passed the starting point in OUDERDOM about 9 a.m. – we were the rear battalion, it was very hot and dusty and the men were pretty tired after their long march from the trenches the night before – we passed through LOCRE and DRANOUTRE and reached our bivouac – a field in C.12.b. – about 2.30 p.m. – a distance of about nine miles.	
DRANOUTRE	21.6.15		We spent a good night in this bivouac. – there being plenty of water available for washing and drinking and a farm handy where we could buy milk, eggs, etc: – the 9th DLI. who marched down with us, were bivouaced in the same field. We received orders about mid-day to march again the rest of the Brigade at NEUVE EGLISE a distance of about 3 miles – we again bivouaced in a field just south of NEUVE EGLISE.	
NEUVE EGLISE	22.6.15		In the morning the C.O, 2nd in Command – Adjutant & the Company Commanders went up to see the trenches that we were to take over. – we were told that we should	

WAR DIARY
or
INTELLIGENCE SUMMARY
(Erase heading not required.)

Army Form C. 2118

Instructions regarding War Diaries and Intelligence Summaries are contained in F.S. Regs., Part II. and the Staff Manual respectively. Title Pages will be prepared in manuscript.

Place	Date	Hour	Summary of Events and Information	Remarks and references to Appendices
NEUVE EGLISE	22.6.15		Found the trenches very comfortable and quiet after being at YPRES — It seemed pretty quiet while we were there and we could go up and down to the trenches anywhere by day — so soon as it was dark that night — we took over the trenches — relieving the 5th SOUTH STAFFORDSHIRE REGT: — The relief was carried out without loss though it took a considerable time.	
	23.6.15		Nothing in particular of interest occurred and it was a quiet day — we found that the trench known as the Diagonal was a good deep and narrow trench — but that the rest consisted of sandbag breastworks which were very worn in parts and consequently not always bullet proof, and looked as if they would stand very little shelling — we had no casualties that day.	
	24.6.15		A quiet day — with a little shelling on both sides — we lost a brave and valuable officer early in the morning in Capt. W. S. Graham who was sniped through the head while looking over the parapet — Casualties 1 Officer killed 2 O.R. wounded — Captain Graham was buried in the evening by the Brigade Chaplain — just outside Battalion H.Q. 2'.	
	25.6.15		A quiet day with the usual shelling — At this time we shared our head quarters which consisted of a farm house, known as ST QUENTIN'S CABARET on the outskirts of the village of WULVERGHEM, with the 6th N.F.	

1875 Wt. W593/826 1,000,000 4/15 J.B.C. & A. A.D.S.S./Forms/C. 2118.

Army Form C. 2118

WAR DIARY
or
INTELLIGENCE SUMMARY

(Erase heading not required.)

Instructions regarding War Diaries and Intelligence Summaries are contained in F.S. Regs., Part II. and the Staff Manual respectively. Title Pages will be prepared in manuscript.

Place	Date	Hour	Summary of Events and Information	Remarks and references to Appendices
NEUVE EGLISE	26.6.15		A quiet day - with no casualties - Col. Edis, who had been staying back at the transport whilst Col. Span (6th NF) was in command of the Fictions rejoined - and the 6th handomee their head quarters to the house opposite which up till then had been used as a dressing station for both battalions - 17 men returned from hospital.	
	27.6.15		A quiet day - the usual German shelling - no casualties.	
	28.6.15		A quiet day - though 1 man of A Coy was shot through the head and killed whilst looking over the parapet - and Sergt Hay of B coy was rather badly wounded whilst on a recconnoitring patrol with Lieut Ellis - the following night.	
	29.6.15		A quiet day - a certain amount of shelling of C2 & C3. - 1 man being wounded.	
	30.6.15		A quiet day - usual German shelling 3 times a day - 1 man of D coy hit through the head and killed.	

149th Bde.
50tg Div.

1/5th NORTHUMBERLAND FUSILIERS.

J U L Y

1 9 1 5

WAR DIARY
or
INTELLIGENCE SUMMARY.

Place	Date	Hour	Summary of Events and Information	Remarks and references to Appendices
	1.7.15		A quiet day. One man of A Coy hit through the head and killed.	
	2.7.15		A quiet day - Officers of the 7th N.F. came to look at the trenches in the morning preparatory to relieving us that night - the enemy shelled C3 and C4 with shrapnel and caused several casualties amongst the 6th N.F. and one of our D Coy men was hit and died shortly afterwards of his wounds. The relief was carried out in the evening, though it took a long time and we returned to ALDERSHOT CAMP well after midnight.	

WAR DIARY
or
INTELLIGENCE SUMMARY
(Erase heading not required.)

Army Form C. 2118

Place	Date	Hour	Summary of Events and Information	Remarks and references to Appendices
NEUVE EGLISE	3/7/15 to 5/7/15		We had a quiet time in the camp, doing the usual physical drill, parade before breakfast and a parade in the morning or a short route march — the men are not supposed to be worked hard when out of the trenches but a certain amount is necessary to keep them fit.	
	6/7/15		On the night of the 6th after 14 days rest — we went back into the same trenches, the relief was carried out quite successfully without casualties.	
	7/7/15 to 9/7/15		These three days were fairly quiet and uneventful, though I man was killed — while looking over the parapet on the 9th. There was a good deal of firing on our left on the night of the 9th when we blew up a defensive mine which successfully upset the German mining operations in front of D IV trench.	

Army Form C. 2118

WAR DIARY
or
INTELLIGENCE SUMMARY
(Erase heading not required.)

Place	Date 1915	Hour	Summary of Events and Information	Remarks and references to Appendices
NEUVE EGLISE	10.7.15		The Battalion was relieved by the 7th N.F. — a quiet night — the relief was carried out in good time without any casualties — the Batt. returned to ALDERSHOT CAMP.	
	11.7.15		The usual inspections of rifles, equipment, smoke helmets etc took place — we supplied a digging party of 6 Officers and 150 men to work in the trenches — no casualties.	
	12.7.15		The men rested all day and at night we supplied a digging party of 8 officers & 200 men for work on the trenches — no casualties.	
	13.7.15		Usual inspection and physical drill parade before breakfast — while in camp 10% of the men have been allowed passes into BAILLEUL each day.	
	14.7.15		Usual inspection and physical drill parade. — The C.O. inspected the Batt'n in marching order. —	
	15.7.15		Usual inspection and early morning parade. — Leave to England has started for the Brigade 2 men went on the 12th and 4 more are going to-day — they get 4 days. Very heavy rain during the night of the 14th — we should have returned to the trenches to-night — but the Brigade was relieved by a Canadian Brigade and we are under orders to move to ARMENTIÈRES and take over a line of trenches there. — the Border Regt. being relieved by the Canadians too to-night — came into the camp and so we have had to double up a bit.	

WAR DIARY or INTELLIGENCE SUMMARY

Army Form C. 2118

Place	Date	Hour	Summary of Events and Information	Remarks and references to Appendices
NEUVE EGLISE	16.7.15		We got orders to move in the evening to a new line of trenches South of ARMENTIÈRES. — We marched out of the hut camp about 8 p.m. and got to ARMENTIÈRES (4 miles) about 10 p.m. In accordance with our usual luck when going into new trenches it was raining — we were met by guides there and after many delays, got into our new trenches about 2 miles the other side of the town — to relieve part of the 3rd K.R.R. and part of the 4th Rifle Brigade. It was a very dark night and the guides didn't know their way too well, and they led some of the companies a long way out of their way, before taking them to their right trenches — The relief was eventually completed about 1.30 a.m.	
ARMENTIÈRES	17.7.15		A quiet day — We found the trenches fairly good — though there is a nasty corner at L'EPINETTE — on the whole they are very like the ones we have at NEUVE EGLISE, We have two and a half companies (C & D and part of (A)) in the firing line the (B) in support and the remaining half of (A) dundid amongst the supporting points. — Sgt Hopper the Pioneer Sgt: was wounded whilst walking down the road by a piece of shell and 3 men of D.coy were wounded by a trench mortar shell — none of them badly though.	
	18.7.15		A very quiet day — There was a little shelling, though mostly on buildings behind our trenches — particularly a building which was once a distillery near the Border Regt. HQrs on our right — One man of B coy was killed — being shot through the head whilst looking over the parapet. — The trenches are still very muddy after the recent rain	

WAR DIARY or INTELLIGENCE SUMMARY

Army Form C. 2118

Place	Date	Hour	Summary of Events and Information	Remarks and references to Appendices
ARMENTIERES	19.7.15		A quiet day – very fine – The Germans shelled the town and the Ecivelling early in the morning – The Brigadier went round the trenches in the morning and when we were on our way round we met General Bush who is temporarily commanding the Division who also made a tour – The trenches are considerably drier to-day – Capt North commanding D Coy was unfortunately wounded in the evening by a rifle grenade, though only slightly and he was able to walk down to the Dressing Station – But he was a very energetic and capable officer, and his loss will be greatly felt. The aeroplanes of both sides were active early in the morning.	
	20.7.15		Very fine with a good south westerly breeze – The Germans again shelled the DISTILLERY in the morning & succeeded in bringing down the chimney which had already been hit several times – They must have thought it was used as an observing station – However a quiet enough day – though a couple of shells came over S.P.2. towards evening killing our man of A Coy & wounding another – D Coy was relieved from the front line changing places with B Coy who had been in the support line – and the two platoons of A Coy were relieved by the other two platoons from S.P.Y. and S.P.2.	
	21.7.15		Quiet day, fine and sunny – Casualties nil – the enemy displayed a good deal of activity during the night with their machine guns – Trying to catch our ration and carrying parties, but were not successful.	

WAR DIARY or INTELLIGENCE SUMMARY

Army Form C. 2118

Place	Date	Hour	Summary of Events and Information	Remarks and references to Appendices
ARMENTIERES	22/7/15		A pretty quiet day - fine in the morning, but very wet towards evening and during the night. The enemy were pretty active with whiz-bangs during the afternoon and knocked in a bit of our parapet in 76. — But caused no casualties — we were firing rifle grenades at them, but only one hit the parapet.	
	23/7/15		The trenches are in a horribly slushy condition owing to the rain — showery weather all day, though pretty fine towards evening and a good strong working party — Lord Gavan went round the trenches in the morning and noticing the place where the parapet had been mended after being knocked in the previous evening — he ordered our howitzers to retaliate which they accordingly did at 6 o'clock in the evening — though only firing eight shots. In the afternoon officers of the 6th D.L.I. visited the trenches to have a look round before relieving us tomorrow night.	
	24/7/15		A quiet day - with no casualties — Wilson our M.O. Keiffer the afternoon to go back to a Base Hospital — M.O's don't seem to take in to they never stay long — Wilson was the seventh since we have been out here, but we were genuinely sorry to lose him — We were relieved by the 5th D.L.I. The relief as usual taking a long time and we did not get our billets in the town till about 12.30 a.m.	

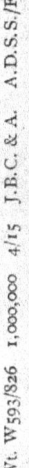

Army Form C. 2118

WAR DIARY
or
INTELLIGENCE SUMMARY
(Erase heading not required.)

Instructions regarding War Diaries and Intelligence Summaries are contained in F.S. Regs., Part II. and the Staff Manual respectively. Title Pages will be prepared in manuscript.

Place	Date	Hour	Summary of Events and Information	Remarks and references to Appendices
ARMENTIERES	25/7/15 to 31/7/15		The Brigade is out for eight days – During this time we carried out the usual routine in Billets, Physical Drill before breakfast – Drill & Route marches in the morning on alternate days – Special attention was paid to the training of bombers – and for the first time we got some live bombs for practice – Very good use was made of these. Colonel Cobb who had commanded the Battn. since it came out, left us on the 26th to take command of the 37th Base Depot – The command then devolved on Major Tuke.	

149th Bde.
50th Div.

1/5th NORTHUMBERLAND FUSILIERS

AUGUST

1 9 1 5

WAR DIARY
or
INTELLIGENCE SUMMARY.

Army Form C. 2118.

Place	Date	Hour	Summary of Events and Information	Remarks and references to Appendices
	1.8.15 to 4.8.15		On the 1st of August the Brigade relieved the 157th Brigade in a section of trenches immediately on the right of those we had previously occupied – the other 2 Batt[alion]s of the Brigade went in, but we were left out for another 4 days as we had been in the whole time before – However we changed our billets and went into a big school in the middle of the town – excellent billets after what we have been accustomed to. – The officers were all billeted in good class houses and we slept in beds. I had in fact every luxury.	
	5.8.15		On Thursday night we relieved the 4th Batt[alion] – quite good trenches – A, B & D Coys went into the firing line, with C Coy in the supporting trenches behind, the relief was carried out very quickly without any trouble.	

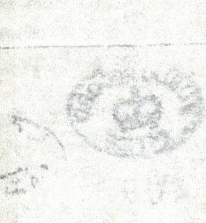

Army Form C. 2118

WAR DIARY
or
INTELLIGENCE SUMMARY
(Erase heading not required.)

Instructions regarding War Diaries and Intelligence Summaries are contained in F. S. Regs., Part II. and the Staff Manual respectively. Title Pages will be prepared in manuscript.

Place	Date	Hour	Summary of Events and Information	Remarks and references to Appendices
ARMENTIERES	8.8.15		A fairly quiet day. Dull and stuffy — a certain amount of German shelling in the morning to which our guns replied — the men were very slightly wounded — machine guns were active at night, especially German — about 9.30 p.m. the Germans turned a powerful searchlight on to our trenches, which made everything as light as day — their object was evidently to try & catch our working parties and put a machine gun on to them, but they didn't catch any of us — two flanges were taken on the searchlight and we judged it to be on a motor-car or lorry on the PREMENCHIES road. There was a tremendous bombardment up north (probably at YPRES) which commenced	
	9.8.15		about 2.30 a.m. and lasted till about 4 a.m. — about 3 a.m. the bombardment seemed to have been taken up all down the line. — In our sector it seemed to be all German and we had about 70 or 80 shells over our trenches — though luckily very little damage was done and no one was hit, which was astonishing considering the amount of stuff that was put over — some of it fairly heavy (probably 4.2 howitzer). We subsequently heard that an attack was being made by the VI Division up in the neighbourhood of Hooge & that it had been successful in taking back the trenches lost by us a week or two previously. The remainder of the day was fairly quiet, nothing particular of note occurring — the searchlight was turned on again in the evening, but one of our machine — guns fired 250 rounds at it and it didn't bother us any more that night. Major Brown returned from his leave & retook command of his company (C.)	

Army Form C. 2118

WAR DIARY
or
INTELLIGENCE SUMMARY

(Erase heading not required.)

Instructions regarding War Diaries and Intelligence Summaries are contained in F. S. Regs., Part II. and the Staff Manual respectively. Title Pages will be prepared in manuscript.

Place	Date	Hour	Summary of Events and Information	Remarks and references to Appendices
ARMENTIERES	10.8.15		A quiet day - very hot. nothing much of interest occurred - a small mountain gun was brought up so as to replace the German Howitzer at L'EPINETTE - it registered a few rounds in the morning. In the evening there were several of our aeroplanes about - one which had been firing at a Tot while coming back over the German lines, appeared to come gradually down somewhere on the N.W. side of the town, but whether it was hit or not we haven't heard - a search then flew right over to and over the town, being fired at quite ineffectually by our anti-aircraft guns - The Huns are our chief pests now - they simply swarm on the trenches and it seems impossible to get rid of them.	
	11.8.15		A very quiet day - rather cooler than yesterday - there being a good south westerly thing - the German aeroplanes were particularly active, during the afternoon and evening - two being up at once - we heard that the aeroplane which we saw coming down yesterday was a Frenchman, and that it landed near the canal at the PONT DE NIEPPE BRIDGE - having a hole through the petrol tank - Imam of Bez was killed to-day, being shot through the head while looking over the parapet.	
	12.8.15		The enemy bombarded our trenches quite heavily between 10 & 10.30 am this morning using chiefly whizz-bangs - but also 4.2" howitzers and French mortars - they went mostly over the trenches and a lot of it fell in the neighbourhood of LITTLE and GRAND PORTE EGALÉ FARMS, this was absolutely frightening - but as the only result was one man slightly wounded no one minded much and the men	

1875 Wt. W593/826 1,000,000 4/15 J.B.C. & A. A.D.S.S./Forms/C. 2118.

WAR DIARY or INTELLIGENCE SUMMARY

Army Form C. 2118

Place	Date	Hour	Summary of Events and Information	Remarks and references to Appendices
ARMENTIERES	12.8.15		were in high spirits afterwards, some 250 shells must have been sent over altogether, and the ground everywhere is littered with bits of high explosive.	
	13.8.15		The officers of the 5th DLI came up to look over the trenches prior to relieving us tomorrow night and as soon as things had quietened down we took them round. A very quiet day after the disturbance of yesterday - fine night - the relief was carried out successfully without casualties - although it took unnecessarily long, owing to part of B Coy getting separated from the rest - we went back to billets in the BLUE FACTORY and got settled in by 12.30 a.m.	
	14.8.15 to 18.8.15		The usual Routine in Billets - nothing unusual occurred while we were out - the HOUPLINES end of the town was shelled fairly heavily once or twice, but otherwise things were quite quiet.	
	19.8.15		On the night of the 19th we returned to the left sector - trenches 78 and 79 this time - only our Batt. Hd.Qrs. were at the same place as they were before when we were at L'EPINETTE - It was a fine light night and the relief was carried out without difficulties and without casualties. A, B and C Coys were in the firing line (78 and 79), D Coy in S.78 and S.P.Y and S.P.Z.	

Army Form C. 2118

WAR DIARY
or
INTELLIGENCE SUMMARY
(Erase heading not required.)

Instructions regarding War Diaries and Intelligence Summaries are contained in F.S. Regs., Part II. and the Staff Manual respectively. Title Pages will be prepared in manuscript.

Place	Date	Hour	Summary of Events and Information	Remarks and references to Appendices
ARMENTIERES	20.8.15		A very quiet day - with very little firing of any kind. The trenches appear to be fairly good and our chief work at present is renewing and thickening the parapet - where possible this is done by truing up front sandbags on the rear and then renewing the trench as well - the trenches are rather complicated thru being too many communication trenches near - some of them disused and which should if possible be filled up as they might nearly form a source of danger if the enemy got a footing in the front line - no casualties on this date.	
	21.8.15		A dull day - with an hours rain in the morning, making the trenches very wet and slushy, some of the communication trenches are not properly drained, and a great many french boards will be required to make them all good - No casualties.	
	22.8.15		Fine and very quiet - the enemy put a few whiz bangs into the town in the morning - No casualties - things have dried up a good deal - A lot of good work has been done on the front line in the way of rebuilding the parapets, and several new traverses are in course of construction. - No casualties.	

Army Form C. 2118

WAR DIARY
or
INTELLIGENCE SUMMARY
(Erase heading not required.)

Instructions regarding War Diaries and Intelligence Summaries are contained in F. S. Regs., Part II. and the Staff Manual respectively. Title Pages will be prepared in manuscript.

Place	Date	Hour	Summary of Events and Information	Remarks and references to Appendices
ARMENTIERES	23.8.15		A fine day, pretty quiet — the Brigadier came round the trenches in the morning and expressed himself very pleased with the work that has been done — in the evening two Majors belonging to the 24th Bat.n arrived, to be attached to us for a few days for instruction — The German machine guns were very active after dark and one fired continuously down the L'EPINETTE ROAD between 8 and 10 P.M. — causing several casualties though why one not our men not our men fortunately — a Lance Corporal of ours was unfortunately accidentally shot by one of our own men in front of the trenches	
	24.8.15		In the afternoon we received the good news that 11 German warships had been sunk in the Gulf of RIGA, and several transports of troops in an attempt to make a landing a hundred miles to the north of RIGA — this is the first good news we have had for some time from the Eastern Front and everyone is much elated — the men have been cheering all along the line, much I think, to the astonishment of the "Boches" — whose only reply was a few uncomplimentary remarks & a good deal of rapid fire.

A quiet day — fine and warm — the flies are a great pest these days and it is difficult to keep them down, owing to the quantity of refuse & odd tins that is scattered about the country — however we do our best by keeping the trenches scrupulously clean and allowing no scraps of food to remain unburied and by spraying the trenches with Creozol. | |

WAR DIARY or INTELLIGENCE SUMMARY

Army Form C. 2118

Place	Date	Hour	Summary of Events and Information	Remarks and references to Appendices
ARMENTIERES 24 A/5	25.8.15		Major Jones and Major Prior - Tyneside Irish arrived last night to be attached to us for trench training. An unfortunate accident occurred late on the night of the 24th scouting in the floor of a very promising officer - a patrol which 2/Lt Winkworth took out from trench 78 was spotted by the Germans who turned a machine gun on to them. 2/Lt Winkworth was hit in the elbow and the stomach - Sgt Topluck who was with him came back and took out stretcher-bearers and successfully brought him in - I am afraid the doctor doesn't express much hope for him. The enemy put over a hundred whiz-bangs and trench mortars over trench 80 this morning about 9.30 a.m. - luckily practically no damage was done - we replied with field guns and howitzers - the latter putting several shells into the German trenches opposite 79. Major Jones and Major Prior fell in the turning to go back to their Battn in England and reported themselves very pleased with what they had seen and learnt. 2/Lt Phillips returned from hospital - 1 man was slightly wounded during the day. The Brigadier agreed to fill up pay of QUEBEC ROAD which runs from Bn Hd Qrs to the Junction of 79 and 78 and the work was commenced to-day.	
	26.8.15		A fine hot day, fairly quiet - we received the sad news that Winkworth died in hospital at BAILLEUL about midday - he was a very keen and promising officer & will be greatly missed.	

WAR DIARY or INTELLIGENCE SUMMARY

Army Form C. 2118

Place	Date	Hour	Summary of Events and Information	Remarks and references to Appendices
NE NTIER/ES	26.8.15		Fauxwalker got on leave	
			Lt. 2nd Lieut 10th Hussars arrived in the evening to be attached for two days to learn trench work. We heard what we took to be an Airship passing over, going west about 10 pm – we could not see anything although it was a bright moonlight night. It [illeg.] have been very high up – 1 man was wounded to-day.	
	27.8.15		Very quiet to-day – fine and hot – Capt Stirling returns from leave – 1 man was wounded to-day – by striking a detonator with his pick while digging – his wounds were very slight.	
	28.8.15		Another quiet hot day – no one seems inclined to do much on a day like this – our howitzers put just shells into the German trench opposite 79 – when the enemy have been working lately. The Brigade bombing officer has given instructions that all bombs are in future to be kept in the support trenches and in future there will be no bomb stores in the front line. – There were no casualties on this date.	
	29.8.15		Very quiet day indeed – the General held a meeting of C.O.s at the 7th NF Headquarters and he gave instructions concerning some new shell shelter trenches to be adopted – these are to consist of T's in the communication trench, each to hold 16 men. We are starting to make one of these to-day, also a new means of holding communication trenches leading into supporting trenches by rifle fire – in order to do this at least 30 yards of the C.T. nearest to the support trench must be straight – there were no casualties on this date.	

1875 Wt. W593/826 1,000,000 4/15 J.B.C. & A. A.D.S.S./Forms/C. 2118.

Army Form C. 2118

WAR DIARY
or
INTELLIGENCE SUMMARY
(Erase heading not required.)

Instructions regarding War Diaries and Intelligence Summaries are contained in F. S. Regs., Part II. and the Staff Manual respectively. Title Pages will be prepared in manuscript.

Place	Date	Hour	Summary of Events and Information	Remarks and references to Appendices
ARMENTIERES	30·8·15		A quiet day — rather cloudy & looking like rain — no casualties. Nothing particular of interest occurred.	
	31·8·15		Our last day in — having been in for 12 days everything is looking forward to getting out. Word for the relief came up to HdQrs of the 4th YORKS REGT. & the 4th EAST YORKS respectively came up to HdQrs at the trenches they are relieving us in, in the morning — we feel that our 12 days have not been wasted, as the men have worked very well indeed, especially in T8 Trench, where a large part of the parapet has been rebuilt as well as several new traverses made — we have also almost completely fixed up QUEBEC AVENUE — which it was decided was to be done as there were so many C.T.'s in that neighbourhood — in addition to this a deep ditch which runs in front of Trench T8 for some 250 yards has been well filled with fascines until. The relief was carried out very quickly & the Battalion returned without mishap to billets in the BLUE FACTORY again.	

149th Bde.
50th Div.

1/5th NORTHUMBERLAND FUSILIERS.

S&E&P T E M B E R

1 9 1 5

Army Form C. 2118

WAR DIARY
or
INTELLIGENCE SUMMARY
(Erase heading not required.)

Instructions regarding War Diaries and Intelligence Summaries are contained in F. S. Regs., Part II. and the Staff Manual respectively. Title Pages will be prepared in manuscript.

Place	Date	Hour	Summary of Events and Information	Remarks and references to Appendices
ARMENTIERES	1-9-15 to		The usual routine in trenches was carried out during this period — physical drill, etc — we had to supply a digging party of 2 Officers & 100 men on the 1st instant. The Brigadier was going to have inspected the Battalion at the Brewery on the 3rd instant, only it was put off owing to the rain. On the night of the 4th a concert was given at the ECOLE PROFESSIONELLE by the JESMOND JESTERS — in which Capt. Phillips & Pte Batt. Woolston took part. The show was much enjoyed by everyone, & it served as a refreshing contrast to life in the trenches & was in general — it is to be hoped to continue these concerts every Wednesday & Saturday throughout the winter if the war lasts long enough? & the Boches permit.	
	5-9-15		On the night of the 6th instant the Brigade returned to the trenches — we however were put in Brigade Reserve for 4 days & so has a further 4 days rest, only we had to change our billets to the ASYLUM — we had to supply large working parties on the nights of the 7th, 8th & 9th respectively — and everyone was so fed up with digging trenches & working parties that they were almost glad to return to the trenches on the night of the 10th.	
	6-9-15 to 10/9/15			

Army Form C. 2118

WAR DIARY
or
INTELLIGENCE SUMMARY
(Erase heading not required.)

Instructions regarding War Diaries and Intelligence Summaries are contained in F. S. Regs., Part II. and the Staff Manual respectively. Title Pages will be prepared in manuscript.

Place	Date	Hour	Summary of Events and Information	Remarks and references to Appendices
ARMENTIERES	10-9-15		On the night of the 10th instant we relieved the 6th N.F. in 67 Trench and its supports — the Trench has its right on the LILLE ROAD & to the right flank of the 50th Division & the whole 2nd Army — on our right are the 1st Bn LEINSTER REGT which is the left Battalion of the 27th Division — the relief was carried out quite quickly & without incident — D Coy & part of C Coy were in the front line (Trench 67) — A Coy & the remainder of C Coy were in the CLOSE SUPPORT & MAIN SUPPORT Trenches — B Coy at LILLE POST where Battalion H.Q. were situated —	
	11-9-15		A very quiet day — very fine & warm — most of the day was spent as usual in looking round & finding out what wants doing — no casualties — the front trench is fairly good though in rather poor repair — the support trenches fairly good though there is lots to be done in the way of wiring — both in the front line and behind.	
	12-9-15		Very fine & would have been quiet — except for the fact that some KITCHENER BATTERIES attached to the Division on our right — were carrying out a War with some new H.E. Ammunition & were firing pretty hard	

WAR DIARY or INTELLIGENCE SUMMARY

Army Form C. 2118

(Erase heading not required.)

Instructions regarding War Diaries and Intelligence Summaries are contained in F. S. Regs., Part II. and the Staff Manual respectively. Title Pages will be prepared in manuscript.

Place	Date	Hour	Summary of Events and Information	Remarks and references to Appendices
ARMENTIERES	12.9.15		Most of the day — the shelling seems to be pretty effective judging from the stuff that was thrown up from the German trenches — the Germans did not shell us in retaliation as we expected — there were no casualties on this date.	
	13.9.15		We were woken about 4.30 a.m. by fairly heavy enemy shelling just on our right — this was no doubt in retaliation for yesterday's performance — however it only lasted some time - quarter of an hour & by all accounts did very little damage — during the day the 29th Division continued its ammunition taking & shelled the German trenches quite heavily at different periods throughout the day — there was no further retaliation on the part of the Germans — there were no casualties on this date.	
	14.9.15		On the 14th the weather changed slightly, having been very fine for over a week with an East wind — the wind went round to the West & there was slight rain in the morning — however it brightened up & now is 3 Officers from Kitcheners Army Division which has just come out from England — were attached to us this evening & left to rejoin their Battalion	

WAR DIARY or INTELLIGENCE SUMMARY

Army Form C. 2118

Place	Date	Hour	Summary of Events and Information	Remarks and references to Appendices
ARMENTIERES	15.9.15		This afternoon — a very short stay — and they found everything very interesting & approved trenches coming to go past 00 room.	
	16.9.15		A quiet day — fine again. The Divisional Commander came round the trenches this morning — he did not stay long as he was going round the whole sector, but he seemed very pleased with the work that had been done.	
	17.9.15		Another very quiet day. We are to be relieved by the 150th Brigade tomorrow night. Some of the officers of the 4th EAST YORKS have been round the trenches today — 1 man was slightly wounded today.	
	18.9.15		This is the quietest period we have yet had in the trenches — only 1 man too has wounded the whole tour & we have hardly had a single shell near the north done has been good although not so noisome as in the last. We have been greatly handicapped by the shortage of bombs for the trenches — we have been greatly handicapped by the shortage of bombs & got the loading of the shell. Cordite trenches — though we have finished one & got well on with another. The relief was carried out very quietly and right — all the trenches being relieved by 9.0 P.M — & we returned to our new billets in the 104th — in the neighbourhood of the O.Chim.	
			The wound received in trenches — The Brigade was inspected by Sir Hubert Plumer G.O.C. 2nd Army on the 20th — it was a very small parade 200 men being	
	23.9.15		early on a working party.	

Army Form C. 2118.

WAR DIARY
or
INTELLIGENCE SUMMARY.
(Erase heading not required.)

Place	Date	Hour	Summary of Events and Information	Remarks and references to Appendices
ARMENTIERES	23/9/15		In the morning we received orders that we were to return to the trenches that night, instead of the night of the 24th — we accordingly took over our trenches 74 & part of 75 with their supports from the 6th D.L.I. — A & B Coys & part of C in the front line — D & the remainder of C in support.	
	24/9/15		The relief was successfully & quickly carried out — it rained during the night & consequently the trenches were in a beastly mess this morning — Orders have been received that there is to be a Big French & English Offensive in the South on the morning of the 25th & that we are to make a demonstration here — to this effect tonight we are going to put pierrots & lamp chars in front of our parapet, to be lit in the morning with the idea that the smoke produced may make the enemy think we are going to start a gas attack — this is being done all along the Divisional front.	
	25/9/15		In the morning everyone was about very early, waiting for the order to light the chars, however the wind was absolutely unfavourable & we decided not to light ours — however on the left the chars was lighted apparently before the appointed time, which was 5.6. a.m. probably accidentally & also on the right where it appeared to be lit by one of the enemy's flares. Our guns bombarded the enemy's lines for a short period at 5 a.m. but I don't think the enemy were much taken in as they came down so much [locs?]	

WAR DIARY or INTELLIGENCE SUMMARY

Army Form C. 2118.

Place	Date	Hour	Summary of Events and Information	Remarks and references to Appendices
	26/9/15		Inspect the whole thing fresh off very lonely — perhaps a nasty sniping moving & an impregnate sniper accounts for this — By now every thing was normal again — we had no casualties except two men accidentally hurt. After this things were fairly quiet, although we had orders to keep active as possible & send out bombing patrols at night etc. Accordingly on the night of the 26/27 I sent out a bombing patrol consisting of himself, Serg. Larson & a Pte.c. — they succeeded in throwing our bombs into the German trench when they were apparently accounted & fire was opened on them — Both the men went wounded at once — Lgtlemsen Senvely — the other men Osceda in crawling back to our trench & getting help, while Linsvan very pluckily stayed with Serg. Larson by the Surrebarne.	
	27/9/15		They were eventually all gotten in about daybreak, thanks by Capt P.P. Phillips & 3 stretcher bearers, who gallantly went out to their assistance. A fairly quiet day — though much ent'd eomplacent. The trench's are in a heavy mess, though we have done our best to make a few drains, & there is one seems to have thought of storm depot — a good deal of work also wants doing to the parapet & trench qu — but every little work can be done in this wretched weather.	

Army Form C. 2118.

WAR DIARY
or
INTELLIGENCE SUMMARY.
(Erase heading not required.)

Instructions regarding War Diaries and Intelligence Summaries are contained in F. S. Regs., Part II and the Staff Manual respectively. Title pages will be prepared in manuscript.

Place	Date	Hour	Summary of Events and Information	Remarks and references to Appendices
	28/9/15		A quiet day — things have eased up a bit — no casualties — 1 man was wounded	
	29/9/15		A quiet day — have been able to do a certain amount of work in building up the parapet & traverses of 7th trench — & also to get on with the shell shelters at the top of Plant avenue — Capt. R. D. Yourt rejoined for duty from the 3rd line on the 28th instant — he was gassed on May 24th at YPRES & has only just been sent out again.	
	30/9/15		Some officers & N.C.O's arrived this morning to be attached to us for training in trench work — they belong to the 8th L.N.L. Regt. & their whole Division is up here for trench training before taking on a bit of the line of their own. Capt. J. M. Lowery was unfortunately wounded through the knee this morning while stamping with a tenaspe & so we have lost the services of a useful Lieutenant officer — another officer however joined in the evening — 2d Escher who has come out from the 3rd Line.	

149th Inf. Bde.
50th Division.

1/5th NORTHUMBELAND FUSILIERS

OCTOBER

1 9 1 5

WAR DIARY
or
INTELLIGENCE SUMMARY

Army Form C. 2118.

Date	
1/10/15	We are to be relieved on the night of the 1st by the 2nd N.F. – Our orderlies were hit at B.Q. by a whiz-bang on the morning, but otherwise the day was quiet. Time for a change – this has been an unsatisfactory tour in the trenches. We continued wet during the first 5 days making it rotten for the men & impossible to do much work, we have been cheered up however by the news of the progress of our own people and the French further South. The relief was carried out quite early after waiting sometime for one of the relieving companies which had gone astray & we returned to billets in the Hospice Civile near the GRANDE PLACE.
2/11/15	We have lost for the present anyway another very useful officer as Captain Syms had to go to hospital yesterday – he has been unwell for sometime. Our billets are good & the time there all too short, as we go back to the trenches after 4 days – we have had to provide a working party of 150–200 men every evening & consequently the men have not been made to do very much during the day. On the night of the 1st we received a draft of unmatched officer 2 Lt Trotman & 16 men

WAR DIARY
or
INTELLIGENCE SUMMARY.

(Erase heading not required.)

Army Form C. 2118.

Place	Date	Hour	Summary of Events and Information	Remarks and references to Appendices
ARMENTIERES	1915 3rd to 5th	Oct 2	The usual routine in billets	
	6th		On the night of the 5th we returned to the Trenches, taking over 80 chiefly of 79 from the 6th Batt. The relief was carried out quickly without any accidents — H.Q. in SPAIN AVENUE, comfortable but small. D.A.C. boys in the firing line & B in supports. 80 Trench being next to us, we were rather interested in it — it consists of a small salient, approaching to within about 100 yds of the German Trench — the trench is well built up & on the whole fairly safe — 1 man of C Coy was killed early in the morning while looking for a good sniping place.	
	7th		It has been decided that the DURHAM Brigade on our left shall take over Trench 80 — & its Support — This leaves us only holding half of 79 & supports — Accordingly on the night of the 7th we were relieved in 80 by the 6th D.L.I. & B & D coys half of A went back into the town, billeting in the CONVENT, also the M.G. section — no casualties.	
	8th		Very quiet.	
	9th		On the night of the 9th we companies that were in the town returned and we took over the whole of Trenches 79 & 78 & their supports from the 7th Batt. — These are held by the mass trenches in the whole line — C, B & D coys were put in the firing line — A remaining	

WAR DIARY
or
INTELLIGENCE SUMMARY.

Army Form C. 2118.

Place	Date	Hour	Summary of Events and Information	Remarks and references to Appendices
ARMENTIERES	Oct 9th		in support with the company bombers — whilst B & D Coys were at the CONVENT a draft arrived of 2 Lt DAGLEISH & 44 O.R. — These were apportioned to the different Coys & came up this Evening — some of them were returned wounded men, but the majority were new — 1 O.R. was wounded on the 9th.	
	10th		On the night of the 10th 2 platoons of the 1st D.L.I. were attached to us for trench training — one was attached to D Coy in 78 Trench & one to C Coy in 79 — one platoon of A & one of C went back to the billets in the CONVENT to make room for them: — a very quiet day & no casualties — Lt SEYMOUR joined on this date from the 3rd line.	
	11th		On the night of the 11th the two platoons of 1st D.L.I. were replaced by two other platoons — the men seemed pretty fair took an interest in things — they were not however hands through — as they had been in the Battle of LOOS & had suffered severely there — one man was wounded on the 11th.	
	12th		On the night of the 12th — all four platoons of the 1st D.L.I. came in as a company. They took over the trench between B & D Coys — the remainder of C Coy except their bombers, went out into billets to make room for them — the platoon of A Coy in billets was brought back to strengthen the support line — some new batteries	

Army Form C. 2118.

WAR DIARY
or
INTELLIGENCE SUMMARY.
(Erase heading not required.)

Place	Date	Hour	Summary of Events and Information	Remarks and references to Appendices
ARMENTIERES	1915 Feb 12		2 18 pounders which have come up were registering on the enemy's trenches & wire this afternoon — as their shooting was liable to be somewhat erratic, our men had orders to go into the shell shelters — but no accidents occurred, & there was not much reply to our fire — There were no casualties on this date & although a few along-range came over — things were fairly quiet.	
	13		We received orders that a demonstration was to be made on our front in the afternoon — all our men were put into the shell shelters except a few sentries — The artillery commenced to bombard the German trenches at 2.30 p.m. & went on in bursts till 3.30 p.m. — They bombarded practically the German wire infront of 60 — the whole idea was to make the enemy think we were going to attack — the Germans did not seem very worried by our artillery fire & did not make much return on our trenches — at 3.30 p.m. smoke bombs were thrown out by the bombers all along the front — this made a big wall of white smoke & caused the Germans to open fire pretty heavily with whizz-bangs & machine Gun & rifle-fire — our trenches however didn't suffer very much & the men were pretty safe in the shell shelters — we had no casualties at all & were pretty lucky considering the amount of stuff	

WAR DIARY
or
INTELLIGENCE SUMMARY.
(Erase heading not required.)

Army Form C. 2118.

Place	Date	Hour	Summary of Events and Information	Remarks and references to Appendices
ARMENTIERES	1915 Oct 13th		That was flying about — the Demonstration seemed to be fairly successful on the whole, though things soon quieted down when it was over. The company of the 14th D.L.I. went out that night & C Coy returned. In spite of yesterdays activity the day was fairly quiet — we had two men wounded early in the morning however — we received orders that we were to relieve the 4th Batt'n that evening in trenches 74, 75 EPINETTE — we were relieved in 78, 79 by the 7th N.F. early on (it is most dark about 5.30 p.m.) & carried out the relief of the 4th without much difficulty — 2 men were hit on the EPINETTE road carrying rations that night, so our casualties were heavier than usual.	
	"14th"			
	"15th"		We have not been in the EPINETTE Salient since we first came to this part of the line in July — though 76 Trench is considerably improved stairway remains 2 hasty corner — Both 75 and 76 were found to be very badly knocked about as a month of the enemys retaliation to our bombardment on the 13th — & we shall have to spend all our time rebuilding the parapet again & making the place moderately safe — at present there are great holes in the parapet which of course	

WAR DIARY
or
INTELLIGENCE SUMMARY
(Erase heading not required.)

Army Form C. 2118.

Place	Date	Hour	Summary of Events and Information	Remarks and references to Appendices
ARMENTIERES	1915 Oct 15th		You can't pass without being fired at — The day was quiet & we had no casualties though the Boches sent over shells over about 6 o'clock as usual.	
	" 16th		We are have some more Kitcheners attached to us, we never seem to be left alone those days — This time it is the 12th NORTHN — 2 platoons came on the evening — one was put under the care of Capt PHILLIPS in No 6 & the other with Capt FORREST in No 5 — to make room some of our own men were put into the close Support Trench — A man of D Coy was unfortunately killed in the evening while on a listening post in House 6 by a shrapnel which the enemy sent over.	
	17th		Two more platoons of the company of the 12th N.F. relieved their others two platoons in the evening. — A man of C Coy was killed early in the morning by a killer while raising up the parapet in the salient. Quiet on the whole — The C.O. & a.adjutant of the 12th came up & spent the night with us, departing the following afternoon. We are to be relieved tonight — no one will be sorry, we are always glad to get out of EPINETTE — we were relieved by the 7 N.F. & returned to billets in the CONVENT.	
	18th		The C.O. Col. LUARD goes away on six days leave today — The command reverting	

WAR DIARY
or
INTELLIGENCE SUMMARY.
(Erase heading not required.)

Army Form C. 2118.

Place	Date	Hour	Summary of Events and Information	Remarks and references to Appendices
ARMENTIERES	1915 19th Oct.		on Major A IRWIN — Excellent billets in the CONVENT — the usual routine in billets — though we have no early parades — Each company & all the details were inspected in marching order in turn.	
	24th		We received orders to take over trenches 78 & 79 again on the night of the 22nd but these were subsequently cancelled — we hear that the Batt.n is to go back somewhere to rest — it sounds too good to be true.	
	25th		Orders received that we are to proceed to STRAZELLE, starting tomorrow. We left ARMENTIERES about 2 p.m. Proceeding by companies to LA CRECHE where we billeted in farm houses for the night — quite a short march. 5 miles, but very miserable as it rained steadily all day and the roads were in a horrid mess.	
LA CRECHE	26th		We started again at 8.30 a.m. in the morning & did the rest of the journey about 8 miles arriving at STRAZELLE about 1 p.m. — it had cleared up & was very pleasant after yesterday — the men were pretty tired after their march, though very few fell out & it is several months since they have done anything of a march.	
STRAZELLE	27th		We are billeted in farm houses — the men in farms — very poor billets after	

WAR DIARY or INTELLIGENCE SUMMARY

Army Form C. 2118.

Place	Date	Hour	Summary of Events and Information	Remarks and references to Appendices
STRAZEELE	1915 Jan 27th		our fine houses at ARMENTIERES — but if we are here long enough I daresay we shall be able to improve them.	Mar/
	28th to 31st		At rest! It has not been nothing but rain since we left Mre the place is a sea of mud — the inhabitants say it gets on like this till march — however every one is fairly happy — we have parades in the morning & afternoon, route marches drills etc — the bombers are hard at work training, the machine gunners we hope to train every man as a bomber & also motor machine gun section. On the 27th there was inspection of troops at RAILLEUL by H.M. the King. we sent a platoon of 40 O.R. under Lt PATTERSON, which formed part of a composite company, made up of all the battalions in the Brigade.	

149th Bde.
50th Div.

1/5th NORTHUMBERLAND FUSILIERS.

NOVEMBER

1 9 1 5

Confidential

War Diary

of

5th Bn Northumberland Fusiliers

from November 1st 1915

(Volume 3) III & IV

Army Form C. 2118.

WAR DIARY
or
INTELLIGENCE SUMMARY.
(Erase heading not required.)

Place	Date	Hour	Summary of Events and Information	Remarks and references to Appendices
STRAZEELE	1st November		We are shaking out here doing as much training as the weather will permit – which isn't very much, so it has been almost constantly wet since we came here and the roads & country are always in a bad state – we are however going ahead with the training of specialists – the bombers have been put altogether into a separate billet & we are working as a company of them now under 2nd Lieut HAGGIE	Map ref/ Sheet 29
	2nd		2/Lieut SHAW – A reserve machine gun section has been formed and a reserve signalling section is undergoing training – The companies are doing chiefly drill & short route marches when the weather permits.	
	5th		On November the 5th we had to change our billets to the East side of the village. The barns here as a whole show an improvement.	
	6th		A draft of 140 men arrived from the 1st line & we had some difficulty in finding room for them but we managed to get them in by crowding up.	
	8th		The new draft were inspected by the Brigadier at C Coy's billet	
	10th		Sir CHAS FERGUSON Commanding 2nd Corps inspected the Battalion – the Battalion were inspected separately – He expressed himself very pleased with the turn out of the Batt. & also with the work that had been done in the trenches	

Army Form C. 2118.

WAR DIARY
or
INTELLIGENCE SUMMARY.
(Erase heading not required.)

Army Form C. 2118.

Place	Date	Hour	Summary of Events and Information	Remarks and references to Appendices
STRAZEELE				Map. ref. Sheet 27.
	1st November		During the last few months we supplied a fatigue party to dig a "Chellers" trench on which it is proposed to practise the attack.	
	15th		A programme of Training has been brought out by the Division as follows 15th November to 1st December – Squad & Platoon Training / Company drill & Training / Battalion drill & Training / Brigade Training	
			2nd December to 9th December –	
			10th December to 12th December – Divisional Training	
			From this it appears that we are going to be here some time.	
			A draft of 48 N.C.O's & men from 3rd line arrived	
	18th		A Brigade Route March – Inspection by Sir HERBERT PLUMER who watched the Battalion march past him en route	
	19th		The Battalion has been playing a lot of football – a divisional competition has been got up for which we have entered – also we have had one or two games of Rugby.	

1577 Wt. W10791/1773 500,000 1/15 D. D. & L. A.D.S.S./Forms/C. 2118.

Army Form C. 2118.

WAR DIARY
or
INTELLIGENCE SUMMARY.
(Erase heading not required.)

Instructions regarding War Diaries and Intelligence Summaries are contained in F. S. Regs., Part II. and the Staff Manual respectively. Title pages will be prepared in manuscript.

Place	Date	Hour	Summary of Events and Information	Remarks and references to Appendices
STAPLE ELE	24th November		A bombing competition was held between battalions in the Brigade – we succeeded in winning the Honour Competition gaining 1st 2nd & 3rd places – prizes were given by the Brigadier. A class of bombs has been commenced 2 lectures on the subject are being given by Major BATTYE Q.S.O & 20th Division – 2nd Lieut. EASTEN has been appointed Bomb Officer	Nil ret Sheet 27
	25th – to –		The weather has taken a decided turn we have had both frost & snow which is preferable to the continual wet & mud. On the 23rd Captain N.M. NORTH rejoined from the 3rd Line – he was wounded when we first went to L'EPINETTE at the end of July & has been at home since then.	
	26th – to 30th		Nothing of importance until the end of the month.	mcl.

1577 Wt.W10791/1773 500,000 1/15 D.D.&L. A.D.S.S./Forms/C. 2118.

149th Bde.
50th Div.

1/5th NORTHUMBERLAND FUSILIERS

DECEMBER

1 9 1 5

Army Form C. 2118.

WAR DIARY
or
INTELLIGENCE SUMMARY.
(Erase heading not required.)

Instructions regarding War Diaries and Intelligence Summaries are contained in F. S. Regs., Part II. and the Staff Manual respectively. Title pages will be prepared in manuscript.

Place	Date	Hour	Summary of Events and Information	Remarks and references to Appendices
STRAZEELE	1st November		Tom was to the 10th. just now we are to do Battalion & Brigade training — that is so far as the weather permits. At present we are busy doing practice attacks on the skeleton trenches that have been dug — who gives excellent practice in organising the attack — filling off the various bombing parties — pont. work & ammunition carrying parties. First we are by companies — afterwards as a Battalion. Orders are written by the officer in charge of each line of the attack & these are afterwards criticised on the ground. We have had two fairly long Brigade Concentration Route marches.	Map ref. Sheet 29
	10th November		We have also practiced an attack in the open, which was made very difficult by the wet state of the country & also its enclosed nature. We are daily expecting to hear when we are going back to the trenches. We originally thought we were going back to ARMENTIERES, but we now hear the unwelcome news that we are to go back to the Ypres salient again. which means the dear old YPRES salient again.	

MCU

WAR DIARY or INTELLIGENCE SUMMARY

Army Form C. 2118.

Place	Date	Hour	Summary of Events and Information	Remarks and references to Appendices
STRAZEELE	16/2/15		We received orders that we were to relieve the 9th Division in the YPRES Salient an unpleasant surprise for everyone, so up till a short time ago we had been told that we were certain to go back to ARMENTIERES — We are to go by train from STRAZEELE to POPERINGHE — very busy packing up & getting everything ready for the move.	Street
	17/2/15		The Battn marched down to the station & left about midday — The Brigadier, the Divisional Commander & Sir Charles Ferguson commanding the 2nd Corps were all at the station to see us off. & Sir Charles to say good-bye to us on leaving his corps — we arrived at POPERINGHE & marched through the mud to CANADA HUTS near DICKEBUSCH — where we were to billet for the night. The mud round these huts was the worst I have ever seen — you literally had to wade to get into them & as we arrived just as it was getting dark, it took a long time to get settled in.	
YPRES	18/2/15		The next morning the Colonel, Adjutant & Company Commanders had to go up to see the positions in Brigade Reserve, that the Battalion was to occupy that evening. Which were dug-outs for two companies at H30a, near the DICKEBUSCH — YPRES main road — Headquarters & one company at BEDFORD HOUSE I26a, 9 or 8	Sheet 28. Sheet 29

Army Form C. 2118.

WAR DIARY
or
INTELLIGENCE SUMMARY.
(Erase heading not required.)

Place	Date	Hour	Summary of Events and Information	Remarks and references to Appendices
YPRES.	15th Sept.		Company at BLAWEPOORT FARM I 27 6. The Battalion occupied their positions that night – B & C coys going to H 30 a, A Coy & H.Q. to BEDFORD HOUSE & D Coy to BLAWEPOORT FARM – relieving the 5th Cameron Highlanders. To-morrow night we are to take over trenches 36, 37 & 38 from the 26th Brigade – these trenches are on the right of the Brigade sector.	Sheet 28.
"	19th		We were woken up at 5 a.m. by hearing heavy rapid rifle & guns firing – over it was taken up all round & it was evident that there was something on as the fire became very heavy – shortly after we got a message telling us to "stand to" that the Germans were making a gas attack. Soon we were able to smell the gas which was apparently coming out from the north side of the salient, where the attack seemed to be taking place, as the guns on our old door quietened down. The gas was not strong at BEDFORD HOUSE & we did not put on our helmets, though our eyes were affected probably by gas-shells & we had to put on our eye-protectors. In the meantime the intense gun-fire by both sides was being kept up, the Germans shelling everywhere indiscriminately – all round BEDFORD HOUSE & the roads & there seemed to be shells dropping everywhere we looked – about 12 noon we got	

WAR DIARY or INTELLIGENCE SUMMARY

Place	Date	Hour	Summary of Events and Information	Remarks and references to Appendices
YPRES	19th Decr.		Start to "stand down" which I must say was a relief & we heard that the Gas attack had been made on the 6th & 49th Divisions who were holding the line in the neighborhood of POTIJZE & WIELTJE & that no infantry attack had followed the gas. The Germans kept up the bombardment all day, still shelling all the road & environs extremely & we thought towards evening that another Gas guessed down a bit. We should not be able to carry on the relief — however the Company Officers & the C.O. went up to look at the trenches we were taking over & we got orders to "carry-on". The 6th Battalion relieved us in Brigade Reserve & we got up to the trenches without any casualties, which I think was very lucky considering the amount of shell fire there was all through the night. We relieved the 8th GORDONS in trenches 36 to 38 — the companies being distributed as follows A Coy 36. B Coy 37 R. C Coy 37 L. D Coy 38 — Each coy having one or more platoons in outpost — the relief was completed by 8 pm. The trenches had been quite heavily shelled in the afternoon & consequently were a good deal knocked about & it took all our time to get the holes in the parapet patched up before the morning — The shelling continued during the night & our losses were	Sheet 28.

1577 Wt.W10791/1773 500,000 1/15 D. D. & L. A.D.S.S./Forms/C. 2118.

Army Form C. 2118.

WAR DIARY
or
INTELLIGENCE SUMMARY.

(Erase heading not required.)

Place	Date	Hour	Summary of Events and Information	Remarks and references to Appendices
YPRES.	19th Dec.		Came in for it again once or twice & we had in all about 12 O.R. wounded during the night of the 19th & the 20th including 2/Lt BELL who was only slightly touched in the foot & came back 3 days later.	Shel 28
"	20"		We were all I think thoroughly expecting to have another gas attack this morning, but nothing happened & things are a little quieter — though the Germans have kept up their bombardment & shells seem to have been pouring into our heads into YPRES & dismal all day — In the afternoon our trenches were shelled at intervals but it caused no casualties — During the night our cyclists were pretty quiet.	
"	21"		Wet — misty & nasty — Quiet all round this morning — what we thought was going to develop into the 3rd Battle for YPRES seems to have died a natural death & we hope it won't reawaken — it continued quiet all day — Casualties 2 O.R. wounded. Our trenches are not so bad so those of us who have had previous experience of the YPRES Salient in winter might have expected — Excepting 38 they are fairly dry — the front line anyway — the support line is on the whole bad — and only excellent parts — the front line at 36 & 37 is fairly good. 38 is the NTOC trench it holds the	

Army Form C. 2118.

Instructions regarding War Diaries and Intelligence Summaries are contained in F. S. Regs., Part II. and the Staff Manual respectively. Title pages will be prepared in manuscript.

WAR DIARY
or
INTELLIGENCE SUMMARY.
(Erase heading not required.)

Place	Date	Hour	Summary of Events and Information	Remarks and references to Appendices
YPRES	21st	Noon	Both sides of the Railway cutting 9 is exactly opposite Hill 60 which commands all the surrounding country & too on an old C.O/O leading into the German trench from a point where the opposing trenches are only 18 yards apart — Part of 38 is very wet. The whole of our efforts are at present centred on drainage — later on perhaps we shall be able to improve the trenches — all the men have gum boots & are very cheerful in spite of the wet Plea condition's.	Feb 28
	22nd		A quiet night followed by a fine morning which is a relief — a little machine gun fire during the night but not so much as one would have expected considering the number of holes there are in the parapet still to be built up — though they are mostly mended now. It started raining again about afternoon & continued all night — making the trenches very wet in spite of our efforts at drainage — D. Coy were bombarded with "whiz-bangs" for half an hour in the evening — but they had no casualties.	
	23rd		Fine bright day — artillery & aeroplanes active on both sides — turned out in the evening — we were relieved in the evening by the 7th N.F. & marched back to CANADA HUTS. a good eight-mile march & everyone was pretty done up by the time	MOU

Army Form C. 2118.

WAR DIARY
or
INTELLIGENCE SUMMARY.

(Erase heading not required.)

Place	Date	Hour	Summary of Events and Information	Remarks and references to Appendices
YPRES.	23rd Dec.		They got thick. A Coy had two men sent out on the wire out. Our present arrangement is at go back to the same trenches each time & which will make things easier as we shall always know the trenches — Casualties 1 O.R. killed — 3 O.R. wounded.	Mat 28
"	24th "		We found a CANADA HUTS in just the same state of mud — but much improved by trench-boards laid on freeze having been put down alongside the huts so that it is now possible to get in and out without wading. Col. VAUX the pioneer company of the 7th D.L.I. seem to be doing all they can to make the place habitable. Spent the day trying to get dry — all the men being well though.	
"	25 "		XMAS DAY 1915 — cold, showery towards, but everyone seemed very cheery for all that — a lot of plum puddings had been sent out to the Battalion & the men had a good feed — Likewise the Officers with the help of a few bottles of champagne sent for from BAILLEUL & a turkey though away captured from STRAZEELE, managed to suitably celebrate the occasion — morning parade service in Y.M.C.A tent. Cold & showery — like yesterday we had a Divisional service in the Y.M.C.A tent in the Camp.	
"	26 "			
"	27 "		We go back to the trenches tonight — Left Camp about 3 p.m. — The Companies	MCW

Army Form C. 2118.

WAR DIARY
or
INTELLIGENCE SUMMARY.
(Erase heading not required.)

Instructions regarding War Diaries and Intelligence Summaries are contained in F. S. Regs., Part II and the Staff Manual respectively. Title pages will be prepared in manuscript.

Place	Date	Hour	Summary of Events and Information	Remarks and references to Appendices
YPRES.	1915 27th Dec.		marching up independently — No casualties going up & the relief carried out peacefully — found trenches O.K. about as wet as when we left — The Coys reverted to the same trenches as last time	Sheet 28
"	28"		Fine bright day — artillery & aeroplanes active on both G.A.S. — Casualties 3. O.R. wounded	
"	29"		Fine day — send a party to for a German gas attack — our guns fired on Hill 60 in the afternoon for an hour — not very much reply — a number of our 8 inch shells failed to burst — otherwise fairly quiet. — Trench Mortars bothered 38 again in the evening — tn/ were eventually shut up by our field guns. — quiet night. Casualties 5 O.R. wounded.	
"	30"		Fine & rather colder — was a oril unforinance S.E. — but the expected gas attack is not yet forth-coming — A lot of artillery fire in the afternoon — Our guns fired a lot in the night in reply to Enemy Trench Mortars which were as usual worrying 38 — Casualties 1. O.R. Died of Wounds. 2. O.R. wounded.	
"	31st "		Our artillery carried out a "strafe" on the enemy trenches in front of 36 & 37 & those on our right — we seem to go for them every day now — however we got a good deal of fire in reply this time — particularly near Batt. H.Q. & in the buring — one shell unfortunately dropped just inside the door of station killing A/Cpl Goodwin of D Coy	

Place	Date	Hour	Summary of Events and Information	Remarks and references to Appendices
YPRES.	1915 31st Dec.		& wounding 5 others amongst whom whose our doctor Lt BIRNIE. R.A.M.C & Sergt GRAY the medical Sergeant, who has done consistently good work all the time the Bn. has been out here. This is a great loss & one not easily replaced. In the evening we were once more relieved by the 7th N.F. & went back to Brigade Reserve — the same companies going to the same places. Casualties killed 1. O.R. — Wounded Lt BIRNIE R.A.M.C. & 5. O.R. Well so ends perhaps the most memorable year in history — most of us I think hope that in this case history wont repeat itself.	Ap. 128. MCU.

Confidential
War Diary
of
5th Bn Northumberland Fusiliers
from January 1st 1916 to January 31st 1916.
(Volume IV.)
V

WAR DIARY
or
INTELLIGENCE SUMMARY.
(Erase heading not required.)

Army Form C. 2118.

Place	Date	Hour	Summary of Events and Information	Remarks and references to Appendices
YPRES.	1916. January 1st		Nothing to be done except to attain amount of work on the dug-outs at the various places — very wet — no casualties.	Ahed 28
	2nd		Wet & Stormy — work on dug-outs at H30a & BLAWEPOORTE FARM.	
	3rd		Fine day — very quiet — no shells near our dug-outs — "The New Year notof" mentioned in despatches" arrived — The following are to be congratulated upon being mentioned — Colonel Coles C.M.G. D.S.O. — Lt Col Fulvis — Major A. Irwin — Capt. D. Hill (Staff Capt.) Capt. A.M. North — Capt. Y.H. Lyons — Capt. S.M. Yoxeay — Lt Ellis — Lt Keen — Lt Soran Quartermaster & Hon. Lieut. R.J. Holloway. Regimental S.M. Offord W.J. no 4475 — C.S.M. Quan no 2258 (Killed) — L.Cpl. Dawson R no 2562 Private Moar A. no 1914.	
	4th		Returned to the night sector & relieved the 7th Bn. or so — no casualties — Clear, fine day — a lot of Artillery fire on both sides — our 5" howitzer's fire impressive —	
	5th		a hundred shells round about Hill 60 — our aeroplanes very active — Some officers sent out from England for a couple of days to gain a little actual experience taken round the trenches — Casualties 2 O.R. wounded —	
	6th		Quiet day on the whole — 3 O.R. accidentally wounded by a rifle going off.	ACH

1577 Wt.W10791/1773 500,000 1/15 D.D.&L. A.D.S.S./Forms/C. 2118.

Army Form C. 2118.

WAR DIARY
or
INTELLIGENCE SUMMARY.
(Erase heading not required.)

Place	Date	Hour	Summary of Events and Information	Remarks and references to Appendices
YPRES.	1916. January 7th		A lot of artillery fire on both sides — the Germans had a small bombardment of our Battalion H.Q. with strong bangs — but they could only hit the top of the mound & could not touch us — Another unlucky accident, 3 men were wounded by the premature bursting of one of our rifle grenades. We were relieved by the 7th in the Evening this time returned to CANADA HUTS for our four days out.	Sheet 28
	8th		Cold windy day — did nothing except clean up.	
	9th		Sunday — the usual services in the Y.M.C.A. Hut.	
	10th		The whole Battalion bathed at POPERINGHE — where there are excellent baths — & whose Major Brown got up a change of clothes — Major Brown got up a concert mild evening for the men which was reported to have been much appreciated —	
	11th		Returned to "trenches" — left Camp about 3.30 p.m. — of course it started to rain just as we were leaving — & kept it up most of the march — Very quiet going up — no casualties — later it cleared up into quite a fine night.	
	12th		Very cold — strong north West Wind — quiet — no casualties.	
	13th		Cold & Quiet — Enemy seem particularly quiet & are doing very little sniping & putting up.	1004

1577 Wt.W10791/1773 500,000 1/15 D. D. & L. A.D.S.S./Forms/C. 2118.

Place	Date	Hour	Summary of Events and Information	Remarks and references to Appendices
YPRES	1916 January	13th	very few flares — the general opinion is that a relief has taken place & that the Boches are firing them just before becoming offensive —	Sheet 28
		14th	Fine, bright day & consequently a good deal of artillery activity on both sides — our howitzers "strafed" Hut 60 continuously — so much in fact that the Boche's at last got thoroughly roused & they sent out eight very large minenwerfer (and to be aerial torpedoes by reports) which shook the booming for miles round & frightened us all to death — but did no other particular damage except to make an enormous hole in JOHNSON'S TRENCH where landed — the next time we "strafed" the Hut I came upon Lieut-Adams glaring up at our blue air with a whistle in his mouth & shouting to his men "If I blow one whistle run like Hell to the right & if I blow two run like Hell to the left" The explanation of this is that you can see those Sausages coming with the air, & if you can judge where they are going to fall, you can run, and of the way, but if you judge wrong you are as likely as not to run right into the beastly thing.	
		15th	We are relieved in the evening — this time by the 4th N.F. — as the 7th N.F. have gone to the left sector, where we shall relieve them next time — went back to BEDFORD HOUSE, BLAUWEPOORTE FARM, & H.30 a. — no casualties.	MCW

Army Form C. 2118.

WAR DIARY
or
INTELLIGENCE SUMMARY.
(Erase heading not required.)

Place	Date	Hour	Summary of Events and Information	Remarks and references to Appendices
YPRES.	1916 January 16th		Quite Quiet & no casualties — Nothing much of interest occurred except that one of our aeroplanes came down near H 30 a, the pilot being shot through the leg — the machine however was undamaged.	Sheet 28.
		19th	A long list of decorations came out on the 15th — Amongst the names were the following who received the Military Cross.	
			Captain N. M. MORTH.	
			Captain D. HILL	
			Lieutenant R. ELLIS.	
			The following received the Distinguished Conduct Medal.	
			No. 559. C.S.M. McDONALD. W.	
			" 732 Sergeant GRAY J. (R.A.M.C. T.F.) Dismissal Sergeant.	
			" 1732 Corporal FITZGERALD C.J.	

Army Form C. 2118.

WAR DIARY
or
INTELLIGENCE SUMMARY.

(Erase heading not required.)

Instructions regarding War Diaries and Intelligence Summaries are contained in F. S. Regs., Part II. and the Staff Manual respectively. Title pages will be prepared in manuscript.

Place	Date	Hour	Summary of Events and Information	Remarks and references to Appendices
YPRES.	1916			
	19th January		Relieved 7th N.F. in left sector – quiet night – got in without casualties	See S 28
	20th "		Very fine clear day – pretty quiet – no casualties	
	21st "		Mild day – some Sausages over S.9 in the morning – but no casualties – dark night and we were able to get some wiring done – A mine was apparently blown up some distance on our right about 2.30 a.m. 9 rapid fire was opened – but soon died down	
	22nd January		Quiet morning – a good deal of artillery fire on the afternoon – some shrapnel hit our R.9. on the afternoon wounding four men. – Very fine moonlight night – motorcycle to Div Check evening	
	23rd "		Very foggy early – Got some good wiring done – some "silent knives" put onto the cutting near H.Q. in the afternoon	
	24th – 26th "		Relieved by 7th N.F. & returned safely to CANADA HUTS. Usual routine at CANADA HUTS	
	27th Jan.		Returned to left sector & relieved 7th Bn N.F. very dark night – 1 man wounded on way up.	
	28th "		A bad day – 39 was ordered continually by Sausages & rifle Grenades – 2 men being killed 9 eight wounded during the day	

Army Form C. 2118.

WAR DIARY
or
INTELLIGENCE SUMMARY.
(Erase heading not required.)

Instructions regarding War Diaries and Intelligence Summaries are contained in F. S. Regs., Part II. and the Staff Manual respectively. Title pages will be prepared in manuscript.

Place	Date	Hour	Summary of Events and Information	Remarks and references to Appendices
YPRES	1916 29th January		A fairly quiet day - except for rifle Grenades - Casualties 1.O.R. killed and 2.O.R. wounded - Wind favourable for gas.	Sheet 28
	30th	"	Another bad day - with rifle Grenades & whizz bangs - 1.O.R. died of wounds. 9. Lt. DIGBY SEYMOUR also rather badly wounded.	
	31st	"	Fairly quiet day. - Relieved by 4th N.F. - New system of inter-brigade reliefs starts - we go into close support, with H.Q. at SQUARE WOOD. This last period in the trenches has been the worst we have had for a very long time - Total casualties Killed or died of wounds - 9.O.R. Wounded 1 Officer 30.O.R.	

5/5.37

J Foster Lt Colonel
Commanding 5th Batt
Northumberland Fusiliers

Confidential
War Diary
of
5th Bn Northumberland Fusiliers
from February 1st 1916 to February 29th 1916
(Volume VI)

WAR DIARY or INTELLIGENCE SUMMARY

Army Form C. 2118.

Place	Date	Hour	Summary of Events and Information	Remarks and references to Appendices
YPRES	1916 1st FEBRUARY		Elta Support — SQUARE WOOD etc — fairly comfortable — working parties supplied to the front line from every company — fine and cold — we hear that the 4th are having a bad time in the right sector.	Sheet 28
	2nd		Still fine & very cold — working parties supplied to front line — officers look more like trenches — very little doing — Capt Rawson and Wedd go off on leave — lucky men. Capt Eric Joins the 2nd Field Ambulance prior to go "locum" while he is away.	
	3rd		Quiet day — until June & cold — in the evening we moved into the left sub-sector of the right sector trenches 49-51 F.3, and relieved the 4th N.F. — 2 O.R. wounded.	
	4th		Relieve our companies one in the front line — trenches good — one the left — open or the right — Quiet day — 1 O.R. wounded (we reckly the ashes of 3 Glasgow Chaps to A.3 advance)	
	5th		A bad day for us — Captain P.D. FORREST being killed & 2/Lt PHILLIPS being wounded by a shell which burst just outside the door of their dugout — By this we lose not only a valuable officer but one who has been associated with the Bn for many years. Phillips died in 2:10	
	6th		Fine day — 1 O.R. in the evening — We hear today that from PHILLIPS died in 2:10 CCS at POPERINGHE & one Infantry lost another Brave & Promising officer — his	

Army Form C. 2118.

WAR DIARY
or
INTELLIGENCE SUMMARY.
(Erase heading not required.)

Instructions regarding War Diaries and Intelligence Summaries are contained in F. S. Regs., Part II. and the Staff Manual respectively. Title pages will be prepared in manuscript.

Place	Date	Hour	Summary of Events and Information	Remarks and references to Appendices
YPRES	1916 6th FEBRUARY		was a good deal of shelling in the afternoon - especially 29 French & round B"H.Q. at MOUNT SORREL. In the evening we were very thankful to be relieved by the 5th YORKS. The relief was not carried out till fairly late however and we had all the extra trouble of loading up & parting back some five hundred pairs of gum boots - The Battalion eventually got back to DUKEBUSCH HUTS between 1 am & 2 am in the morning.	Huts 28
		7h --	Cleaning up - inspections etc	
		8h --	Fine day - training carried out in accordance with programme laid down by the Brigade	
		9h --	Corps Commander Visits the Huts - No B'n at DUKEBUSCH BATHS - Lt ADAMS goes off on leave	
		10h --	Musketry - has rate of 31st Range - Concert on the Sergeants Mess in the evening.	
		11h --	Wet day - Excellent concert in the Y.M.C.A (by Martin Bruce Low & party from 24 Field Ambulance - heavy firing to the north of YPRES during the night.	
		2h --	G.O.C. Review relieves from Cave & Cpl Bruce Low goes back to the Field Ambulance. A lot of firing all day - We Joephane to go back to the trenches - Both attacks somewhere in the north part of the Salient. Orders dinner out. The Brigade relieves the 151st Bn. - we relieve the 6th D.L.I. in Railway dugouts with one Coy in MAPLE COPSE	

1577 Wt. W10791/1773 500,000 1/15 D. D. & L. A.D.S.S./Forms/C. 2118.

WAR DIARY
or
INTELLIGENCE SUMMARY
(Erase heading not required.)

Army Form C. 2118.

Place	Date	Hour	Summary of Events and Information	Remarks and references to Appendices
YPRES	1916 13th February		Fine day with very little shelling.	
	14th " "		Fine day — heavy shelling — German attack on several places round the salient & succeed in taking Trenches 30-34 from the 14th Division who are hanging on to the bit of 1. Counter-attacks by 14th Division in early morning fail. All attempts to advance in one Divisional front repulsed.	
	15th " "		Fine day & cold — Trenches 30-34 still in hands of the Boche — our officers go up to front line to look round the Clear Sector — a good deal of shelling — Counter-attack by 14th Division in early morning fails, except to take back a small position on Trench — May guns — Bulln moves up to relieve 9th N.F.	
	16th " "		in right sub sector of left sector. Trenches A.H. to R.12. 14th Division hand over the lost trenches on the evening — A few whizz bangs over our trenches (9.H. to R.11.) but inclusive at stand to — otherwise quiet day. S.C.Rumnell.	
	18th " "		Wet day — very quiet — no shelling. Bright moonlight samples sent on Corse. and Watching — Our Patrols are constantly sent out to ascertain if the Germans are working in their new posts in front of CLONMEL COPSE. 1 O.R. killed. 2 O.R. wounded	
	19th " "		Dull wet day — Enemy fired a number of Rainbow rockets A.H. ? about the bottom	

WAR DIARY or INTELLIGENCE SUMMARY

Army Form C. 2118.

Place	Date	Hour	Summary of Events and Information	Remarks and references to Appendices
YPRES	19th February		Trenches handed off 4th N.F. in several places have to work all night building up etc — a lot of ruining done all along the front.	
	20th		Quiet day. Battn relieved by 9th N.F. Moved into close support in MAPLE COPSE — Lt. SWAN goes to hospital & Lt. ADAMS returns from leave.	
	21st		Battn is distributed amongst supporting points & dugouts in SANCTUARY W., ARMAGH WOOD — H.Q. in MAPLE COPSE. 1 O.R. killed.	
	22nd		Some snow — working parties & carrying parties supplied by all coys — Line	
	23rd		Snow & frost — very cold. — A few shells into MAPLE COPSE in morning — otherwise quiet	
	24th		Bn is relieved by 11th Yorks & returns to DIKEBUSCH HUTS — very troublesome walking owing to the french roads as they are covered with a coating & ice & no lights all over the place.	
	25th		Battn bathes at DICKEBUSCH & POPERINGHE baths.	
	26th		Practice in Bombing Range — over those two limbs who have not already.	
	More so — Heavy bombardment of enemy's position on BLUFF in evening.			
	27th day — Sunday — usual services in Y.M.C.A. tent. — 4th N.F. are moved from SCOTTISH LINES to DIKEBUSCH HUTS and we and the 6th have to crowd up to make room			

WAR DIARY
or
INTELLIGENCE SUMMARY.

Army Form C. 2118.

Place	Date	Hour	Summary of Events and Information	Remarks and references to Appendices
YPRES	1916 27th FEBRUARY		For them - we expect to be moved up at any time on to Plackhart - the 9th Division to going to retake the BLUFF and the first trenches & we have to be ready in case of counter attack on the part of the Boche.	Sheet 28.
	28th		Hot day - Battn confined to camp - Lectures.	
	29th		Fine day - still confined to camp - Receive orders that we are not moving to trenches that night -	

Confidential

War Diary

of

5th Bn Northumberland Fusiliers

from 1st March 1916 to 31st March 1916.

(Volume ~~X~~ VII)

Charles Turner
LT. COLONEL
COMDG. 5th. NORTHUMBERLAND FUSILIERS

WAR DIARY
or
INTELLIGENCE SUMMARY.

Army Form C. 2118.

Place	Date	Hour	Summary of Events and Information	Remarks and references to Appendices
YPRES	1916 1st March		Bn. in DICKEBUSCH HUTS in Divisional Reserve – In the ordinary course of events we should return to the trenches tonight, but owing to the coming attack on the Bluff, reliefs are postponed. The Bn. is ordered to be ready to move at an hours notice. Tomorrow is allowed to dress the vicinity of the huts - The weather remains fine & our artillery is very active during the day, particularly during the afternoon when enemy's trenches on the Bluff, were heavily bombarded.	
	2nd		4.30 am. attack on the Bluff took place with great success. Tom seemed to reveal all the first trenches are retaken by the Division on our right, who also succeeded in taking a salient of the enemy's original front trench with 5 officers & 246 prisoners – In the evening the Bn. moved up to the night-held section of the Right Brigade into Hill 60. One company of the 6th 8th Midds trenches 34L & 34L Lulford. A Coy 58 Trench C Coy 39 trench B Coy 40 Trench & N Coy 41S & 44b. The enemy had established a barrage across the Railway Cutting & we had some difficulty in carrying out the relief. Fortunately our casualties were very small considering the amount of hostile shell fire. A box bar I man killed & 2 wounded – The 6th Bn. attack! 2 killed & 1 wounded – Bn. H.L. behind the DUMP had been heavily shelled for 2 hours & the shelling continued throughout	A.V.

WAR DIARY or INTELLIGENCE SUMMARY

Army Form C. 2118.

Place	Date	Hour	Summary of Events and Information	Remarks and references to Appendices
YPRES	2nd March		The night without casualty. The trenches especially the support lines have been very badly knocked in & the 8th D.L.I. whom we relieve have been unable to remove the dead who unfortunately number about 40. There are also about 50 wounded left - to be evacuated, but owing to the enemy's barrage this cannot be done. Relief complete about 11pm.	
	3rd March		Shelling of Bn. Headquarters commenced 11am. Enemy's Artillery does not trouble front line & work of burying dead & evacuating wounded is carried on all day. Parties are also busy rebuilding damaged parapets in front line & endeavouring to drain off accumulated water. Heavy snowstorm in the afternoon. Owing to the number of dugouts which have been blown in & as the support line is untenable there is little shelter for the men - most of whom are soaked through. Their spirits however are excellent & they are remarkably cheery - A Coy. strength of 36 which joined last week & which now numbers about 20 - The remainder having one sick - one killed & two wounded - is experiencing life in the trenches for the first time - Ration Parties have great difficulty in getting up lines owing to the railway line having been daily punished during the recent shelling & consequently the ration could not be worked. Rations & stores had to be	

WAR DIARY or INTELLIGENCE SUMMARY

Army Form C. 2118.

Place	Date	Hour	Summary of Events and Information	Remarks and references to Appendices
YPRES	1916 3rd March 4th		Carried by hand from ZILLEBEKE STATION 1/4 to the trenches – Very heavy snow storm – makes already wet trenches very uncomfortable – The Hun however is very quiet – undoubtedly devoting his energies to repairing his very badly wrecked trenches – Our artillery bombardment has been most effective as can be seen & as reported by prisoners captured on our right. Enemy blew in one of our mine galleries, killing two of our miners who were in the act of preparing to blow in enemy's gallery – Explosion forms crater in front of 39 trench. The Bn has now evacuated all the wounded left by the 8th D.L.I. 9th D.L.I. & 7th D.L.I. – Total number of wounded evacuated during the last two days is over seventy & together with assistance of close supporting Coy of 6th Bn we have turned twenty four – This together with the clearing of the front line trenches has taken up all our time & labour – Lieut A.H. TOPHAM Signalling Sergt is gazetted 2nd Lieutenant in the Battalion joins us as Signalling Officer with Headquarters.	W.
	5th March		A fine sunny morning giving the men an opportunity of getting somewhat dry, the Hun remains very quiet which is exceptional for a Sunday which he	

WAR DIARY or INTELLIGENCE SUMMARY

Army Form C. 2118.

Place	Date	Hour	Summary of Events and Information	Remarks and references to Appendices
YPRES	1916 5th March		generally makes a day of plate & shapes us accordingly — undoubtedly he is still slowly recovering from his shock of last week. Work on the support lines was commenced. Thumping as engaged in — No casualties — Heavy fall of snow at night	
	6th March		Snowing — but a quiet day — little battle shelling — no casualties. Bn. (less one to Brigade Reserve) is relieved by the 4th Bn N.F. Headquarters & H. & D. Coys are quartered in BEDFORD HOUSE. "A" Coy very congested in dugouts just behind a battery which fortunately seldom fires. B & D Coys in the stables also very cramped — Incidentally these are famous mining stables of Baron Rosendahl who according to rumour was shot as a Spy on the doorstep of the house. C Coy is quartered in camp at SWAN CHATEAU late Brigade Headquarters of the 149th Brigade — the officers are in comparatively luxury, their Messroom containing a fire place, arm chairs & other luxuries. BEDFORD HOUSE containing a dressing station for Brigade on our right — many cases of trench feet can be seen — men who have been up to their waist in water for two days in our trenches on the Bluff. Brigade stand all day — Battalion resting & drying. Feet infections?	IV/1

WAR DIARY or INTELLIGENCE SUMMARY

Army Form C. 2118.

Place	Date	Hour	Summary of Events and Information	Remarks and references to Appendices
YPRES	1916 7th March		Nothing - We see quite a number of jets of Trench Gas from Ypres on our right & their defences seem to be intense - Working parties supplied for the evening to road head at SHRAPNEL CORNER to carry Engineers stores from ZILLEBEKE STATION to the trenches. No shells near our billets or dugouts & two bivvied heavily all night & the ground is there a four inches thick in mud. Fine day however & brilliant sunshine. Men still resting & cleaning up after our toil in the trenches. We move up to close support of the trenches again. Br. Headquarters to SQUARE WOOD. B. Coy. to Trenches 8½ & 9½. C.Coy. to H.Q. support. A9. & GLASGOW CROSS - D.Coy. to X Trench 9 & Coy. to LARCHWOOD DUGOUTS & R.7.	
	8th			
	9th		A fine clear day taken advantage of by the enemy who shelled our trenches to a certain amount of damage. A Coy. have two men killed in R.7 & Machine Gunners from the Battalion are killed in M.5. The enemies a Machine Gun in the air placed at large road opposite "Forster" machine & Enfiled trenching to plane of ours. The Forster have also two trays but a point over a hanger - suddenly diving down with two machine guns in action - Cloudy	

WAR DIARY
or
INTELLIGENCE SUMMARY.

Army Form C. 2118.

Place	Date	Hour	Summary of Events and Information	Remarks and references to Appendices
YPRES	1916 9th March		machine guns & attempts to escape – but the Fokker recovering perfectly circles round its foe many above are more carbonic the fight – our plane does not appear to be armed and is so slow as unable to find any resistance. The "Fokker" does again & the British Plane falls over long to the ground – both observer undoubtedly killed. The Fokker rises into the air again but instead of making for home immediately it continues to reconnoitre our line – About six Fokker & German anti-aircraft guns about 50 minutes from a Lewis Gun in MAPLE COPSE is all the hate it causes from us. Two other many other onlookers what we have witnessed leads us to doubt the statistical statement that we hold the superiority in the air. Our 8 inch guns bombarded the DOGS TOOTH fact there are many duds. "We go over late, the one for German that goes into a tramcar."	
	10th March		From again – On the move once again – A Coy goes to 39 Trench – B to 38, C to 40, D to H1, H5, H45 – two companies of the H. 9th N.F. attached – are goes to 34L & the other to LARCHWOOD DUGOUTS & P.7 Two OCCs	

Army Form C. 2118.

WAR DIARY
or
INTELLIGENCE SUMMARY.
(Erase heading not required.)

Place	Date	Hour	Summary of Events and Information	Remarks and references to Appendices
YPRES	1916 10th March		Officers arrive at 8th N.L. posted to A boy. Another officer 2/Lieut A.E. KENDELL reports at the hut but unfortunately has to go back. 2/Lieut DODDS departs to hospital sick. Our heavies & 18 pounders bombard Hun lines throughout the night — no retaliation from the Hun.	
		11th	A fine morning & quiet up till 11pm. Our bombardment continues 9.2 Howitzers, Trench 4.5 & 18 pounders. At 11 pm Enemy's artillery opened fire at Trenches heavily bombarded the cutting of the YPRES/MENIN Railway at "BRIDGE" & Trenches 392 to 11/5 — This bombardment continued without a lull throughout the night — 9th Headquarters at the "DUMP" being heavily strafed. 2/Lieut TOVEY goes to hospital sick —	
		12th	Fine day — Enemy's bombardment continues till 4am exactly twelve hours. Robin Yankees unable to get down the railway until 11.15 am. During the remainder of the day enemy (a few stray guns) — we are able to get an idea of the damage done to the trenches & work of repairing same is immediately begun. LOVERS LANE is cleared?	𝓊

WAR DIARY
or
INTELLIGENCE SUMMARY
(Erase heading not required.)

Army Form C. 2118.

Place	Date	Hour	Summary of Events and Information	Remarks and references to Appendices
YPRES	1916 12th March	—	Work pushed on BENSHAM AVENUE, JOHNSONS TRENCH – JACKSON STREET – The support lines are absolutely wrecked. Parapets in the front line where there are any breaks are repaired – Work continued throughout the whole of the night. Other men have been killed & about 14 wounded (yesterday) 2/Lieut TOPHAM who only joined us as an officer a few days ago as badly wounded in the face this morning – We find the barby two wounded his ration of ammunition will (at us not in peace for the last two days – The men badly need rest & a change – but are remarkably cheery & in splendid spirits –	
YPRES	13th	—	A fine morning and work at obtaining our badly damaged trenches is continued – Communication trenches BENSHAM AVENUE, LOVERS LANE, and JOHNSONS TRENCH, are cleared – and the support line trenches are cleared but far from being in a fightable condition – a large amount of water has accumulated in this line & will only be got away with difficulty. With the exception of about half a dozen whizz-bangs over H1 the enemy remained quiet for the rest of the day.	

WAR DIARY
or
INTELLIGENCE SUMMARY

Army Form C. 2118.

Place	Date	Hour	Summary of Events and Information	Remarks and references to Appendices
YPRES	1916 15th March		A magnificent day - brilliant sunshine and hot - weather like this does us a world of good. Still laid at Scott Copse in support line trenches. The enemy artillery quiet, undoubtedly during spent all his ration on us on Saturday night. We are relieved by the 8th D.L.I. and march to the YPRES-VLAMERTINGHE road, where at 2 am we entrain for POPERINGHE.	
POPERINGHE	16th		Arriving POPERINGHE at 3.30 am. Companies found billets awaiting them then slept till midday, then had dinners & during the afternoon new clothing was issued to those who had need of same and equipment was overhauled and cleaned up. — A beautiful day - Battalion at the baths - washed and arrayed in clean new clothes, the men look very spick & span and the arrival of the GUARDS division in POPERINGHE today - blended looking fellows - helps to still further smarten them up - everyone trying to look (not a Guardsman) the "Francais" & other attractions in the town claim attention in the evening - the change west is doing everyone a tremendous amount of good.	

WAR DIARY
or
INTELLIGENCE SUMMARY.

(Erase heading not required.)

Army Form C. 2118.

Place	Date	Hour	Summary of Events and Information	Remarks and references to Appendices
	1916			
POPERINGHE	17th March	—	Another fine day — The Brigadier inspected the Companies at their billets & expressed himself satisfied with the good pieces out & smart appearance. He received the sad news that Capt BARRETT, lately of & 4th commanding A Coy 8th YORKSHIRE REGT has been killed — The News will known to us as Adjutant of the 6th Battalion N.F. Lt. BAINBRIDGE, Adjutant of the 6th Bn. N.F. has also died of his wounds.	
POPERINGHE	18th	—	Stay six days in POPERINGHE, so we at first arranged has been too good to last — and now at the end of four we are ordered back to the mud at DICKEBUSCH. Leaving POPERINGHE at 4 o'clock arrived at our old huts at 6 p.m. Three new officers arrive 2/Lieut LAWSON (B Coy) 2/Lieut NORRIS (A Coy) 2/Lieut BOULTON (A Coy)	⚑
DICKEBUSCH	19th	—	Fine day — Services in Y.M.C.A.	
HUTS	20th	—	Company parades & bombing practices carried out — A good deal of heavy shelling during the day & one or two get party close to the huts	
	21st	—	Wet day — Battalion practices the attack with bombers in the morning on the "dummy trench" — Return to trenches in the evening. March off from huts	

WAR DIARY
or
INTELLIGENCE SUMMARY.
(Erase heading not required.)

Army Form C. 2118.

Place	Date	Hour	Summary of Events and Information	Remarks and references to Appendices
DICKEBUSCH HUTS	1916 21st March		about 6.30 p.m. — Allotrihution. A+D. Coys GLASGOW CRoss & X Trench — C.Coy H.I. ? H.I.S. & H.S. & B. Coy R.Y. & LARCHWOOD DUGOUTS — H.Q. SQUARE WOOD — Quiet night — no trouble going on	
YPRES	22nd "		Fairly quiet day — no casualties — 2/Lt GILL to hospital sick — News is received that Colonel LUHRS is to be called home for munition work.	
	23rd "		Very quiet day. No casualties — a few "sausages" over H.I. in the morning	
	24th "		Quiet day up till 11am when the enemy broke out and started shelling all round — particularly on H.I.S. H.I.S. — which was heavily shelled for a time — Our C. Coy was being relieved by a Coy of the 2nd N.F. & luckily succeeded in getting away without any casualties — C.Coy went to dugouts in ARMAGH WOOD. Some dozen fair sized shells were put into SQUARE WOOD — 2/Lt. RIBSON being slightly wounded value I.O.R. — all quiet again about 9.30 p.m.	
	25th "		In the morning ARMAGH WOOD was crumped rather madly 20 R. being killed & 2/Lt ELLIS being wounded — The dugout in which ELLIS was sitting was hit by the shell who was lucky in not being killed, as it was his leg was fractured and we look a very valuable officer for an important period. Lieut-Col. F.C. TURNER C.M.G. took over command from Lt. Col. J.L.R. Glasson	

Army Form C. 2118.

WAR DIARY
or
INTELLIGENCE SUMMARY.
(Erase heading not required.)

Place	Date	Hour	Summary of Events and Information	Remarks and references to Appendices
YPRES	1916 25th April		LUHRS reconnoitering zone on Divisional Front. 2/Lieut BLACKBURN & 2/Lieut WINTON to hospital sick.	
	26th		The one was lamentably short of officers – our trench strength being 11. A quiet day, no casualties.	
	27th		Turned up at 4.15 am by very heavy bombardment to the south – soon found out that our trenches were not affected – though some shells were put over X trench. Killing one man of 10 Bn. – Bombardment continued until about 9 am. – More information that the 3rd division have made a small attack near ST ELOI having up two mines. Remainder of day fairly quiet. Interchanged trenches with 4th N.F. that night – we took over A3 to A9. Mostly Bat. right – Relf. Coy completed till 3.30 a.m. Lieut Day – I.O.R. attd. The fd trenches much improved since we were last in them.	
	28th		Quiet day – Relieved in the evening by the 16th CANADIAN REGT – no long letter for Divisional Relief at last – returned safely to DICKEBUSCH	

WAR DIARY
or
INTELLIGENCE SUMMARY.
(Erase heading not required.)

Place	Date	Hour	Summary of Events and Information	Remarks and references to Appendices
YPRES	1916 29th March		HUTS for the last time we hope – very cold night – got in about 3 a.m.	
	30th		Got up about 9.30 a.m. when the Bosche suddenly began shelling near the camp – after one shell had gone into the camp it cleared all the men out – and it was lucky we did so – as after that some large calibre shells were put right amongst the huts as it was, damaging several huts, but doing no other damage After this little entertainment all was quiet for the rest of the day	
	31st		Did nothing but rest and prepare for the (march tomorrow. We are due to march out of camp at 8.30 a.m.)	

Confidential

War Diary

-of-

5th Bn Northumberland Fusiliers. T.F.

from 1st April 1916 to 30th April 1916.

(Volume 7) VIII

30th April. 1916.

Arnold Nixon Major
for Lieut Colonel
Comdg 5th Bn Northumberland. Fus.

Army Form C. 2118.

WAR DIARY
or
INTELLIGENCE SUMMARY.
(Erase heading not required.)

Instructions regarding War Diaries and Intelligence Summaries are contained in F. S. Regs., Part II. and the Staff Manual respectively. Title pages will be prepared in manuscript.

Place	Date	Hour	Summary of Events and Information	Remarks and references to Appendices
	1916.			
In the Field	April 1st		Battalion marched from the huts at DICKEBUSCH to billets in farms near BERTHEN — The weather was delightfully fine & sunny, & the march a pleasant one — for the second time we bid goodbye to the YPRES Salient & all hunt we shall never have to live in it again — Major Irwin & 2 hired Worlds return to the Battalion after being sick in hospital.	Sheet 28
LOCRE	April 2nd		Another beautiful day — making the country look very charming — Bn attended Church Parade in the morning & in the afternoon marched to billets in LOCRE VILLAGE — staring taken over billets from the 11th Bn N.Z. who arrived the previous night, we are now in Divisional Reserve to the new Divisional Front.	
	April 3rd		Our billets are comfortable & the men enjoy a day resting & cleaning up. Officers visit our new trenches, which we are to take over on the 8th, and which we regret to find are not good ones — Apparently the 2nd Canadian Division has not been seriously troubled by the enemy during its existence here, for the trenches chiefly consist of breastworks without parados — giving little protection to shell fire — The same is particularly good & very strong — WATLING STREET is the only communication trench leading to our sector of the front line & this is overlooked by the enemy on WYTSCHAETE RIDGE and in the PETIT BOIS. The enemy have excellent observation posts on the RIDGE, in the HOSPICE and in the HOLLANDSCHESCHUUR FARM. These posts look down	

1577 Wt. W10791/1773 500,000 1/15 D.D.& L. A.D.S.S./Forms/C. 2118.

WAR DIARY
or
INTELLIGENCE SUMMARY.
(Erase heading not required.)

Army Form C. 2118.

Place	Date	Hour	Summary of Events and Information	Remarks and references to Appendices
LOCRE	1916. April 3rd		into our trenches & are no doubt most useful to the enemy as no serious attempt appears to have been made to conceal the ruins from them — Battalion HeadQuarters is in a farm known as YORK HOUSE which is little damaged considering its position & very comfortable, but a considerable distance from the line. The front line we hold consists of what are known as the K Trenches & the L Trenches — On the Battalion right is K2 Trench which is isolated & only held by night. Next come Trenches K2H, & K2B both of which are also isolated, there being gaps between them & no communication trench to them. L1, L2, L3, L4, & L5 all connected up, complete the Battalion "front line" — On our immediate left are the 151st Brigade — & on our right another Battalion of our own Brigade — The Support trenches consisting chiefly of breastworks are very close to the front line and are known as K25, which stands by itself but is accessible by day, L5, L6, & L7R, all of which are joined up, & L7L an isolated Trench, which can only be reached by night. The civilian inhabitants are living very close up to the line & few farms behind Battalion HeadQuarters have been seriously damaged — Ploughing the land is being carried on by the local farmers in front of our 18 Pounder Battery Positions — 2 Lt Gill returns to the Battalion from hospital.	Sheet 28

WAR DIARY
or
INTELLIGENCE SUMMARY.
(Erase heading not required.)

Army Form C. 2118.

Place	Date	Hour	Summary of Events and Information	Remarks and references to Appendices
LOCRE.	1916. April 4th		Battalion commences a course of training – Beautiful day & men thoroughly enjoy a short route march – The change of scenery after the YPRES salient, does one good.	Sheet 28.
"	April 5th		Fine weather continues – Companies march to WESTOUTRE & enjoy baths & a clean change of under clothes. Very heavy firing heard coming from the vicinity of ST. ELOI & continuing all the afternoon & night	
"	April 6th		Col. Turner takes command of the Brigade during the absence of General Clifford who is gone on leave. Major Irwin temporary in command of the Battalion. – Training continues – Physical Drill from 7a.m to 8 a.m. – Coy. work from 9 a.m to 10 a.m. From 11 a.m to 12 noon – Lectures during the afternoon from 2 pm to 3 pm. – Very heavy cannonade heard during the night coming from ST ELOI – Another beautiful day.	
"	April 7th		Cloudy but fine day – Battalion spent morning route marching – Church parade in the evening.	
"	April 8th		A delightfully fine day. – Morning spent in preparing for the Trenches – 2nd Boulton gn's to hospital sick – In the evening we moved to the trenches. A Coy occupy. K2, K2A & K2B – B Coy S.P.13, L6, L7R, L7L. – C Coy L2, L3, L4, L15 – D Coy L14, L15. We relieved the 14th N.F. & the relief was completed by 11:30 p.m. – Heavy shelling going on at ST. ELOI. The Bn is very short of officers in the line – A Coy commanded by 2 Lt Easten has only	

Army Form C. 2118.

WAR DIARY
or
INTELLIGENCE SUMMARY.

(Erase heading not required.)

Instructions regarding War Diaries and Intelligence Summaries are contained in F. S. Regs., Part II. and the Staff Manual respectively. Title pages will be prepared in manuscript.

Place	Date	Hour	Summary of Events and Information	Remarks and references to Appendices
LOCRE.	1916 April 8th		One other officer 2/Lt Morris — B Coy Capt Pattison, 2/Lts Bizot & Hanson — C Coy 2/Lt Adams, 2/Lts Gill & Thomas — D Coy. Capt North being on leave, Capt Hart is in command, & 2/Lt Dodds. Headquarters consist of Major Irwin & Capt Yate.	Nos 18.
	April 9th		All our trenches have been very heavily shelled today — an a our artillery retaliation has been very poor — Two men have been killed & 5 wounded.	
	April 10th		A very fine day — of which the enemy's artillery took full advantage. The bombardment of our trenches has gone on all day & all night & we are fortunate only to have five men wounded during the 24 hours. We had hoped that this would be a peaceful part of the line — but are disappointed.	
	April 11th		Another fine day — The bombardment of the trenches shews no signs of abating — going on by day & by night — 171 is untenable by day, & we have decided only to occupy this trench by night — The K trenches have had a very bad time as a result of which B Coy relieved A Coy tonight — Enemy have established a barrage across WATLING STREET doing considerable damage to the trench — Again our casualties have been remarkably low, considering the severe bombardment — one man killed & 7 wounded. The shelling is making it impossible to do any work & there is a considerable gap in the line	

1577 Wt.W10791/1773 500,000 1/15 D. D. & L. A.D.S.S./Forms/C. 2118.

Army Form C. 2118.

WAR DIARY
or
INTELLIGENCE SUMMARY.
(Erase heading not required.)

Instructions regarding War Diaries and Intelligence Summaries are contained in F. S. Regs., Part II. and the Staff Manual respectively. Title pages will be prepared in manuscript.

Place	Date	Hour	Summary of Events and Information	Remarks and references to Appendices
LOCRE.	1916. April 11th		Between L5 & the 151st Brigade, which cannot be built up — Lt. Thomas goes to hospital sick —	Sheet 28
"	April 12th		Heavy shelling of our trenches still going on, but the Battalion on our right seems to be having an even worse time. — Our Artillery retaliation certainly shows signs of improving, but is unable to force the enemy's fire to slacken. 2 L/Cpls have been killed & a man wounded	
"	April 13th		It had been intended to keep us in the line for 6 days, but owing to the rough time the 6th Bn 9 Outshires have had, the Brigade are going to relieve the front line tonight & the 4th & 7th Bns will take our places — So add to our troubles — all leave has suddenly been stopped & all officers & men on leave are to be back by the 18th — The enemy has not shelled us so badly today & there have been no casualties — Relief by the 4th N.F. was carried out by 9.45 p.m. & A.Q. A & B coys proceeded to R.C. Farm, C coy to SIEGE Farm & D coy to WAISONVILLE DUG-OUTS — We are now in Brigade Reserve.	
"	April 14th		A beautifully fine day & the men obtained a well earned rest — Large working parties were supplied at night however to the R.E.s & Pioneer Bn. — 2 Lis MAGEE & ALDER, two new officers arrive & are posted, the former to C coy & the latter to A coy.	
"	April 15th		Another delightfully fine day — men resting all day and on working parties at night	

Army Form C. 2118.

WAR DIARY
or
INTELLIGENCE SUMMARY.
(Erase heading not required.)

Instructions regarding War Diaries and Intelligence Summaries are contained in F. S. Regs., Part II. and the Staff Manual respectively. Title pages will be prepared in manuscript.

Place	Date	Hour	Summary of Events and Information	Remarks and references to Appendices
LOCRE.	1916 April 16th		Fine day. Church Parades in the afternoon for A & B Coys at R.C. Farm & C Coy at SIEGE Farm. Large working parties supplied at night after which C Coy relieved D Coy in WATSONVILLE DUG-OUTS — the latter Coy coming back to SIEGE FARM — WATSONVILLE DUG-OUTS are just behind the support line & are often heavily shelled — SIEGE FARM on the other hand is occupied by civilians who are unperturbed by the authorities as pro German — Mein farm has never had a shell near it despite its close proximity to the line — Col. Turner resumes command of the Battalion.	Sheet 28
"	April 17th		A miserable wet day. The C.O. second in command & officers of D Coy inspect the subsidiary line trenches — which though very wet are well sighted the wire in front is strong & good. The whole of the Battalion are out on working parties at night — Capt North returns from leave.	
"	April 18th		Another miserable wet day. The Battalion returns to the trenches & relieves the 4th N.F., companies occupying the same positions as those they left on the 13th instant. — During the relief, enemy's machine guns were unpleasantly active, but no casualties occurred. Relief carried out by 9.30 p.m. — Lt Holloway returns from leave having been recalled after only a few days at home.	
"	April 19th		A showery day — Enemy fairly quiet all day & no casualties. Lr Matthews arrives &	

WAR DIARY
or
INTELLIGENCE SUMMARY.
(Erase heading not required.)

Army Form C. 2118.

Place	Date	Hour	Summary of Events and Information	Remarks and references to Appendices
	1916.			
LOCRE.	April 19th		Reports to the Battalion – is appointed Batt's Transport Officer which enables Capt. Kinsella to devote the whole of his attention to Brigade Transport Duties.	Sheet 28
"	April 20th		A wet day – fortunately little shelling on Batt's front, our neighbours on the right and left are, however, being heavily shelled. No casualties.	
"	April 21st		Good Friday & a fine morning of which the enemy's artillery took full advantage & bombarded us heavily – WATLING STREET – and Bn. BATTLE HEADQUARTERS are severely shelled – several direct hits have been made on Battle HeadQuarters which fortunately are empty. They are apparently marked down by the enemy – Most of the enemy's shelling passed just over the front line – bursting either in front of the support line or just behind it. Considering the severity of the bombardment, the damage done was extraordinarily small & we have been exceedingly fortunate in having no casualties. 2Lts Winton & Snelect arrive – the former from hospital & is posted to B Coy, the latter goes to A. Coy.	
"	April 22nd		A miserable wet day – The K trenches have a bad time from an enemy trench mortar at "Stand to" – 4 men killed & 3 wounded in K2A. There was not much shelling during the rest of the morning, but about 5 p.m. in the afternoon the enemy suddenly opened a tremendous shell fire on our parapets – damaging same in several places – so severe	

WAR DIARY or INTELLIGENCE SUMMARY

Army Form C. 2118.

Place	Date	Hour	Summary of Events and Information	Remarks and references to Appendices
LOCRE	1918 April 22nd		was the bombardment we were led to believe an infantry attack was likely to be launched. Our artillery retaliation was splendid & the enemy's trench was badly damaged. Again fortune favoured us in the matter of casualties there being no others than those already mentioned. The Battalion was relieved by the 14th N.F. & proceeded to billets in Divisional Reserve at LOCRE. We understand that the Division is to be relieved & we hope not to see front line trenches again for at least a month.	Sheet 28
"	April 23rd		St George's Day & beautifully fine. Battn attended Divine Service – Red & White Roses were distributed & worn – The Battn Commander & Coy Officers spent the day on KEMMEL HILL viewing our new trenches on the hill side – Lt Winton departs to hospital again sick.	
"	April 24th		Battn moved in the morning to YORK HUTS, new huts hardly yet completed & on the LOCRE/BAILLEUL ROAD – In the afternoon A, B & C Coys moved out to the KEMMEL defences & relieved coys of the 14th Bn Royal Fusiliers, 12th Northumberland Fusiliers, & 13th Kings Liverpool Regiment respectively – These Battalions belong to the 9th Brigade of the 3rd Division & are taking up their position in the trenches we have just left – Battn Headquarters, Battn Bombers & D Coy are remaining at YORK HUTS.	
"	April 25th		Another delightful day – the weather is very hot – L.O. & 2nd in Command visited the	

WAR DIARY
INTELLIGENCE SUMMARY.

Army Form C. 2118.

Place	Date	Hour	Summary of Events and Information	Remarks and references to Appendices
LOCRE.	1916. April 25th		Companies on KEMMEL. They all look very happy & are enjoying the rest & change — D Coy spend the day resting & cleaning up the camp. 2nd Lts "Thomas & Smith arrive — the former from hospital goes back to C Coy, the latter posted to D Coy.	Sheet 78
"	April 26th		Another hot beautiful day — D Coy spend day improving & cleaning up camp. In the evening B & C Coys, who had been relieved by Coys of the 1st & 14th Bns N.F. respectively, returned to YORK HUTS.	
"	April 27th		The glorious weather continues. Today is the hottest day of this year — Coys employed on fatigue improving the camp. 2nd Lt Winton returns from hospital.	
"	April 28th		Another delightful day — Companies enjoy baths & clean change of under garments at LOCRE Baths — Inter company football matches are being played each afternoon — Enemy dropped several large shells unpleasantly near to the huts.	
"	April 29th		Still beautiful weather — Men are enjoying a thorough rest & doing no parades — 2nd Lieut Thompson arrives with a draft of 26 men — he is posted to A Coy & appointed Battalion Bombing Officer.	
"	April 30th		We were disturbed at 12.50 a.m by the gas alarm & sounds of very heavy shelling coming from vicinity of KEMMEL — The Battalion immediately "stood to" and at 1.10 a.m	

Army Form C. 2118.

WAR DIARY
or
INTELLIGENCE SUMMARY.
(Erase heading not required.)

Instructions regarding War Diaries and Intelligence Summaries are contained in F. S. Regs., Part II. and the Staff Manual respectively. Title pages will be prepared in manuscript.

Place	Date	Hour	Summary of Events and Information	Remarks and references to Appendices
	1916			
LOCRE	April 30	4¢	was ordered to occupy KEMMEL DEFENCES — Companies were very soon on the way & had taken up their positions in the trenches by 2.15 a.m. — By this time however the shelling was not so severe and a later died down considerably — It transpired that the enemy had attacked with gas in the vicinity of the MESSINES/WULVERGHEM road but had failed to occupy our trenches — We were ordered to return to YORK HUTS at 3.15 a.m. & were back by 4.30 a.m. Although the Battalion did nothing beyond occupying the trenches, this proved an excellent practise in case we have to conduct this operation again under more serious conditions. The remainder of the day was spent resting, the only parade being in the evening for Church — Lieut Willis arrived & is posted to D Coy.	Sheet 28

Army Form C. 2118.

WAR DIARY
or
INTELLIGENCE SUMMARY.
(Erase heading not required.)

Place	Date	Hour	Summary of Events and Information	Remarks and references to Appendices
LOCRE	1916. April 30th		NOMINAL ROLL OF OFFICERS	
			Head Quarters Lt Col. C. Turner. C.M.G. Major A. Irvin. Capt. P. Manson. (Medical Officer) Capt. V.A.C. Yate (adjt)	
			A. Coy. 2 Lieuts Gaskin, A.S. Winton, R. Boulton, A. Morris, C.V. Allen, and J.P. Thompson (Bombing Officer). 4 R.G. Smith. L. Surplice.	
			B. Coy. Capt. W.A. Patterson, 2 Lts. C. Bissett, M.W. Lawson,	
			C. Coy. Lt. N.V. Adams, 2 Lieuts A.W. Gill, L.A.S. Thomas, S.S. Magee.	
			D. Coy. Capt. L.M. North, Capt. W.N. Peek (kuis Gun) 2 Lieuts A.G. Dodd, O. Willis.	
			Transport Lieut S.W. Mathews. Quartermaster Lieut. R.J. Holloway.	

Confidential

War Diary

of

5th Bn Northumberland Fusiliers

From 1st May 1916 to 31st May 1916.

(Volume 8) 9

W. Watt Captain, Acting Adjutant
Jos [?] Lt Colonel.
Comdg. 5th Bn Northd Fus.

WAR DIARY
or
INTELLIGENCE SUMMARY

Army Form C. 2118.

Place	Date	Hour	Summary of Events and Information	Remarks and references to Appendices
	1916			
LOCRE	MAY 1st		The Month of May has chiefly been devoted to resting and training — the Battalion	See Sheet 28
LOCRE	MAY 14th		moved on the 11th from York Huts at LOCRE to rest billets on the BAILLEUL/ST JANS CAPELLE Road. (About a quarter of a mile from BAILLEUL) With the exception of D Coy who remained behind in our sector of the KEMMEL DEFENCES. This Company was relieved on the 11th inst by C Coy and on the 18th B Coy took their turn. — We were favoured with splendid weather during our period of rest and the men thoroughly enjoyed the change of scenery — the opportunities of visiting BAILLEUL and plenty of undisturbed sleep. Daily routine consisted of physical drill - bayonet fighting and running. Exercises from 7 to 4.45 am when breakfast was served. Company or Battalion parades from 9.30 am till 12.30 pm and lectures and inspections from 2 to 2.30 pm. Men were allowed into BAILLEUL from 4 pm till 4.30 pm. Many team football matches were played and each Company is now in possession of its own football colours and garments. The Battalion team defeated the 1/2 NORTHUMBERLANDS. by one goal to nothing after a draw and so	

WAR DIARY / INTELLIGENCE SUMMARY

Army Form C. 2118.

Place	Date	Hour	Summary of Events and Information	Remarks and references to Appendices
			Qualified for the final of the Brigade Football Competition. Unfortunately we were defeated in the match for the Cup by the 4th Batt. A great deal of time has been devoted to the training of officers and non-commissioned officers in special duties – Many of these were attached to various schools of instruction for brief periods, including the Divisional Defensive Gas school, Grenade school, Signalling School etc. All non-commissioned officers went to the N.C.O's School. Other courses which officers and men attended were on firing – Barbed Wiring – Gas – Engineering – Physical Training – and Bayonet Fighting – Various Schools of Instruction for Senior Officers were arranged by the Division and many officers visited, in a pleasant round in a motor bus, such places of interest as the Aerodrome at BAYEUL – Railheads – Ammunition Trains – Divisional workshops – Entraining, Grenade and Non-Commissioned officers schools etc. One or two officers were also attached for a few days to a Battery of R.F.A. – Several new officers have arrived from England and the Battalion is now well off for numbers – Below is a list of officers at present on the strength – Lt-Col C Yurver. C.M.G. Commanding	Sheet 28

Sheet 28

Major A. Sheun Second in Command. Capt. H.W. Hale. Adjutant. Capt. H. Leete. Intelligence Officer. 2nd Lt. Thompson. Bombing Officer. 2nd Lt. Alden. Signalling Officer. 2nd Lt. Matthews Transport and Lt. & Q.M. Holloway. – A Coy Commanded by 2nd Lt. Carter and 2nd Lt. Martin, Lieutts Boulton and Morris – B Coy Commanded by Capt. D. Patterson and 2nd Lts Bryett, Lawson, Winton, Wolfe, and Marriell – C Coy Commanded by Lt. Adams and Lts Gibson & 2nd Lts Gell, Thomas and Mc.Gee – D Coy Capt. North, and 2nd Lts Wells, Kendall and Bennet, – in addition Capt. Kinsella is Brigade Transport Officer, Lt. Keep Brigade Bombing Officer & Lt. Lagge Acting Staff Captain attached to the Inf. Brigade. – On April 22nd Battalion Carts were held which proved most successful and the services of the Divisional Band were much appreciated – The Battalion Transport was inspected on two occasions – Once by the Brigadier and Later by the Divisional Commander and most satisfactory reports were obtained –

Army Form C. 2118.

WAR DIARY
or
INTELLIGENCE SUMMARY.
(Erase heading not required.)

Instructions regarding War Diaries and Intelligence Summaries are contained in F. S. Regs., Part II. and the Staff Manual respectively. Title pages will be prepared in manuscript.

Place	Date	Hour	Summary of Events and Information	Remarks and references to Appendices
	1916			Sheet 25
BAILLEUL	23rd MAY		We were sorry when on the 23rd of the month we left the rest area and marched to LOCRE. – The Battalion visited here for two days and had tea – later proceeding to Brigade Reserve – B & D Coys to SIEGE FARM. Headquarters and A & C Coys to R.E. Farm. – Battalion relieved the 10th WEST YORKS of the 3rd Division	
LOCRE	24th MAY		Battalion moved into the front line taking over the same sector occupied in April. – A Coy took over S.P. 13 and WATSONVILLE DUGOUTS. B Coy L 2,3, +5. – C Coy K3, K2A a K2B. and D Coy L10 L1,S – Battalion Headquarters at YORK HOUSE. There was some shelling and machine gun fire during the relief but fortunately no casualties occured and the 13th KINGS LIVERPOOL REGIMENT was relieved by us by 11.30 pm.	
	25 MAY		A beautifully fine day. The 9th Brigade who were relieved was completed the linking up of the the trenches making it possible to walk from L1 K2A by day. – WATLING STREET has also been considerably improved, and L5 and the N trenches are linked up.	

1577 Wt. W10791/1773 500,000 1/15 D. D. & L. A.D.S.S./Forms/C. 2118.

WAR DIARY or INTELLIGENCE SUMMARY

Army Form C. 2118.

Place	Date	Hour	Summary of Events and Information	Remarks and references to Appendices
LOCRE	14/6			
	25th MAY		About 3 p.m. in the afternoon the enemy commenced a very heavy bombardment of our front trenches with shrapnel - gas, explosive and lachrymatory mortar bombs - all the trenches were badly damaged - particularly K2 A - L1 and L4 - and unfortunately we suffered many casualties - the Principals of which were 2/Lt Adams, 2/Lt Cohen, 2/Lt Gardell, 2/Lt Winterburn, Coy Sgt Major RAY of B Coy and JONES of C Coy and amongst others Sgts NIEL and NESBITT - All of whom were wounded. Total casualties to the day numbered 5 killed + 40 wounded including 5 officers. Sheet 28	
	26th MAY		Another quiet day: The enemy continues to annoy us at intervals with heavy mortar bombs and during the night our machine guns were very active - playing on to WATLING STREET and the advanced R.E. DUMP near SP13 - The enemy also sent over several small shells into WATLING STREET and the road near YORK HOUSE during the night - but no serious damage was done all of them were large	

WAR DIARY
or
INTELLIGENCE SUMMARY.

(Erase heading not required.)

Army Form C. 2118.

Remarks and references to Appendices

Sheet 2

Place	Date	Hour	Summary of Events and Information	Remarks
	1916			
HOOGE	27 MAY		working parties about a the line. Work of wiring & gun damaged trenches was continued throughout the day and night. Fine weather continues – Enemy's activity fifty. Consists in sending over large and small trench mortar bombs. This Artillery is comparatively quiet – During the night the German machine guns were again troublesome and our snipers were eventually called upon to put an end to his annoyance – Cpl KEEN of the Bedfords and Brigade Bombing Officer wounded.	
	28 MAY		A comparatively quiet day – and beautifully fine – the 1st Battalion of the Regiment relieved us during the evening and we returned to Brigade Reserve at SIEGE FARM & R.E. FARM. Despite the heavy machine gun fire this relief was carried out without a casualty. During the four days in the trenches our total casualties amount to 4 killed and 59 wounded. 2nd Lt. Y. Thomas goes to hospital and is we hear likely to be away for some time.	

(Note: we are to be retired tonight by the 4th R.F. & go into Brigade Reserve – 2 coys & 4 Hd)

WAR DIARY
or
INTELLIGENCE SUMMARY

Army Form C. 2118.

Place	Date	Hour	Summary of Events and Information	Remarks and references to Appendices
	1916			
LOCRE	28 May		at R.C. Farm. Troops at SIEGE FARM do not go — relieved on ??? they use to Billets	
	29		not have to [illegible] in ??? in Dug outs	
	30		The usual working parties at night (about 110) — 100 Rifles.	
			We have commenced digging shallow Trenches at R.C. Farm + SEIGE FARM in case of shelling — the above working parties (about 140) — one of the working parties was unfortunately caught by Trench Mortars somewhere in the I Trenches — 5 Rank being killed + 5 wounded.	
	31		Shallow trenches continued — working parties as usual — no casualties.	

On the field
June 1st 1916

[signature] Lieut Col
O/C 3/11 N?H [illegible]

£50
Vol 10.

95/n.7

Confidential

War Diary
of
5th Bn Northumberland Fusiliers
from 1st June 1916 to 30th June 1916
(Volume 9)

M White Capt. Adjutant
for Major
5th Northumberland Fusiliers

WAR DIARY
or
INTELLIGENCE SUMMARY.

Army Form C. 2118

Place	Date	Hour	Summary of Events and Information	Remarks and references to Appendices
LOCRE	10/6			
	June 1st		The following officers having come up from the Base, reported for duty on the 30/5/16	CASUALTIES. June 1st – June 5
			2ND LIEUT T.G. GARRARD.	
			2ND LIEUT O.R. BROWNE	KILLED 2.O.R.
			2ND LIEUT A.R. PARK	WOUNDED. 12.O.R.
			2ND LIEUT K. McDONALD.	
			2ND LIEUT A.E. MOORHOUSE.	
			The Battalion relieved the 11th N.F. in the left sector on the night of the 1st June – Relief complete about 11 p.m. – no casualties.	
	" 2nd		Quiet day – Casualties – Killed 1 O.R. – Wounded 2 O.R.	
	" 3rd		Quiet day – At 12:30 a.m. on the morning of the 4th our Guns bombarded the trenches opposite us heavily – the Division on our right were executing a raid – the Germans replied fairly heavy on our trenches, but our casualties were slight – 3 O.R. wounded. All was quiet again by 1:30 a.m.	
	" 4th		Quiet day – except for some 30 to 40 H.2."s fired around the "Laitrie" about lunch time – Headquarters very busy digging for nose-caps for the rest of the afternoon.	
	" 5th		1 man killed during the night – Fairly quiet day – except for some trench mortaring	

WAR DIARY
or
INTELLIGENCE SUMMARY.
(Erase heading not required.)

Army Form C. 2118.

Place	Date	Hour	Summary of Events and Information	Remarks and references to Appendices
LOCRE	1916. JUNE 5		Shelling in the afternoon — Casualties 1 O.R. wounded.	
			Relieved by 1st N.F. & return to DONCASTER HUTS, LOCRE.	
"	6		Wet day — Battalion bathing at WESTOUTRE.	
			Our casualties from May 24th to June 5th am as follows:—	
			Killed or died of wounds 19 O.R.	
			Wounded 5 Officers 15 O.R.	
			Total 5 Officers 94 O.R.	
"	7		Usual routine in camp — We find DONCASTER HUTS which were to be known as YORK HUTS much improved — particularly the Officers Quarters — which were not complete when we were there before.	
			No 2212 L/Cpl STRAUGHAN. J. awarded the Military Medal for gallantry on 25/5/16.	
"	8		2150 Pte. FANNAN E.L. } join for duty from 3rd line.	
			2nd LIEUT FORSTER	
"	9		Return to left Subsector — Companies leave LOCRE 8pm — Relief complete 11.30pm — Quiet night.	
"	10		Enemy blew up a mine in front of K1 about to sump forming a crater crater —	

WAR DIARY
or
INTELLIGENCE SUMMARY.
(Erase heading not required.)

Army Form C. 2118.

Place	Date	Hour	Summary of Events and Information	Remarks and references to Appendices
LOCRE	1916 June 10th		Quiet day – a good deal of shelling going on but our trenches were left alone. 1 O.R. sniped killed in the evening	CASUALTIES JUNE 10 – JUNE 19 KILLED 1 O.R. WOUNDED 3 O.R.
	" 11th		A quiet day – no casualties	
	" 12th		Very wet – quiet – Enemy trench mortars active in the evening – 3 O.R. wounded – Wet night.	
	" 13th		Still wet – Quiet – no casualties – Relieved by 4th NF – Go back to R.C. & Siege Farms as usual.	
	" 14th		Heavy cold shower day – about 200 men out on working parties in the evening.	
	" 15th		Dull & cold – Working parties at night – The huns dropped on "hour" at 11 p.m. on 14th	
	" 16th		"Fine day" – about 12.30 a.m. on 17th Enemy opened a heavy bombardment on our front – our own "Bingos" front was however reported clean – Gas was chiefly afterwards reported by 3rd Division – but it did not come out way – though Gas alert was put into force – all quiet by 2 a.m. – Heard afterwards that no attack took place. Returned to left Sub Sector – Quiet night.	
	" 17th			
	" 18th		Sunday – Quiet – though the Right Sub Sector was badly "draped" with T.M.S	
	" 19th		Very Quiet day – A few T.M.s over towards dusk	

WAR DIARY
or
INTELLIGENCE SUMMARY

Army Form C. 2118.

Place	Date	Hour	Summary of Events and Information	Remarks and references to Appendices
	1916			
LOCRE	June 20		Enemy sent over some T.M's about 10 a.m causing 3 casualties – 2/Lt O'WILLIS was killed by an unlucky shell which landed at the door of a dug-out about the same time – He was buried in the Cemetery near YORK HOUSE	CASUALTIES June 1st – June 21st KILLED fl. OFFICER 1. O.R. WOUNDED T.O.R.
	" 21		No casualties during remainder of day.	
	" 22		Sunday – quiet – no casualties – Relieved by 4th N.F. – Major P.P.PHILLIPS rejoined from England, having been away since December – Went back to DONCASTER HUTS	
	" 22		Naval review – Baths for battalion at WESTOUTRE	
	" 23		Capt. TURNER goes on leave – Major P.P.PHILLIPS takes over command.	
	" 24		Very fine & warm – Thunderstorm in afternoon.	
	" 25		Very fine day – Return to left sector.	
	" 26		Enemy bombards "L" & "K" with T.M's from 11 a.m til 12.30 p.m – causing rather a lot of casualties – though many of them were slight (1 Officer & 25 O.R wounded) Rest of day quiet – Heavy bombardment by our guns during the night	
	" 27		Fine day – fairly quiet – our artillery active all day – During Wire etc.	
	" 28		3 casualties in the morning from trench mortars – Our artillery again active all day cutting wire etc	

WAR DIARY or INTELLIGENCE SUMMARY

Place	Date	Hour	Summary of Events and Information	Remarks and references to Appendices
LoCRE	19/15			
	June 28		There was carried on by 150ᵗʰ Brigade on our right on night of 28ᵗʰ – there was a heavy bombardment – but it hardly affected our front & became a kind of diversion shewing we were not affected at all – It became very quiet by night	CASUALTIES June 25ᵗʰ – June 29 Wounded 10 Other ran — 38 O.R.
	29ᵗʰ		A quiet day – there was a certain amount of shooting, but our artillery were fairly quiet & the enemy for once left our trenches alone – there was some heavy enemy shelling however on our right about 9 p.m. – which was kept up till late into the night – however it did not affect our front. We were relieved by the 4ᵗʰ N.F. without mishap & went into Brigade Reserve at R.C. Farm.	
	30ᵗʰ		Rest !!!	

10/5127

Vol XI

50

CONFIDENTIAL.

WAR DIARY

OF

5TH BN NORTHUMBERLAND FUSILIERS.

FROM JULY 1ST TO JULY 31ST 1916

(VOLUME XI)

[signature]
Major
Comdg. 5th Bn. Northld. Fus.

1st Aug. 1916.

WAR DIARY or INTELLIGENCE SUMMARY

Army Form C. 2118.

Place	Date	Hour	Summary of Events and Information	Remarks and references to Appendices
LOCRE	1916			
	1st JULY		Very fine + hot — usual routine at R.C. Farm — about 200 men out on different working parties at night.	
	2"		Sunday — service in one of the huts in the afternoon — Enemy shelled a battery about 700 x away in the evening — for about an hour — no damage done however — same working parties at night.	
	3"		2/Lieutenant MOORHOUSE was unfortunately (wounded) last night while on working party getting a bullet through the thigh — he has only been out a few weeks. In the evening (3") we were relieved at R.C. Farm by the 4th EAST YORKSHIRE REGT — the 150th Bde is relieving the whole of our Bde & we are to do pioneer work for a week or so. We went into Camp near BRULOOZE.	
	4"		Fine day — resting + cleaning up — Turned wet in the afternoon — no working parties to night.	
	5"		Fine day — working parties about 250 under R.E. + Burying Cable — we have received a draft of 37 men from the 1st B' N.F. — very useful with some of them — the majority being specialists have gone to the Lewis Gun Regimental Sections.	

1577 Wt. W10791/1773 500,000 1/15 D. D. & L. A.D.S.S./Forms/C. 2118.

WAR DIARY
or
INTELLIGENCE SUMMARY.

(Erase heading not required.)

Army Form C. 2118.

Place	Date	Hour	Summary of Events and Information	Remarks and references to Appendices
LOCRE	1916			
	6 JULY		Same working parties.	
	7"		Showery day — The Divisional Band played in the camp in the afternoon but it was rather interrupted by the rain — The B" team played a football match against the 1st Entrenching Battalion who are in Camp next door to us.	
	8"		Fine & hot again — Same working parties.	
	9"		Church parade on the football ground — Same day — Same working parties at night.	
	10"		Fine but windy — We send 50 men to be attached to 2" Field Coy R.E. relieve the Brigade Working party — 2Lt LETTS & 2Lt JOHNSON join from the 3" Line — No working parties tonight	
	11"		We send a further 50 men to tonight the relief of the B" working party — the whole to stay under command of 2Lt MORRIS — No working parties again tonight — the men are getting a few days rest not.	
	12"		Drill parade for coys before breakfast — in the morning — No working parties.	

Army Form C. 2118.

WAR DIARY
or
INTELLIGENCE SUMMARY.
(Erase heading not required.)

Instructions regarding War Diaries and Intelligence Summaries are contained in F. S. Regs., Part II. and the Staff Manual respectively. Title pages will be prepared in manuscript.

Place	Date	Hour	Summary of Events and Information	Remarks and references to Appendices
GRE	13th JULY		Cold + cloudy — We hear we are to relieve a battalion of the 151 Brigade in the M+N Trenches on night of 15/16th. The 100 here return from the Brigade working party — 250 men out trenching cable at night.	
	14th		Wet — Col O — Officers go round new trenches.	
	15th		We hear that we are to carry out a raid on the HOLLANDSCHESCHAUR SALIENT with 2 Coys on or about the 23rd instant. We relieved the 15th 13th Bttn 5th D.L.I. In trenches M1 to N2 A — Relief carried out successfully by midnight — We were able to get the men gun relieved in the afternoon.	
	16th		We found the new front line considerably better than the L+K Trenches — but there is no support line — and only one C.T. which leads up some little way on the left of our trenches. Batt. H.Q. is a very long way back: it takes 45 minutes to walk up from there to the front line. Rather a noisy day — our artillery were cutting — Enemy "shafts". No MA with T.M's badly wounding 3 men of D Coy.	

Army Form C. 2118.

WAR DIARY
or
INTELLIGENCE SUMMARY.
(Erase heading not required.)

Instructions regarding War Diaries and Intelligence Summaries are contained in F. S. Regs., Part II. and the Staff Manual respectively. Title pages will be prepared in manuscript.

Place	Date	Hour	Summary of Events and Information	Remarks and references to Appendices
LoCRE	17th JULY		Quiet day in our trenches — though hoeing on the right — we get a draft of 3 officers & 183 men who are staying down at the Transport at present — A & B Coys who have been chosen for the raid — busy patrolling etc in front of HOLLANDSCHESCHUUR to learn the ground.	
	18th		Fairly quiet day — a few T.M's on front but no damage — 2Lt MATHEWS severely wounded (slight-maya bullet through the face).	
	19th		Fairly quiet day — fine shot — head T.M. Staffe in afternoon — 1 O.R. wounded.	
	20th		Sea not to get to know the ground thoroughly we are staying in six days & then going out six days — Lt Q.M. HOLLOWAY was thrown from his horse & damaged his head — & sent to the Base.	
	21st		Fine & hot — Quiet day — get word that a Canadian Brigade is taking over our Brigade front — Canadian officers come round the trenches — Relieved by 31st Canadian Battalion & go to RIDGEWOOD.	
	22nd		Receive word that our Brigade is taking over a sector south of the 1st Bn towards NEUVE EGLISE — are relieved in RIDGEWOOD in the afternoon by the Canadian Bats — march to camp at DRANOUTRE — it is our turn for Divisional Reserve — 4th & 7th Bats have gone into the line in the new sector.	

WAR DIARY
INTELLIGENCE SUMMARY

Place	Date	Hour	Summary of Events and Information	Remarks and references to Appendices
DRANOUTRE	23 July		Resting in Camp — Camp quite good — Decoy is a slack Camp from remainder of Battalion.	
	24 July		Battalion Bathing — our new Brigade front is almost exactly the same as that held by us in July of last year.	
	25		The following officers have joined during the last few days — 2Lt HARMER G.L. 2Lt OLDHAM J 2Lt JONES C 2Lt SARGENT E.V. 2Lt MEEK T.H.B. 2Lt BEATON P.I. 2Lt WILSON T.B. 2Lt ARMSTRONG H. The Brigadier having gone on special leave — Lt Col C. Turner CMG assumes command of the Brigade during his absence — the command of the Battalion Hereby devolving upon Major A. IRWIN. Owing to the move of the Brigade of course our "raid" is off — for which we are rather relieved — as these winds opposed to move are "much to latter. You can catch the enemy napping." We got a sudden order about 5pm to send 16 officers + 200 men out at 9pm on looking party — this after a little difficulty in starting up the men was accomplished allright — the party did not return till 5 a.m.	

WAR DIARY
or
INTELLIGENCE SUMMARY.
(Erase heading not required.)

Army Form C. 2118.

Instructions regarding War Diaries and Intelligence Summaries are contained in F. S. Regs., Part II. and the Staff Manual respectively. Title pages will be prepared in manuscript.

Place	Date	Hour	Summary of Events and Information	Remarks and references to Appendices
DRANOUTRE	25th JULY		Hot morning — having been employed in carrying "gas cylinders" out of our trenches.	
	26th		Men resting after last night's efforts.	
	27th		Officers busy going round new trenches.	
	28th		Relieved 4th N.F. in trenches D3 D4 D5 D6 — Art corps in Trenches D5 D6 — Art corps in front line — B coy in Sp'g & No 5 Minwerps — D coy in support at R.E. Farm — H.Q. COOKER FM — Relief carried out quite quietly.	
	29th		2 men snipers & killed in the early morning — very quiet for the rest of the day — Trenches fairly good front line — support trenches being constructed but not yet complete.	
	30th		Very fine hot — very quiet day indeed — no casualties.	
	31st		Very fine hot — Divisional General visits trenches in morning — Exceptionally quiet day — no casualties. There is a tremendous amount of machine gun rifle fire at night which causes a good deal of trouble to the transport & people coming up the roads. —	MU

(CONFIDENTIAL.)

WAR DIARY

OF

1/5TH BN NORTHUMBERLAND FUSILIERS.

FROM 1ST AUGUST TO 31ST AUGUST '16

VOLUME IX

Vol 12

11/5 N 7

[signature] Lieut. Colonel.
Comdg. 5th Bn Northd. Fus.

Army Form C. 2118.

WAR DIARY
or
INTELLIGENCE SUMMARY.
(Erase heading not required.)

Instructions regarding War Diaries and Intelligence Summaries are contained in F. S. Regs., Part II. and the Staff Manual respectively. Title pages will be prepared in manuscript.

Place	Date	Hour	Summary of Events and Information	Remarks and references to Appendices
	1916			
DRANOUTRE	1st AUGUST		Fine - hot - very quiet - Enemy shelled North mine saps with 5.9's for about an hour in the afternoon - No Casualties.	
	2"		Fine - hot - Colonel Turner return from Brigade - the General having come back from leave - 5 men wounded last night - Major P. Phillips slightly wounded in head by a splinter from his periscope which was "holed" by a Bosch Sniper. Enemy shelled mine saps vigorously between 4 pm + 5 pm - no serious damage or Casualties.	CASUALTIES 1st - 3rd KILLED 10 O.R. WOUNDED -:- Major Phillips + 11 O.R.
	3"		Fine - very hot - Quiet day - Corps Commander visited trenches - Relieved by 4th N.F. Relief complete 11:30 pm - Returned to Brigade Rooms as follows. H.Q. T3A 3.8 (Farm) A Coy N35 6.2.3 (Dugouts) B Coy N32 B.2.2 (AIRCRAFT FARM) C Coy T10C 9.9 (Farm) D Coy T4C 7.7 (Farm).	
	4"		Fine but windy - Resting as usual the first day after coming out of the trenches Supplies working party of 2 officers + 100 men in the evening.	
	5		Supplies working party of 1 officer + 50 men early in morning. Enemy tried to find a 60 pound Battery in neighbourhood of the H.Q. Farm - but did no damage. C.D. Corps had to move from their farms owing to another Division coming into that area	

WAR DIARY or INTELLIGENCE SUMMARY.

Army Form C. 2118.

Place	Date	Hour	Summary of Events and Information	Remarks and references to Appendices
DRANOUTRE	5th AUGUST 1916		D Coy joined B Coy in AIRCRAFT FARM & C Coy was put in another farm between H.Q. & AIRCRAFT FARM — From 4 pm to 6 pm our guns bombarded the German trenches — During the bombardment one of our hits 240 AB Trench Mortars (Aerial-Torpedo) was fired from the neighbourhood of R.E. Farm —	
	6th		Lovely Day — Enemy again shelled in neighbourhood of HQ with 5.9s but did no damage — Great aeroplane activity on both sides — The Division is being relieved by the ULSTER Division & we receive orders to march tomorrow to the Rest Area in the neighbourhood of METEREN — Capt. Lyle as billetting officer is sent on to find out about billets etc. — Very busy making arrangements for march.	
	7th		Left Brigade Reserve about 9 am & marched through LOCRE (companies marching independently) to MONT ROUGE where we had an hours halt for breakfast — the Q.M. having been sent on with the cookers to prepare same — Finally reached our billets in the area between METEREN & STRAZELLE about 10 a.m. — This is practically the same area as that occupied by the Battalion which visiting last Novbr. &c. A cool cloudy day — but excellent for marching — all arrangements worked well & men marched well.	

T2134. Wt. W708—776. 500000. 4/15. Sir J.C. & S.

Army Form C. 2118.

WAR DIARY
or
INTELLIGENCE SUMMARY.
(Erase heading not required.)

Instructions regarding War Diaries and Intelligence Summaries are contained in F. S. Regs., Part II. and the Staff Manual respectively. Title pages will be prepared in manuscript.

Place	Date	Hour	Summary of Events and Information	Remarks and references to Appendices
STRAZELLE	8th August	—	Resting after march — We expect to be here only a few days before proceeding to join one of the Armies in the South — Major P. P. PHILLIPS rejoined yesterday.	
	9th	—	Very hot indeed — Companies have inspections + practice of gas cold drill — Receive orders that we shall entrain at BAILLEUL on the early morning of the 11th + proceed to the neighbourhood of BERNAVILLE (Département de SOMME) to join the IVth (RESERVE) Army.	
	10th	—	Cooler — getting packed up ready for move to-morrow — Our spare kit has been sent to a Divisional Dump at BOESCHEPE + all officers kits have been reduced to 35 lbs.	
	11th	—	Left billets about 3 a.m. — marched to BAILLEUL station — Entrained + left about 6.25 a.m. Arrived at DOULLENS about 12.30 p.m. — marched to billets 2 coys at CANDAS - 2 coys + HQ. at FIENVILLERS — Distance 7 miles to CANDAS — 8 miles to FIENVILLERS — Bad march — Very hot — after the early start + journey the men marched badly — Delays of an hour on the road waiting for water carts — Everyone in by 6.30 p.m. — Fairly good billets in the village.	
	12th	—	Fine + hot — Resting — Everyone rather weary after yesterday — Large British aerodrome	

T2134. Wt. W708—776. 500000. 4/15. Sir J. C. & S.

WAR DIARY or INTELLIGENCE SUMMARY.

Army Form C. 2118.

(Erase heading not required.)

Instructions regarding War Diaries and Intelligence Summaries are contained in F. S. Regs., Part II. and the Staff Manual respectively. Title pages will be prepared in manuscript.

Place	Date	Hour	Summary of Events and Information	Remarks and references to Appendices
FIENVILLERS	12th August		Near FIENVILLERS – having a continued hang in the air.	
	13th		Dullish day – short battalion route march (5 miles) – The following officers joined from the Base – : 2nd Lieuts. D. ARMSTRONG, B. HEAD, G. McCREE, G.J. BANFIELD, S.A.T. KERR.	
	14th		Dull day – rain at intervals – Drill parade by Coys – We commence our march up country to-morrow to join the IVth Army on the SOMME.	
NAOURS	15th		Marched off from billets 4.45 a.m. – reached our destination NAOURS at 8 a.m. – about 8 miles – good march – cool – none fell out – Went billets in village – We go on to-morrow	
PIERREGOT	16th		Marched off from billets 9.50 a.m. – reached PIERREGOT about 12 noon – short march – about 7 miles – marched quite well – rather poor billets in village – Rooms airy – With the greatest regret that Lt. Quarter-Master R.J. HOLLOWAY has died in London as the result of his fall out here – 2/Lt A. MORRIS has been acting most successfully as Q/master. Since Lt. HOLLOWAY left.	
HENENCOURT WOOD	17th		Marched off from PIERREGOT at 5.12 a.m. – reached our destination, camp in HENENCOURT WOOD about 10 a.m. – Long hot march – about 10½ miles – but everyone marched well – a few men fell out but were brought in with the rear guard. Since leaving	

WAR DIARY
or
INTELLIGENCE SUMMARY.
(Erase heading not required.)

Army Form C. 2118.

Place	Date	Hour	Summary of Events and Information	Remarks and references to Appendices
	1916			
HENENCOURT WOOD	17th AUGUST		FUSILIERS We have marched each day as a Brigade with 70th internal Relation Battalions. HENENCOURT is about 4.5 miles from ALBERT — We now belong to the III Corps IV Army — We have been told we may expect at the most 3 weeks training before being shoved into the Battle.	
	18th		Huts in the wood — rather crowded, specially officers — whole camp very dirty. Commence training — Training ground is Fresherit — country consists of open chalk downs — with occasional patches of woodland. Camp cleaned up.	
	19th		Very heavy showers — which make Camp in a horrid mess — Hard at work training — Hours of parade are as follows — 6.30am — 7.30am 9am — 12.30pm 5.30pm — 7.30pm — So most of our time is fill up Ration Cols & damp.	
	20th		Practising new formation for attack in morning — church parade in afternoon — wet & cold.	
	21st		Usual training parade — Col Turner & other O.C of Brigade went up to trenches round the front held by the 15th Division.	

Army Form C. 2118.

WAR DIARY
or
INTELLIGENCE SUMMARY.
(Erase heading not required.)

Instructions regarding War Diaries and Intelligence Summaries are contained in F. S. Regs., Part II. and the Staff Manual respectively. Title pages will be prepared in manuscript.

Place	Date	Hour	Summary of Events and Information	Remarks and references to Appendices
	1916			
HENENCOURT	22nd AUGUST	—	Training – Very hot and muggy – parties for Brigade Field day tomorrow.	
WOOD.	23rd	—	Brigade Field day – not unlike Aldershot – followed by the usual boss-loors.	
	24th	—	Usual training – Fine hot – C.O. went round front of 1st Division.	
	25th	—	Trial of signalling system between our signallers & an aeroplane – which was on the whole successfull – heavy rain in afternoon.	
	26th	—	D/vn rehearsal for Medal Presentation Parade which is to be held on Monday 28th.	
	27th	—	Very wet day – Suspicion of Transport which had been ordered for 10 a.m. cancelled. Church parade also cancelled.	
	28th	—	Battalion drill in morning – Sports by rain as usual – Owing to the weather the Presentation parade was confined to the 149 Brigade – Lt General W.P. Pulteney Commanding III Corps presented the medals. The following 4 NCOs & men of this Bn. received the "Military Medal" for gallantry &c during the last few months. No 1642 Sergt T. BARRAS, No 1439 L/Cpl. W. MERTON, No 2150 L/Cpl. E.L. FANNAN, No 3302 Pte J. BELLFIELD.	

J. BELLFIELD.

WAR DIARY
or
INTELLIGENCE SUMMARY.
(Erase heading not required.)

Army Form C. 2118.

Place	Date	Hour	Summary of Events and Information	Remarks and references to Appendices
HENENCOURT WOOD	29th AUGUST	9/6	Fine in morning — B" practised attack on trenches — very heavy thunderstorm train in afternoon making camp in a miserable state.	
	30th		Very wet + stormy — morning parades had to be cancelled — raining all day — impossible to do much.	
	31st		Cleared up + was a very fine day — though very wet + slushy under foot — Company practised the attack + the whole B" battn) at HENENCOURT CHATEAU, where some in the have been rigged up in the stables. The Battalion carried out practice night operations and did a successful Company march followed by taking up battle formation.	

149th. INFANTRY BRIGADE

50th. DIVISION

5th. NORTHUMBERLAND FUSILIERS

149th. INFANTRY BRIGADE

SEPTEMBER 1916.

CONFIDENTIAL

WAR DIARY

OF

5TH Bⁿ NORTHᴸᴰ FUSILIERS.

FROM 1ˢᵀ SEP. TO 30ᵀᴴ SEP. '16

(VOLUME ~~12~~)

Vol/3

1-10-16.

Arnold Twin
Major
for O.C. 5th Bⁿ N.F.

WAR DIARY or INTELLIGENCE SUMMARY.

(Erase heading not required.)

Place	Date	Hour	Summary of Events and Information	Remarks and references to Appendices
HENENCOURT	1-9-16		Fine day — Usual training	
Sheet 57D	2-9-16		Fine day — Usual training	
(X.26.b.)	3-9-16		Holiday	
	4-9-16		Training interfered with by rain	
	5-9-16		Battalion route march	
	6-9-16		Usual training	
	7-9-16		Rehearsal field day — Battalion had dinners in the field after	
			operations were over.	
	8-9-16		Moved from HENENCOURT WOOD at 1:30 p.m. & marched through ALBERT to the	
			QUADRANGLE — QUADRANGLE reached. No Battn went into dug outs round	
			LOZENGE WOOD.	
CONTALMAISON	9-9-16	9 a.m.	Moved to QUADRANGLE — receive orders from 44th Brigade — 15th Division whom we	
Sheet 57D			are relieving in the line, and another whose orders we are temporarily, that 3 boys	
(X.22.B.)		9 p.m	H.Q. are to go up, commencing 4 pm, to relieve the 8th BLACK WATCH in the line.	
		4pm	This relief carried out	
		6:45pm	1st DIVISION on our right attacked HIGH WOOD — attack failed — considerable	

WAR DIARY
or
INTELLIGENCE SUMMARY.
(Erase heading not required.)

Army Form C. 2118.

Place	Date	Hour	Summary of Events and Information	Remarks and references to Appendices
nr MARTINPUICH Sheet 57c (S.3 Central)	9-9-16		Shelling lasting most of the night.	CASUALTIES:— 12 noon 9th – 12 noon 10th
		7.30 pm	Our remaining lorry came up & went into the front line practically without casualties.	wounded CAPT. P. RANSOM & 3 O.R.
		10.30 pm	Relief complete.	
		12 m.n.t	Shelling slackened off.	
			Dispositions now as follows:— D Coy — CLERK'S TRENCH and BETHELL'S SAP.	
			B " — BRECON TRENCH.	
			A " — ARGYLE STREET	
			C " — CHESTER STREET.	
			HQ — MILL STREET.	
	10-9-16	Noon	Intermittent shelling during day — Quiet at night.	CASUALTIES:—
		11 pm	Orders to take over some more front line on the left — accordingly B Coy	12 noon 10th – 11th
(S.2.b.2.)			sent to SWANSEA TRENCH — A Coy to support trenches behind.	wounded 7 O.R.
			Relief carried out successfully by 1 a.m.	
		1 am	We are ordered to move our Headquarters to the QUARRY — which was accordingly	
			done at 2 a.m.	

WAR DIARY
or
INTELLIGENCE SUMMARY.
(Erase heading not required.)

Army Form C. 2118.

Place	Date	Hour	Summary of Events and Information	Remarks and references to Appendices
YPRES Sheet 57C.	11-9-16		During the morning Brig. Genl. CLIFFORD was unfortunately killed whilst reconnoitring the new assembly trenches.	
		11am	Owing to the death of Genl. CLIFFORD — Lieut Col C. TURNER C.M.G. temporarily took over the command of the Brigade — Major A. IRWIN came up to command the Battalion.	
		5pm	B Coy in CLARKS TRENCH heavily shelled from 3pm to 5pm.	
(S. 9d.)		9.30pm	Germans after heavy barrage on front line followed by machine gun fire which was kept up for an hour. Enemy apparently laid an attack. This unfortunately caught "C" Coy passing through CLARKS TRENCH and they suffered some casualties.	
		11mdn't	4th DIVISION who have relieved 1st DIVISION on our right, take over strong point on extreme right of CLARKS TRENCH — they also take over CHESTER STREET. — C Coy completing D Coy in BETHELL'S SAP tonight. Our C Coy, — 91 moved to BRECON TRENCH	
(S. 3.b.)	12-9-16	7.30pm	D Coy eventually relieved and returned to BRECON TRENCH — Light N.M. NORTH wounded (not severely) on his way out	CASUALTIES 12 noon 11th, 12th Killed 13 O.R. wounded Bathurst 2/Lt SINCLAR 23 O.R.

T2134. Wt. W708—776. 500000. 4/15. Sir J. C. & S.

WAR DIARY
or
INTELLIGENCE SUMMARY.
(Erase heading not required.)

Army Form C. 2118.

Place	Date	Hour	Summary of Events and Information	Remarks and references to Appendices
MARTINPUICH Sheet 57c.	15.9.16	5pm	Despite several efforts, we failed to retrieve Genl. CLIFFORD'S body last night. French quarter quiet.	
		4pm	A Coy relieved B Coy in CLARK'S TRENCH	
	13.9.16		Usual intermittent shelling over whole area.	CASUALTIES:- 12 noon 12th-13th Killed. I.O.R. wounded 5 O.R.
		1.15pm	BRECON TRENCH shelled for 2 hours by our own guns – D Coy had to evacuate trench and luckily suffered few casualties – Trench was badly damaged.	
		5pm	Our two Coys in support (B+D) relieved by 2 Coys 6th M.F. and coming back to neighbourhood of H.Q.	Genl. CLIFFORD'S body recovered.
	14.9.16	12 noon	CLARK'S TRENCH sector heavily shelled causing some casualties. Battn. stands tomorrow – very busy making preparations.	CASUALTIES:- 12 noon 13th-14th Killed 2 O.R. wounded 11 O.R.
			Our 2 Coys in front line are to be relieved tonight – at 6 a.m. tomorrow we shall be in Brigade Reserve as follows:– Hdqrs – QUARRY, "D" Coy – CHALK ROAD, "B" Coy – MILL STREET, "C" Coys – MILL STREET, "A+C" Coys – CHALK ROAD	
S. 8. d.		10pm	Fairly quiet day – A+C Coys successfully relieved	

WAR DIARY
or
INTELLIGENCE SUMMARY.
(Erase heading not required.)

Army Form C. 2118.

Place	Date	Hour	Summary of Events and Information	Remarks and references to Appendices
MARTINPUICH	15-9-16		Attack commenced 6.20am and apparently was successful in taking first objective on strip of HIGH WOOD. Heavy machine gun fire from HIGH WOOD. By 12 noon all our Companies had been ordered up.	
S.H.a.C.			Division on right had first failed to take HIGH WOOD. — attacked again and took it. This considerably cleared up the situation on our front. Position remained obscure all day — We were believed to have taken first of second objective — It was later ascertained that we only held as far forward as the SUNKEN ROAD. Casualties in the Brigade have been heavy — chiefly owing to HIGH WOOD not being taken at the first attack — Estimate at 30 officers 1250 O.R. 151st Infantry Brigade came up during the night	
	16-9-16	9.30am	151st Brigade attacked second and third objectives but did not succeed.	
		3pm	Portion of our Companies as follows — A.Coy — on extreme left of first objective connecting with 2 R.W.F.; B.Coy — on extreme right of first objective connecting with LONDON DIVISION (47th) under orders of 6 N.F.	A
			D. Coy on CLARK'S TRENCH under orders of 10.6 N.F. throughout the duration	

WAR DIARY
or
INTELLIGENCE SUMMARY.

Army Form C. 2118.

Place	Date	Hour	Summary of Events and Information	Remarks and references to Appendices
MARTINPUICH Sheet 57d. (S.8.d.)	16.9.16		B Coy. had been employed as a carrying party under the Brigade. H.Q. has remained at the QUARRY.	
		9 pm	119th Brigade is withdrawn into Divisional Reserve - Our Coys are pulled out as quickly as possible and took up a position in dugouts and old trenches behind CHALK ROAD. A new Brigadier having been appointed, Lt. Col. TURNER returned to the Battalion. Casualties 12 noon 15th to 12 noon 16th — Killed 10.O.R. C.Y. ALDER. 2/Lieuts. J.C.ROBSON, R.L DAGLISH, H.E. MERRITT, and 5 H.O.R. Missing - 8.O.R.	CASUALTIES 12 mm 18 [illegible] wounded [illegible]
	17.9.16		Resting - Ordered to stand-to in case of counter-attack as we are the first Battalion in the Brigade to go up - but we are not pulled out.	
	18.9.16		Very wet and sad - everyone very miserable as there is very little shelter, large carrying parties supplied at night - chefs of 100 men served.	
	19.9.16		to move today. We also during day though ground and men are in a very bad state. Another draft of 50 men came also 2/Lt. R.G. SMITH.	
	20.9.16		119th Brigade is to relieve 151st Brigade today.	

WAR DIARY
or
INTELLIGENCE SUMMARY.
(Erase heading not required.)

Army Form C. 2118.

Place	Date	Hour	Summary of Events and Information	Remarks and references to Appendices
MARTINPUICH Sheet 57.c.	20.9.16	4pm	Left CHALK ROAD. and occupied CLARK'S TRENCH – Relief complete about 9p.m. Trenches in a wretched condition from mud.	
	21.9.16	All day	looks like rain	CASUALTIES:– 12 noon 20th – 21st wounded. 1. O.R
		A/noon	Receive orders to send out two working parties of 200 men each.	
(N.33a to N.36d.)		2.30pm	Information received that STARFISH TRENCH has been evacuated by Germans & that Bavarian on our right have entered it. 11th N.F. ordered to send forward parties to see if the trench is reoccupied in front of us.	
		8.30pm	Our working parties cancelled and two parties of 2 Officers & 100 men each (C & D Coys) (with tools) sent up under orders of O.C. 11 H.N.F. to support the operation –	
	22.9.16	12.15am	"A" Coy ordered to report to O.C. 11th N.F. at SUNKEN ROAD.	
		12.30am	"B" Coy ordered to occupy HOOK TRENCH.	
		8am	We have occupied STARFISH & PRUE TRENCHES without opposition. Thus our final objective is attained. Companies situated as follows:– "A" & "D" Coys – are with 11th N.F. in PRUE TRENCH	A.1.

WAR DIARY or INTELLIGENCE SUMMARY

Army Form C. 2118.

(Erase heading not required.)

Place	Date	Hour	Summary of Events and Information	Remarks and references to Appendices
MARTINPUICH 22.9.16 Sheet 57c.			"C"Coy with 6th N.F. in S/F of STARFISH; "B"Coy – HOOK TRENCH; HQ – CLARK'S TRENCH. Enemy appears to have retired to third line as there is no sniping whatever.	CASUALTIES. 12 noon 21st-22nd wounded 11 O.R.
		8pm	No change, though there has been intermittent shelling during the day. We have had very few casualties. Received orders to construct three strong points in line of road some 200x in front of PRUE TRENCH, with the help of working parties from the other Battalions, who was carried out successfully without any opposition from the enemy of whom no signs are seen - flares being kept up from some considerable distance back.	
M.33a to M.33a.	23.9.16		Usual shelling – nothing in particular occurred. Companies remain in same positions and relieved in the evening by 150th Brigade, with the exception of "B" Coy who were not relieved until the morning of the 24th. After dark Lieut ARMSTRONG and a party of 50 men from "B" Coy completed the strong point they were working on last night.	CASUALTIES. 12 noon 22nd-23rd Killed 10 O.R. wounded 70 O.R. missing 20 O.R. A.I.

Army Form C. 2118.

WAR DIARY
or
INTELLIGENCE SUMMARY.
(Erase heading not required.)

Instructions regarding War Diaries and Intelligence Summaries are contained in F. S. Regs., Part II. and the Staff Manual respectively. Title pages will be prepared in manuscript.

Place	Date	Hour	Summary of Events and Information	Remarks and references to Appendices
MARTINPUICH	24.9.16		Companies on relief returned to original positions in CLARK'S TRENCH. Fine day. Each Co ordered enlarge all shelter slots in its area and to make a dump of them.	
CONTALMAISON Sheet 57.c.		2/pm	Relieved by 8th BORDER REGT. – Battalion returned to QUADRANGLE TRENCH. This is the farthest back we have been since going in on the 9th last	
	25.9.16		Fine day – Large working party of 400 men supplied to work on the roads	CASUALTIES :– 12 noon 24th–25th wounded 6 O.R.
	26.9.16		Battalion succeeded in getting baths for the men at BECOURT, which were most welcome & most needed. Lieut Col. TURNER goes to hospital (sick) The command hereby devolving on Major N.I. WRIGHT Major A. IRWIN	CASUALTIES :– 12 noon 25th–26th wounded 10 O.R.
	27.9.16		Working party of 400 men supplied to work on roads – Major N.I. WRIGHT (2nd Bn. N.F.) joined Battalion and assumed command.	
	28.9.16		Working party of 400 men again supplied. Very wet day – Battalion moves from QUADRANGLE at 8 a.m.	
MARTINPUICH Sheet 57.c. (S.E.d)	28.9.16		relieved 4th Bn. YORKS REGT. in CLARK'S TRENCH – Relief successfully.	A.1.

Army Form C. 2118.

WAR DIARY
or
INTELLIGENCE SUMMARY.

(Erase heading not required.)

Instructions regarding War Diaries and Intelligence Summaries are contained in F. S. Regs., Part II. and the Staff Manual respectively. Title pages will be prepared in manuscript.

Place	Date	Hour	Summary of Events and Information	Remarks and references to Appendices
MARTINPUICH	29.9.16		Served out - only one man being wounded.	CASUALTIES 17 now 28 th wounded.
Sheet 57.C	30.9.16		Heavy bombardment on left during the night - our front quiet. Battalion ordered to attack with 151st Brigade tomorrow morning.	

CONFIDENTIAL

WAR DIARY

OF

5TH BN NORTHUMBLD FUSILIERS.

1ST OCT. to 31ST OCT. 1916

(VOLUME 13)

31-10-16

[signature]
Major for
Lieut Colonel
Comdg 5th B" North" Fus.

WAR DIARY
or
INTELLIGENCE SUMMARY.
(Erase heading not required.)

Army Form C. 2118.

Place	Date	Hour	Summary of Events and Information	Remarks and references to Appendices
EBUICRT L'ABBAYE	1-10-16		Orders were received late last night that the Battalion would attack the following objectives today:— (1) M.22 a.2½ to M.21 b.8.3 and (2) M.22 a.2.3 to M.21 b.8.H. The frontage is about 300 yards and a comrade Battalion (8th D.L.I. & 5th BORDERS) is to be on our right and the 23rd Division on the left. The day was fine and the men in excellent spirits. Unfortunately the assembly trenches were found to be very shallow and in several places there was no trench at all — the men lying out in the open — Lieuts LETTS & BEATON — both of A Coy were wounded neither very severely.	Copy of Bn Orders Order No 354 &c. attached
Sheet 57C. S.W.		3.15 p.m	ZERO HOUR	
		3.14 p.m	D Coy seen extending on top of the ridge.	
		3.15 p.m	Whole line disappeared over ridge and was followed by smoke of bursting shells — own barrage opened very intense and — we afterwards heard — with excellent results. Enemy's artillery opened promptly but the Battalion had already passed their barrage zone.	
		4 p.m	Message received from Capt Easton "Hav gained 1st objective and am in touch with SHERWOOD FORESTERS on my left.	A1

WAR DIARY
or
INTELLIGENCE SUMMARY.

Army Form C. 2118.

(Erase heading not required.)

Instructions regarding War Diaries and Intelligence Summaries are contained in F. S. Regs., Part II. and the Staff Manual respectively. Title pages will be prepared in manuscript.

Place	Date	Hour	Summary of Events and Information	Remarks and references to Appendices
FAUCORT L'ABBAYE (Sheet 57c SW.)	1·10·16		Message from Capt PATTERSON "B" Coy — "Have gained 2nd Objective and am in touch with 23rd Division on my left.	
		7.30pm	One Lewis gun attached to "A" Coy shot out of action — have left reserve gun sent up.	
		8.30pm	Finding further reports — Battalions on right & left reported successful — (LESARS reported taken)	
		9.45pm	Message from 2/Lieut Gill — Does that his Company had gained both Objectives and was in touch with people on his right and left — Four reports our casualties seem to have been small — estimated at about 50. the 2 officers already mentioned. Shelling by enemy slackens a little — No further reports except that CUTTING is believed not to be occupied	CASUALTIES 12 noon 1st to 12 noon 2nd Killed — 1 O.R. Wounded — 2/Lts LETTS, BEATON & 59 O.R. Missing — 3 O.R.
		12 midnt	Orders received from Brigade that we are to advance & occupy the CUTTING. On consultation with O.C. Coys and with BORDERS on the right — who established have found the TANGLE occupied — C.O. decides not to carry out this advance — owing to Coys being very mixed, also B.H.Q. and the relieving of the line — not 2:30 a.m.	A.A.
	2·10·16		Usual shelling all day — especially BATH.Q. and support lines — fairly quiet on frontline	

WAR DIARY
or
INTELLIGENCE SUMMARY.

Army Form C. 2118.

Place	Date	Hour	Summary of Events and Information	Remarks and references to Appendices
EAUCOURT L'ABBAYE (Sheet 57c S.W.)	2-10-16	5pm	119th* Bde. so to relieve 151st Bde. (to which we are temporarily attached) Tonight - are nearly all day. - By night, trenches + C.T's in a very bad state.	CASUALTIES 12 noon 2nd - 12 noon 3rd Killed - 1. O.R. Wounded - 14. O.R.
		10pm	Received orders that 6th N.F. would relieve us in the early morning -	
		11pm	Germans started shelling CRESCENT ALLEY near H.Q. with 5.9's which was kept up till about 8pm on 3-10-16. This very much interfered with the relief owing to all reliefs being very late. The 6th N.F. could not get up the trench to relieve us. till about 6 am with the result that our boys could not get out till daylight.	
	3-10-16	6 am	Fortunately there was a thick mist which enabled them to get out without being seen - though the last Coy had a Machine gun turned on to it coming down 26th AVENUE - All Coys got to their various destinations all night by about 8.30 am. Their positions were as follows - "A" O Coys. CRESCENT ALLEY - "C" Coy - SPENCE ST. - "B" Coy and B" H.Q. - BLAYDON ST. - If it had not been for the mist we certainly could not have been relieved.	
		Noon	Shelling continued in CRESCENT ALLEY which is now badly damaged. Here we are going to be relieved by the 23rd Div. this afternoon, and have sent guides down to guide them	

WAR DIARY or INTELLIGENCE SUMMARY.

Army Form C. 2118.

Place	Date	Hour	Summary of Events and Information	Remarks and references to Appendices
ENVOURT L'ABBAYE (Sheet 57C.S.W)	3-10-16	5 hm	Shelling of B"HQ's BLAYDONS7 all very heavy. 2/Lt D. ARMSTRONG is killed – this young officer died splendidly even with the 8th, showing his all too short stay with us – and though his great courage & cheerful disposition – won the hearts of officers & men – he meets his loss. 2/Lt WILSON & Capt. PATTERSON are both wounded – the latter seriously, but we trust both will recover rapidly. The 11th D.L.I. came up about 4 p.m. but owing to blocks on the C.T.s they could not get in till 9 p.m. We were eventually relieved by them. The men are pretty well done up, but come back singing – they are splendid. The mud & rain during the last few days has been their worst enemy, but the men never lose heart.	CASUALTIES. 12 noon 3rd. 12 noon 4th. Killed. 2/Lieut D. ARMSTRONG. Wounded – Capt C.R.PATTERSON, 2/Lieut J.B.WILSON & 31 O.R. Missing – 1.O.R.
CONTALMAISON (Sheet 57D.S.E) ALBERT	4-10-16	10 p.m	Bn. returned to QUADRANGLE for the night – all boys in by midnight. Bn. marched to ALBERT via BECOURT – leaving QUADRANGLE TRENCH at 2 p.m. – then in very good form – German helmets & other trophies very much in evidence – Good billets in ALBERT.	
Sheet 57D.S.E & 62 D.N.E				
MILLENCOURT (Sheet 57D SE & 62 D.N.E)	5-10-16		Bn. marched to rest camp at MILLENCOURT, arriving about 3.30 p.m, followed at once by official photographer, who took many photographs which duly appeared in the illustrated papers. Col. TURNER returns to the B.L. – Major	

Army Form C. 2118.

WAR DIARY
or
INTELLIGENCE SUMMARY.
(Erase heading not required.)

Instructions regarding War Diaries and Intelligence Summaries are contained in F. S. Regs., Part II. and the Staff Manual respectively. Title pages will be prepared in manuscript.

Place	Date	Hour	Summary of Events and Information	Remarks and references to Appendices
MILLENCOURT Sheet 57D.S.E. 62 D.N.E.	6-10-16		Day devoted to thoroughly a clean up - and the men relieved there well earned rest - were able to enjoy hussefo - beer etc - Congratulations received from Brigade & Division & bn Commander on the splendid results achieved by the Bn in the action of October 1st.	
MILLENCOURT	7-10-16		Commenced training - We hear Division may be here for a fortnight - training programme prepared - Leave orders taken in the day but B.H. has to return to ALBERT tomorrow to work on road repairing. Training scheme cancelled.	
ALBERT Sheet 57D.S.E. 62 D.N.E.	8-10-16		Marched to ALBERT - having put camp at 2pm - Arrived to find our promised billets occupied by CANADIANS, who have no intention of leaving. After various consultations between C.O., 2 i/c Command & Town Major, CANADIANS evacuate Billets & the Bn which was quartered in a wet field for 6 hours, takes over billets & settles down comfortably.	
ALBERT.	9-10-16		Working parties of 350 men supplied from 5.30 a.m to 4.30 pm. A great deal of work required to keep up the roads which owing to the very heavy traffic have to be constantly under repair.	
ALBERT	10-10-16		Similar working parties to yesterday supplied - Our Billets are in close [?] to the Basilica of NOTRE DAME de BREBIERES with its famous virgin & child. The portion of the town so far from healthy when the enemy shells the place but fortunately we have not [?] the [?] for several days.	A.V.

Army Form C. 2118.

WAR DIARY
or
INTELLIGENCE SUMMARY.
(Erase heading not required.)

Instructions regarding War Diaries and Intelligence Summaries are contained in F. S. Regs., Part II. and the Staff Manual respectively. Title pages will be prepared in manuscript.

Place	Date	Hour	Summary of Events and Information	Remarks and references to Appendices
ALBERT	11-10-16		Have large working parties on the roads — We are relieved by the 6th & 8th N.F.'s march back to our camp at MILLENCOURT — Have training subalterns firehand.	
MILLENCOURT Sheet 57D.SE & 62D.NE	12-10-16		Training commenced — boys shooting on the ranges — reduce to officers by Major HOLBROOK on the ford supply for the SOMME area.	
" "	13-10-16		Training continues — a draft of 4 N.C.O's and 86 men go to hospital with SCABIES	
" "	14-10-16		We congratulate the undermentioned N.C.O's & men on being awarded the MILITARY MEDAL for gallantry in the field — Sergt T.H. HORNER "B" coy — Sergt N. HINDMARSH "B" coy — L/Cpl R.O. NEBB - A. coy. Pte W. HENNESSY, A coy — T.H. PAXTON, C. coy. — A. NAKEPEACE, B coy. W.D. PATTERSON, Transport — T. ATKINSON, "A" coy & L/Cpl N. FITTON, Signal Section. Two other N.C.O's have won the medal but they have unfortunately both since been killed in action. — Sgts D. KELLY, B. Coy & L. WOOD. D. Coy. Leave is being granted to one or two officers & N.C.Os each day to proceed to AMIENS.	
MILLENCOURT	15-10-16		He had news that Capt. C.A. PATTERSON has died of wounds two first received as. This gallant officer has been with the 8th for nearly 18 months when he was wounded. By his death we lose a true friend and a fearless soldier — always popular with both officers & men — He 8th Batt. lost in a divisional night attack which	

WAR DIARY
or
INTELLIGENCE SUMMARY.
(Erase heading not required.)

Army Form C. 2118.

Instructions regarding War Diaries and Intelligence Summaries are contained in F. S. Regs., Part II. and the Staff Manual respectively. Title pages will be prepared in manuscript.

Place	Date	Hour	Summary of Events and Information	Remarks and references to Appendices
MILLENCOURT Sheet 57d.S.E. 62 D.N.E.	15/10/16		was cold and satisfactory — It was exceedingly cold however & we were glad to get back to our comfortable billets. Lt. THOMAS demonstrated with a new Stand Training continued — Lecture to Senr Officers by Captain PALMER on "Pivots" &c noted at Bouzincourt — Practical.	
MILLENCOURT	16/10/16			
MILLENCOURT	17/10/16		Training stopped owing to Bn having to supply large fatigue parties at/from Huge at MILLENCOURT. 2/Lieuts KERR, CLEMENTS, & HARNER, go to hospital (sick).	
MILLENCOURT	18/10/16		Whole Bn on fatigues during most of day. B. Inducis might attached with good results "A", "C" & "D" Coys under Major IRWIN. forced to FRICOURT FARM for work on roads. A very wet day. In working camps of tents & bivouacs at FRICOURT into which we moved. A party of 50 men of Bn. under 2/Lieut STOKES, joined to BECOURT to assist in building some hutments. Major PHILLIPS & C/1 ODDS go to Hospital (Sick).	
MILLENCOURT	19/10/16		Only H.Q, half of 15 Coy & Specialists during training are left at MILLENCOURT A very cold day and the men is very but — Coys at FRICOURT busy repairing the CONTALMAISON — FRICOURT Road.	
MILLENCOURT	20/10/16		Bright fine day but very cold — Coys at FRICOURT & BECOURT working hard all day in conjunction with labour Bn. for which there are a great many here now.	

WAR DIARY
or
INTELLIGENCE SUMMARY.
(Erase heading not required.)

Army Form C. 2118.

Instructions regarding War Diaries and Intelligence Summaries are contained in F. S. Regs., Part II. and the Staff Manual respectively. Title pages will be prepared in manuscript.

Place	Date	Hour	Summary of Events and Information	Remarks and references to Appendices
MILLENCOURT	22-10-16		Usual parades at MILLENCOURT. Parties at FRICOURT BECOURT at work all day. Weather continued fine but very cold and it was frosty in the morning.	
ALBERT	23-10-16		Bn. HQ. & MILLENCOURT PARTY, moved to ALBERT & spend night in comfortable billets. Remainder of Bn. hard at work on roads & huts.	
BAZENTIN-LE-GRAND (Sheet 57c. S.W.)	24-10-16		Bn. HQ. ALBERT, all Bn. & jobs joined by FRICOURT } BECOURT detachments at FRICOURT. Marched by CONTALMAISON } BAZENTIN-LE-PETIT Wood to BAZENTIN-LE-GRAND. Reached Reserve trenches. A very wet day & roads in very bad condition. Arrived at 5 P.M. & settled down. Several shells burst in vicinity of Bn. HQ. during the night.	
BAZENTIN-LE-GRAND	25-10-16		Wet cold day – very little available comfortable – the remainder of the Brigade are in front line. 6th N.F. being in front line – attack which was to have taken place today was put off on account of bad weather – large working parties supplied.	
BAZENTIN-LE-GRAND	26-10-16		Weather still wet – not & available – large parties out working at night.	
	27-10-16		Weather continued very bad – attack again put off owing to bad state of ground. 2/Lt. H. ARMSTRONG joined Bn. from 4th (Reserve) Bn.	
	28-10-16		Fine but very cold day – Major WRIGHT – 7th N.F. is attached to the Bn.	
	29-10-16		Very bad day – poured with rain – roads & trenches much in mud & water	

952.
N.1.

Army Form C. 2118.

WAR DIARY
or
INTELLIGENCE SUMMARY.
(Erase heading not required.)

Instructions regarding War Diaries and Intelligence Summaries are contained in F. S. Regs., Part II. and the Staff Manual respectively. Title pages will be prepared in manuscript.

Place	Date	Hour	Summary of Events and Information	Remarks and references to Appendices
BRIENTINLLE GRANDE TO THE (Sheet 57c. S.W.)	24-10-16 to 31-10-16		Working parties supplied as usual. 2nd Lieut JONES wounded. Fine day - cold. So good and strong which we trust will dry up the sodden ground. In order to support lines in the vicinity of the COUGH DROP - Colonel C Turner CMG leaves the Battalion to take over the Command of a Divisional School - Major N.I. Wright 4th Bat Yor R.I. is appointed to the Command of the Battalion.	CASUALTIES 24th - 31st Killed = 3.O.R Wounded - 16.O.R. Missing - 2.O.R. 953 E.B

List of officers with Battalion on 31st October:

H.Q. — Lt.Col. C. TURNER CMG.(Com.g.) - Major R. IRWIN (2nd in Command) - Capt. N.A.C. YATELEY(Adjt.)
Lieut McKENZIE, R.A.M.C. (M.O.) — Capt. LEETE (Intelligence)

A Coy. — Capt. N. EASTEN, 2/Lt. J.N. LOUGH, 2/Lt. S. STONES,

B Coy. — 2/Lt. E. BISSET, 2/Lt. N.W. LANSON, 2/Lt. R.H. FORSTER, 2/Lt. H. ARMSTRONG.

C Coy. — 2/Lt. B. HEAD, 2/Lt. R.R. PARK,

D Coy. — 2/Lt. H.N. GILL, 2/Lt. H. ARMSTRONG, 2/Lt. E.V. SARGENT,

(Transport) Lt. H.T. PAPE, (R.M.) 2/Lt. R. NORRIS, (Signals) 2/Lt. C.V. ALDER, (Lewis Gun) 2/Lt. T.N. MELROSE, (Bom.) 2/Lt. SURFLEET.

CONFIDENTIAL

WAR DIARY

OF

5TH BN NORTHUMBERLAND FUSILIERS

FROM 1ST NOVR TO 30TH NOVR 1916.

(VOLUME 14.)

Arnold Irwin

1-12-16

Major
Comdg 5th Bn North Fus.

Army Form C. 2118.

WAR DIARY
or
INTELLIGENCE SUMMARY.
(Erase heading not required.)

Instructions regarding War Diaries and Intelligence Summaries are contained in F.S. Regs., Part II and the Staff Manual respectively. Title pages will be prepared in manuscript.

Place	Date	Hour	Summary of Events and Information	Remarks and references to Appendices
FLERS. (Sheet 57 S.E.w.)	1-11-16		Fine day – Battalion remained in vicinity of COUGH DROP – Attack postponed until morning of 2-11-16	Casualties 1-11-16 to 3-11-16 Killed 2/Lieut STONES,S. 2. 3. O.R. 16 O.R.
"	2-11-16		Rained during night & all morning – We get orders that we are to relieve the 7th N.F. & will attack on morning of the 3rd. Attack again postponed owing to the bad state of the trenches – Relieved 7th N.F. Relief complete about 5 p.m. – Enemy fairly quiet except for CUTTING which is always shelled – Night fairly quiet –	
"	3-11-16		Fine day – Dull in the early morning. 2/Lieut STONES (A Coy) sniped through the head & killed about 7.30 a.m. By his death we lose an excellent officer – The men cheering at H.Q. & HEXHAM ROAD – Relieved by the 8th B.D.L.I. – Relief commenced at 9 a.m. & completed about 1 p.m. – Luckily no casualties – Went to new camps behind HIGH WOOD.	
HIGH WOOD 4-11-16 (Sheet 57) (S.W.) S.10.a.			Men in canvas huts – very crowded – nevertheless fairly comfortable after the front line	
"	5-11-16	9.10 A.M.	151st Brigade attacked – we are under orders to move at a moment's notice if required. Attack succeeds on the left but not on the right & a counter attack delivered later drives whole line back to the original trenches – We do not move.	

A 5834 Wt W4973/M687 750,000 8/16 D.D. & L. Ltd. Forms/C.2118/13.

WAR DIARY
or
INTELLIGENCE SUMMARY.

(Erase heading not required.)

Army Form C. 2118.

Place	Date	Hour	Summary of Events and Information	Remarks and references to Appendices
HIGH WOOD (Abt 57c.S.W.) (S.10.a)	6·11·16		Remain in the Camp resting. No working parties for a change — Get orders to move to PRUE and STARFISH TRENCHES at 8 p.m. — Move carried out without any casualties — Accommodation in trenches very bad — a quiet night.	
MARTINPUICH (Abt 57c.S.W.)	7·11·16		Rained nearly all day — Trenches in a very bad state — most of the dug-outs fair in wet at intervals and windy — Started making good dug-outs — a lot of artillery activity on both sides during the night —	Casualties 6–7/11/16 Killed 2 O.R. Wounded 1 O.R.
	8·11·16		Very fine cold day — Great aerial activity — German "Planes" seem very keen for a change — Very nearly succeed in driving down one or two of our observation "planes" — Relieved in the evening by the 1st N.F. — A fine moonlight night — We return to the Camp south-east of HIGH WOOD.	Casualties 8–9/11/16 Wounded 1 O.R.
HIGH WOOD	10·11·16		A bright cold day — Plenty of aerial activity on both sides	
	11·11·16		A dull day — Relieved the 1st Bn EAST YORKS in the FLERS LINE — no casualties	Casualties 10·11/11/16 Wounded 1 O.R.
FLERS	12·11·16		Dull day though warmer — Remained in the FLERS LINE 9 am the evening sent out working parties — about 150 men.	Casualties 11–12/11/16 Wounded 1 O.R.
	13·11·16		A dull day — very quiet. Get orders we are to attack tomorrow — Very busy getting up stores &c all day — Relieved the 1st N.F. at night in the right sub-sector — Relief completed by about 11·15 p.m. — Lieut HERD at duty room O.C. about 9 p.m.	Casualties 12–13/11/16 Killed 3 O.R. Wounded 3 O.R.

956

WAR DIARY
or
INTELLIGENCE SUMMARY

Place	Date	Hour	Summary of Events and Information	Remarks and references to Appendices
FLERS.	13.11.16		The 1st N.F. are to attack on our left + the 5th AUSTRALIAN BRIGADE on our right — zero hour is at 6.45 a.m. on the 14th inst — At that time Companies are to be disturbed as follows — B & D Coys in NEW SUPPORT TRENCH — A & C Coys in ABBAYE TRENCH — B & D Coys will form the first lines & waves — "C" Coy will form the 3rd wave & is carrying up 80 sandbags of bombs. At zero hour A Coy will move into SNAG & SNAG SUPPORT TRENCHES (2 platoons in each).	A.
		6.45 a.m.	Zero hour — Attack started.	
BUTTE de WARENCOURT.	14.11.16	8 a.m.	We get news from Capt. GILL (wounded) commanding D Coy on the right that they got to GIRD TRENCH alright but had a lot of casualties going on — chiefly from our own barrage & also machine gun fire from the same right. No news of left Coy (B) yet.	
"	"	8.45 a.m.	We receive news that C Coy are in position but apparently have no officers left — It looks as if the 1st N.F. on our left have not got their objective — although they are holding HOOK SAP.	
"	"	10 a.m.	Men of B Coy coming down wounded say that their Coy got up alright — but we have as yet no news & no definite news.	
"	"	11 a.m.	Note received from Capt. EASTEN that part of A Coy have got up to BUTTE TRENCH.	
		2 p.m.	Definite news is received from 2/Lieut. H. ARMSTRONG (now commanding D Coy) that he is occupying about 100x of GIRD TRENCH with about 150 men composed of B, C & D Coys.	

WAR DIARY
or
INTELLIGENCE SUMMARY.

(Erase heading not required.)

Army Form C. 2118.

Place	Date	Hour	Summary of Events and Information	Remarks and references to Appendices
BUTTE de WARLENCOURT. (Sh: 57c.5.w)	14.11.16	3 p.m.	has established a strong post. - no definite news of the 1st N.F. has yet been received.	A.1
"	"	4 p.m.	S.O.S. signal is put up - Our artillery put up a heavy barrage - Result, however, is not known.	
"	"	6.30 p.m.	1 Coy of 1st N.F. & 2 Coys of 4th N.F. are sent up to make an attack & occupy parts of trenches not taken this morning - This attack did not come off as these Coys were unable to get into position in time.	
"	"	10 p.m.	A party started to dig a communication trench from P. ALLEY to the HOOK but were hampered from the apex of HOOK as the Germans have managed to get back into their end of the HOOK - no other information	
"	"	11 p.m.	Major WRIGHT & hunt Colonel GIBSON (4th N.F.) went up to the line to organise a fresh attack - They have for this 1 Coy of 1st N.F. & 1 Coy 4th N.F. on the left and 1 Coy 4th N.F. This remains of our 1 Coy (now only 30 strong). Strong bombing patrols are sent out - 2 on the left of P. ALLEY & 1 on the right	
"	15.11.16	12.30 a.m.	Both these patrols were repulsed by very heavy (shown by the word fight on SNAG TRENCH) and met by very heavy machine gun & rifle fire from the front - They were forced to return to our trenches - A very heavy barrage was put up by the enemy - He is evidently holding HOOK TRENCH in strength - This shews conclusively that the enemy are holding the BLIND TRENCHES & that they have somehow got in between us & our men - who remain there for he in the GIRD LINE.	

WAR DIARY
INTELLIGENCE SUMMARY

Army Form C. 2118.

Place	Date	Hour	Summary of Events and Information	Remarks and references to Appendices
BUTTE de WARLENCOURT (Sheet 57cS.W.)	15 Nov	1 a.m.	Received a message from 2/Lieut ARMSTRONG (D Coy) that his Company is still holding on the left of the AUSTRALIANS. They had not been counter attacked until an hour ago – when the enemy made a bombing attack from the left which was repulsed.	A1
"	"	1.30 a.m.	Lt Col. GIBSON (4th NF) & Major WRIGHT have examined SNAG TRENCH for defence & have returned to Bn H.Q. – nothing more can be done at present. – Remainder of night fairly quiet –	959
"	"	9 a.m.	SNAG & SNAG SUPPORT trenches are very much damaged by enemy shell fire.	
"	"	12 noon	Received note from 2/Lieut ARMSTRONG that the Germans have been massing on his left & that front line above that he is short of bombs, ammunition etc. – We arrange for getting a carrying party of 35 men from the 5th Bn. YORKS. REGT & sent up with supplies during the afternoon.	
"	"	3 p.m.	2/Lieut ALDER (Signal Officer) & 2/Lieut AITCHISON (Scout) are sent up from H.Q. to find out the exact situation & position of our men – They report them to be holding very much as we thought. 150 yds on the left of SUNKEN ROAD – The AUSTRALIANS being on their left – They have not again been counter-attacked.	
"	"	4 p.m.	We get word that we are to be relieved tonight.	
"	"	7 p.m.	The SNAG FRONT LINE & SUPPORTS are relieved by the 11th Bn YORKS by about 7 p.m. without difficulties – a fairly quiet night – 2 Coys of 4th Bn E. YORKS are relieving our men in GIRD LINE on right – This relief is punctually completed and our men out by 3 a.m. on 15th inst. The casualties during Bulgnieva (14th – 15th) have been very heavy. Capt H.W. GILL, 2/Lieuts L. SURFLEET, A.R. PARK & R. BOULTON being wounded on the 14th & 2/Lieuts T.N. MELROSE, N.W. LAWSON	

WAR DIARY
or
INTELLIGENCE SUMMARY.
(Erase heading not required.)

Army Form C. 2118.

Place	Date	Hour	Summary of Events and Information	Remarks and references to Appendices
FLERS.	15-11-16		& HAROLD ARMSTRONG (all of B.Coy) have been missing since the 14th — They went last seen when going out with their Lewis gun to attack. Casualties amongst N.C.O's heavy (Chiefly 2nd 14th) were KILLED 35 — WOUNDED 138 — MISSING 64. Very little hope is entertained regarding the latter.	
"	16-11-16		All that is left of the Bn returns to FLERS LINE, a total of 7 Officers & 220 O.R. Including some of the enemy altogether the trenches captured by us & the AUSTRALIANS — 4 Officers & 130 men come up from transport —	
"	17-11-16		Very fine, cold, frosty — We spend a quiet time in FLERS LINE — Have brew a 3 Officers & 50 men to be attached to the 6th Bn N.F. until they are relieved — We move from FLERS LINE into FLERS SWITCH going to the 12th Division coming in — We are to be relieved tomorrow.	CASUALTIES. 12 noon 17th – 18th KILLED 1 O.R. WOUNDED 2 O.R. MISSING 2 O.R.
FLERS. BAZENTIN-LE-GRAND. ALBERT	18-11-16.		Very wet — We left FLERS SWITCH at 4.30 A.M. & marched to BAZENTIN CIRCUS STATION — where we were just in time to catch the train — Proceeded in good trucks to MEAULT & marched about 5½ miles to ALBERT — where we went into good billets — Very tired but thankful to get back.	
ALBERT.	19-11-16		Spent the day in cleaning up — Party attached to 6th NF rejoins.	
"	20-11-16		Cleaning up — A number of men rejoin from Brigade Carrying Party.	
"	21-11-16		Cleaning up — C.O. (Major WRIGHT) goes on leave. Command handed over to Major IRWIN.	
"	22-11-16.		Making up the numbers of Lewis Gunners & Bombers 2nd Lieut HARMER rejoins from sick leave in England —	
"	23-11-16		Capt YATE (Adjutant) goes on leave — 2nd Lieut EASTEN acts as Adjutant	

960 —

A1

Army Form C. 2118.

WAR DIARY
or
INTELLIGENCE SUMMARY.
(Erase heading not required.)

Place	Date	Hour	Summary of Events and Information	Remarks and references to Appendices
ALBERT (Sheet 57 D.S.E.)	24.11.16 25.11.16		Whole day the Battn. on working party - Lewis Gunners & Bombers underwent training.	
"	26.11.16		Church Parade in CINEMA with band - most of Battn. on working party.	
"	27.11.16		A very cold day - Battalion less specialists made arrangements - on working party. The town was shelled from 7 p.m. to about 9 p.m. but little damage was done, except a big hole in the part of the Q.M.'s Store - 2/Lieut HEPWORTH returns from leave - 2/Lieuts H.O. JOHNSON & E.V. SARGENT go to hospital sick.	
"	28.11.16		Big working parties supplied to clean up the streets of ALBERT.	
"	29.11.16		More working parties - About midnight a draft of 133 men banded from the Base - Corpl. G.W. DODDS rejoined with this party - The training officer A. SWYNFEN commenced leave A.I.	A.I.
"	30.11.16		Receive orders that we are to move to BRESLE tomorrow - Very busy making preparations for moving -	

961 - EB

A5834 Wt.W4973/M687 750,000 8/16 D.D.&L. Ltd. Forms/C.2118/13.

...cots the 1st Objective.

V. These two parties will form block to counter attack in case the troops on either flanks do not gain their objective.

VI. A patrol of officer + NCOs + 10 men will be detailed by E Coy to examine the dug outs + cellars belonging to ...ing street M.16.5.2

VII. The B. Dump will be at M.11.3.7.2.5 from which all stores will be drawn.

VIII. Each coy will detail 5 men to report to Bn HQ at 4am — A coy to supply NCO to be in charge of this party.

IX. A + D coys will each take 2 Lewis guns. B + C coys one each — B + C coys will each send 1 gun + team to report to Bn HQ at ..... 7 a.m.

X. A + C coys will each take one telephone.

XI. 50 bayonets are to be fixed in the Assembly trenches before 3.10 pm.

XII. Watches will be synchronized at B.HQ at 12 noon — each coy will send an officer

Copy No I

OPERATION ORDER. No. 35 A.

I. The Bⁿ will parade at 4am (Y.O.P. taking coad to N⁰ 5 DURHAM ROAD M22C14.7 to M21D6.8 & M22C14.6 to M21D5.7 respectively
Bⁿ H.Q. will be at M.27.B.7.0

II. The Bn will attack the two following objectives
(1) M22 A 2½   (2) M22 A 2.3
    to   to
   M21.6.8.3   M21 B 9.4
Frontage of about 300 yards.
The A Composite Bⁿ (8ᵗʰ D.L.I. + 5ᵗʰ Borders) will attack on the right & the 23rd Division will attack on the left.

III. The Bⁿ will attack in four waves composed of columns of platoons at 50 yards distance.

IV. The first wave will go straight through to the 2nd Objective.
The second wave will stop at the first objective & clean it out.
The 3rd wave will go through to the 2nd Objective
The 4ᵗʰ wave will stay with the 2nd wave in the first objective.

V. The 1st & 3rd waves will consolidate the 2nd objective — the 2nd & 4ᵗʰ waves will

there at that time.

ARTILLERY

Zero to Zero (3.15pm) Deliberate Bombardment.

3.15pm – 3.17pm Barrage 50 short of German front
line – infantry advance at Zero
under cover of Barrage.

3.17pm Barrage got back to German front line
Infantry continue to advance.

3.19pm Barrage lifts off German front line
onto a line 150ᵗʰ beyond German
Support line.
All wave continue to their objectives.

3.45pm Barrage lifts clear of Cutting M.28.d.9
to M.16.c.3.2.
At this hour patrols from the
leading B⁽ⁿ⁾ will push forward &
ascertain at the earliest possible
moment weather the Cutting is
held by the enemy.

30/9/16   M.C. Wats... Capt & Adjt
                                                        .F.

Copy

OPERATION ORDER No 133.

I. The 50th Division is going to attack tomorrow. The 149th Brigade will be in support. The 5th N.F. will be ready to move from their present camp any time after 6. am tomorrow morning.

II. Companies will be fully equipped for the assault.

III. Breakfasts will be at 5. am. Companies will arrange to have all tomorrows rations except breakfast carried on the man.

Acknowledge.

(Sgd) V.A.C. Yate Captain
Adjt 5 N.F.

4/11/16
5.30 pm

Copy:

OPERATION ORDER No 134

I. The Batt will occupy STARFISH & PRUE TRENCHES as follows tonight:—
C & D Coys PRUE TRENCH from RUTHERFORD ALLEY to the right.
A & B Coys STARFISH from RUTHERFORD ALLEY to the right.
H.Q. STARFISH TRENCH.

II. Coys will march off from here commencing 8 pm in the following order D C B A
An interval of 50x to be kept between platoons
Coys will go down RUTHERFORD ALLEY.

IV. An endeavour is being made to get the water cart refilled tonight — if this can be done — all water bottles to be filled before marching off.

V. Coys will take their cooks & dixies up with them & will arrange to cook in their company areas.

VI. Completion of relief to be reported HQ

6/14/16

Sgd V A C Yate Captain
Adjt 5 NF

OPERATION ORDER No 135

I. The Bttn will relieve the 6th EAST YORKS in the FLERS LINE today - relief to be complete by 4 pm. Companies will relieve their opposite numbers.

II. Companies will move by half platoons & will leave their present camp at the following times:
- A Coy.   11.30 am
- B Coy.   12.30 pm
- C Coy.   1.30 pm
- D Coy.   2.30 pm

Coys will make their own arrangements for dinners, either at this end or the other.

III. 2/Lt Swiflert will issue this morning 500 sandbags for each coy - these will be put round the leg before moving off - all puttees will be rolled up & left in a pile under guard of 1 man per coy to be handed over to the Transport.

IV. C Coy will hand over 12 water tins to A Coy. D Coy will hand over a similar number to B Coy - water tins will be exchanged for full ones as before at the SWITCH DUMP.

V. HQ will be in FLERS LINE at M 29 B 3.0. Completion of relief to be reported here.

VI. Advance parties will meet coys at junction of DROP ALLEY & FLERS LINE.

1/11/16

Syd V A G Yate Capt
Adjutant 5 NF.

CONFIDENTIAL

WAR DIARY

OF

5ᵗʰ Bⁿ NORTHUMBERLAND FUSILIERS

FROM 1ˢᵗ Decʳ 1916 to 31ˢᵗ Decʳ 1916.

(VOLUME 15)

1-1-17

[signature] Major
Wᵗ Lieut Colonel
Comᵈᵍ 5ᵗʰ Bⁿ Northᵈ Fus.

WAR DIARY or INTELLIGENCE SUMMARY

Army Form C. 2118.

Place	Date	Hour	Summary of Events and Information	Remarks and references to Appendices
ALBERT	1-12-16		The Battalion left ALBERT about 10 a.m. & marched along the AMIENS road to BRESLE, relieving the 9th/8th Black Watch in rest billets. The billets are fairly good. Sing Song & Xmas dinner - the officers were in tents.	A1
BRESLE	2-12-16		Day spent in resting & cleaning up.	
BRESLE (Sheet 62DNE)	3-12-16 to		Training commenced - Route march before breakfast, squad & company drill to noon. Afternoon devoted to lectures, gas helmet drill & bombers, under N.C.O.'s, Signallers & Lewis gunners training under the respective specialist officers. A Brigade Concert Party is formed by Capt Snowball A.S.C. & smokers are frequently given in the Brigade Canteen arranged by the Revd J. Snel. Lieut J.H. SWAN reported on 5th inst.	
	5-12-16			
	6-12-16		Owing to rain yesterday the inspection of the Brigade by the Corps Commander is postponed. This inspection was held at noon today on the Brigade training area near BRESLE WOOD. Pouring rain during evening so cancelled owing to rain. Lectures are given by Coy. & Platoon Commanders in billets.	

WAR DIARY
or
INTELLIGENCE SUMMARY.

Army Form C. 2118.

Place	Date	Hour	Summary of Events and Information	Remarks and references to Appendices
BRESLE (Sheet 2D)	7-12-16 to 9-12-16		Training as carried out on the same lines as for first 3 days. A good rifle range is available. Companies not the range on alternate days. The Brigade Grant partly gave their final inspection, which is much approved as, BRESLE is a very dull place. No men per day are allowed leaves to AMIENS	
	10-12-16		Friends B.H. ORMSBY & H.J. BASAN joined on 9th inst. also a draft of 40 O.R. Church Parades. Cleaning arms, equipment, billets &c.	
	11-12-16		Company & Bn drill to 12.30 p.m. Companies on attack or a system of trenches. Proposed night schedules cancelled on account of rain. 2nd Lieut. H.S. MINTON Leaves the Bn. being ordered to proceed to 11° 52.18 D	
	12-12-16 to 16-12-16		Training continues. Companies being exercised in the attack on trenches taken. In artillery formations, outposts to. Training is somewhat interfered with by rain. Brigade lectures for officers are carried out in the afternoons under the Brigade Commander. Great attention to paid to the training of the various specialists. Night schedules arranged for 13th inst are cancelled owing to bad weather.	

WAR DIARY
or
INTELLIGENCE SUMMARY.
(Erase heading not required.)

Army Form C. 2118.

Place	Date	Hour	Summary of Events and Information	Remarks and references to Appendices
BRESLE (Shut 62D)			Stables are held each evening on the Brigade Centre. These stables help to while away the long evenings. Major P.P. PHILLIPS reports on the 15th a draft of 25 O.R. (Young soldiers on 16th inst.)	
	17.12.16		Divine Service. — Captain (A.C. YATE (2nd R.S.L) who has done continuous duty as Adjutant since his appointment on 5th May 1915, leaves us to-day on being appointed Second in Command of the 1st/8th Royal North Lancs Regt. (1st Milstream) We are all sorry to lose him & wish him every success with his new unit.	
	18.12.16		Training continues. — Companies exercise in extended order drill. — Close & open order formation — Artillery formations etc. All specialists receive training separately. The Brigade concert party recurse an ovation (by the inclusion of Major PHILLIPS.	
	19.12.16		Usual training — Night work carried out — cancelling La Marsh by compass on a given portion.	
	20.12.16		Brigade training in progress. Captain G.W. DODDS leaves Bn. for duty with Base Commandant at ETAPLES.	

Army Form C. 2118.

WAR DIARY
or
INTELLIGENCE SUMMARY.
(Erase heading not required.)

Instructions regarding War Diaries and Intelligence Summaries are contained in F. S. Regs., Part II. and the Staff Manual respectively. Title pages will be prepared in manuscript.

Place	Date	Hour	Summary of Events and Information	Remarks and references to Appendices
BRESLE (Sheet 62D)	21.12.16		Usual training – awaiting of Battalion drill attacks on Hayes Trenches – Lectures are given each afternoon by divisional staff officers.	
	22.12.16			
	23.12.16		Inspection of the whole Brigade on the training ground by the Brigade Commander who also presented the M.C. ribbon to 2/Lieut (Temp Capt.) H. ARMSTRONG & the D.C.M. ribbon to 3205 C/Sjt Major P. FAWLEY, who have been decorated for their excellent work during the operations on 14th November.	
	24.12.16		Church Parades & party of 25 O.R. was sent to BOTTOM WOOD to make tables etc for transport when we move forward.	
	25.12.16		Voluntary Church parades. A pleasant day is spent – the men having plenty of Xmas pudding & beer. The Brigade Concert Party gave a good performance at night which was very well attended. The N.O's & Sergeants enjoy a dinner at night. We are fortunate in being out of the line for Xmas day.	A1
	26.12.16		Brigade route march. Night operations cancelled owing to rain. 2/Lieut GRAHAM (sick) to hospital.	

WAR DIARY
or
INTELLIGENCE SUMMARY.

(Erase heading not required.)

Army Form C. 2118.

Place	Date	Hour	Summary of Events and Information	Remarks and references to Appendices
BRESLE (Sheet 62.D)	24/12/16		Visual training – Received orders that we are to move to the forward area tomorrow & according made the necessary preparations. A large number of N.C.O's are detailed for courses & they, with the main of Specialists are to remain behind at BRAZIEUX.	
BECOURT (Sheet 57D S.E)	25/12/16		Battalion moves off from BRESLE at 10 a.m. & marches to Meaulte to hub at BECOURT. – A good day for everything – BECOURT reached by 12.45 p.m.	
HIGH WOOD (Sheet 57C S.W)	26/12/16		Battalion moves off from BECOURT at 9.20 a.m. & marches to HIGH WOOD WEST HUTS – arriving at 11.15 a.m. Preparations made for tomorrows move to trenches.	
FLERS (Sheet 57C S.W.)	27/12/16		Battalion takes over trenches from 2nd Bn. Royal Sussex Fusiliers (1st Division) on the front line trenches from M.18.1 to M.24.4. Leave HIGH WOOD HUTS at 11.p.m & relief completed by 4.30 p.m. This excellent performance is chiefly due to duck boarding which is laid from HIGH WOOD Camps right up to Bn. HQ in TURK ALLEY. The front line is composed of a series of posts each held by a LEWIS Gun and 14 men.	A1

Army Form C. 2118.

WAR DIARY
or
INTELLIGENCE SUMMARY.
(Erase heading not required.)

Place	Date	Hour	Summary of Events and Information	Remarks and references to Appendices
FLERS (See 15/t.S.H)	30/11/16		These posts are in shell holes, which have been improved & strengthened. B & C Coys are in the line. D Coy is in support. Owing to the heavy rain & the previous night the mud is exceptionally bad & communication presents almost impassable types are however laid to the front line across the open. These greatly assisted during the relief. Little shelling during the night & no casualties as there is only room for 2 Companies in the line, A Coy is left behind at a tent camp at N.E. corner of MAMETZ WOOD. to mend & supply rations amongst parties.	A1
FLERS.	3/12/16		Still day. Comparatively little shelling in front. This is a great change to what we have previously experienced in this portion of the line. We sincerely trust that 1917 will be the year of victory for the Allies & do end the war.	

(CONFIDENTIAL)

WAR DIARY

OF

5th Bn. NORTHUMBERLAND FUSILIERS

FROM 1ST JANY 1917 TO 31ST JANY 1917

VOLUME 16

1-2-17

Lieut Colonel
Comdg 5th Bn N.F.

WAR DIARY
or
INTELLIGENCE SUMMARY.
(Erase heading not required.)

Army Form C. 2118

Place	Date	Hour	Summary of Events and Information	Remarks and references to Appendices
FLERS Sheet 57c S.W.	1-1-17		No improvement in trenches, which are still in a very bad state, water and mud up to the knees in most places. The enemy seem inclined to be hospitable so bottles and aims are freely thrown above the parapet. Practically no shelling. Resume enemy are holding New Year's Day in good style. D. by relieve B/C bombing in front line.	Casualties 12 noon 1st 2nd Killed – 2 O.R. Wounded – 2 O.R.
	2-1-17		Raining most of the morning, making conditions a little worse in the front line. Cleared up during the afternoon. COBHAM TRENCH & neighbourhood of FIVE CROSS ROADS, shelled fairly heavily between 2 p.m. & 3 p.m. but no damage done. There are moments very bad had conditions but very cheery and bright.	
	3-1-17		Fine again and trenches looking a little better as men have been working hard. Enemy artillery are more active, mainly around the DUMP & YARRA RESERVE trench. Knocking to shew which was an old German artillery dugout, gives more than its ration of S.O.S. hours. This is an endeavour to get at any time. Relieved by 7th N.Z. relief complete 2.50 p.m. Be change dugouts First Battalion come from into support, to a spot which is very	2294

A5834 Wt. W4973/M687 750,000 8/16 D. D. & L. Ltd. Forms/C.2118/13.

WAR DIARY
or
INTELLIGENCE SUMMARY.

(Erase heading not required.)

Army Form C. 21

Place	Date	Hour	Summary of Events and Information	Remarks and references to Appendices
FLERS	3-1-17		Little better than the front line in regard to condition	
	4-1-17		Rained all day - Men having a well earned rest, but go out at night as carrying party to YARKA BANK. Very little shelling. Weather fine & clear. Aeroplanes very active, several fights but none brought down. Our artillery here a big shoot with heaves on LOUPART WOOD during the afternoon. Enemy who retaliates against FIVE CROSS ROADS fairly heavy. Two companies out on working party, nearly all night laying cable on walk track to YARKA BANK.	Casualties 5 w.6 m Killed - I.O.R. wounded - I.O.R. missing - I.O.R.
	5-1-17		Wet morning - not very much anything activity on either side and really a quiet day. Two companies digging at BANK and carrying material from TURK DUMP.	Casualties 2 w. Killed - I.O.R wounded 2.O.R
	6-1-17		Another quiet day. YARKA AVENUE has a bad branch from lower from H.2 Trosigan, but luckily no one has behaved by 4th East York Regt about 8pm and march back to BAZENTIN LE PETIT where we are billeted in Nissen huts- Lieut Relief.	Casualties 6 - 1 wounded 5. O.R.

2207

WAR DIARY or INTELLIGENCE SUMMARY

Army Form C. 2118

Place	Date	Hour	Summary of Events and Information	Remarks and references to Appendices
BAZENTIN -LE- PETIT	8-1-17	—	Men pulling down & clearing dug-outs. Huts are fairly comfortable. About 240 men out on working parties at all times.	
(Sheet 57cS.W)	9-1-17		Very cold. Continue to supply fatigue working parties. Have 290 men out today.	
	10-1-17		Still cold and damp. What men are left in camp are cleaning up, the remainder – 240 – are out working most of the day. Heavy bombardment during the night seems about THIEPVAL.	
	11-1-17		Rained nearly all day. Again have big working parties out. Fine but still exceptionally cold. Working parties out all day.	
	12-1-17		Major Swan goes to BAIZIEUX to command Meal Camp 2/Lieuts L.W. HOWARD & A.V. DAVIES join the Battalion.	
	13-1-17		Wet day – have big working parties out. Relieve about 80 men from BAIZIEUX – mostly men who have been out here before.	
	14-1-17		Sharp frosty day – have 180 men out on working party. 2/Lieut J.B. WILSON rejoins the B[attalio]n. goes to "B" Coy	

A5334 Wt.W4973 M687 750,000 8/16 D.D. & L. Ltd. Forms/C.2118/13.

WAR DIARY or INTELLIGENCE SUMMARY

Army Form C. 21

232×

Place	Date	Hour	Summary of Events and Information	Remarks and references to Appendices
FLERS (Sh57c(S.w))	15-11-17		Still frosty – preparing to go up to the line. Relieve 4th East Yorks Regt. in the front line. Distribution – C Company (100 men) on right (holding posts 19-22 and YARRA BANK. A Company on left (with 45 men) and D Company in COBHAM TRENCH (115 men). Relief complete about 8 p.m. Quiet night.	Relieved 1.O.R.
	16-11-17		Very cold day and ground quite hard after the frost. Enemy seems in the same markee condition offensiveness but is working hard on his trenches. Enemy artillery fairly active but no enemy in evidence. We fire the opportunity of burying a few harsh Indian tombs fell behind YARRA BANK during the night and also between 12 noon & 2 p.m.	Casualties 12 noon 16.11.17
	17-11-17		A heavy fall of snow in the early hours of the morning, about 4 days by 9 a.m. and still snowing. Practically no shelling and work still progressing. Day relieved by D Coy in left sector. Quiet day.	
			Hard frost at night, making conditions much very dangerous	

WAR DIARY or INTELLIGENCE SUMMARY

Army Form C. 2118

Place	Date	Hour	Summary of Events and Information	Remarks and references to Appendices
FIERS (Sheet 57/28 S.W)	18-1-17		Fine weather. Enemy more active with artillery, giving COBHAM CORNER a little more than its ration. He did that getting no great "shaking."	
	19-1-17		Still foggy all day, but weather clearer. Enemy seems to be becoming more active in regard to sniping. Artillery much the same, fairly active against FIVE CROSS ROADS and during the night, meathead road. Relief went with whizz bangs. Relieved by 4th M.G.F. and King Nos 6.7 coys from BAZENTIN to join C Company in dugout. C Company to go to YORK ALLEY. The Battalion in dugout.	Casualties 12 noon 18th - 19th 31 wounded O.R.
	20-1-17		H.Q. in shelters in NORTH ROAD. Relief complete about 8pm. Companies rest during the morning except A which goes to work on YARRA BANK the whole day. Very little shelling C Coy carrying material to BANK at night. Still foggy.	
	21-1-17		Still foggy all day, and as snow is still lying, Jacko shed up very plainly. A rather sharp burst of shelling against YORK ALLEY caused by enemy's sniping Lewis Gun Coy firing	Casualties 12 noon 20-21st wounded H.O.R

Place	Date	Hour	Summary of Events and Information	Remarks and references to Appendices
FLERS (Sheet 57c SW)	21-1-17		Much Cloud trouble remainder of the day quiet. Too enemy aeroplanes over BANK. Afraid most of our work will be seen. D Company working all day at the BANK and A Company carrying material all night from DUMP.	
	22-1-17		Still freezing, but on the whole a quiet day with very little artillery activity. C Company working all day at the BANK. D Company carrying R.E. Stores till midnight.	
	23-1-17		Still freezing hard. TURK ALLEY shelled during the early morning with H.E. shells, who shuttered Frank Enemy artillery fairly quiet except for several shots which got their daily rest. Battalion relieved by 4th East Yorks Regt about 8 p.m. and move that to BAZENTIN CAMP. Lee H. C Company remain behind to work, but arrives in camp about midnight. A very bad journey from the trenches on account of frost.	

WAR DIARY
or
INTELLIGENCE SUMMARY.
(Erase heading not required.)

Army Form C. 211

Place	Date	Hour	Summary of Events and Information	Remarks and references to Appendices
BAZENTIN-LE-PETIT. Map 57c. S.W	24-1-17		Still very cold. Generally cleaning up and getting ready to move. About 100 men out on working party.	
	25-1-17		Move from Camp No 14, to ALBERT. Leave camp at 8.15 a.m and march via CONTALMAISON - FRICOURT- BECORT. Arrive in ALBERT at 12 noon. Men in good fettle & much fitter. 2/Lieut B.HEAD rejoins the Battalion	
ALBERT.	26-1-17		Generally cleaning up and reorganising specialists etc. C.O. inspects Companies and men generally settling down. Cold but fine. Start training of Companies. Route marches and inspections. Getting ready to move to next spot and fitting up all supplies stores. Capt N.M. NORTH rejoins Bat'n from leave in the morning - French Civilio - cleaning up.	
	27-1-17		Vacated billets at 9 a.m & marched to DERNANCOURT. Some heavy shells fell in ALBERT just as Bn. left the town.	

235/4

WAR DIARY
INTELLIGENCE SUMMARY

Place	Date	Hour	Summary of Events and Information	Remarks and references to Appendices
BERNANCOURT [Sheet 62c NE]	29-1-17		Arrived in bus billets about 10.15 a.m. Rest of day spent in cleaning up. Billets were fairly good.	
	30-1-17		Very cold day. Companies commence training in vicinity of village. Lewis, Hotchkiss Gunners & Signallers under their respective officers.	
	31-1-17		Very cold. Coy. fall. Lewis Parade at intervals. Training continues.	

Vol 18

17/5 N 7

CONFIDENTIAL

WAR DIARY

OF

5TH BN NORTHUMBLD FUSILIERS

FROM 1ST FEBY TO 28TH FEBY 1917.

(VOLUME. 17)

1-3-17

[signature] Lieut-Colonel
Comdg 5th Bn Northd Fus.

Army Form C. 2118

WAR DIARY
or
INTELLIGENCE SUMMARY.
(Erase heading not required.)

Instructions regarding War Diaries and Intelligence Summaries are contained in F. S. Regs., Part II. and the Staff Manual respectively. Title pages will be prepared in manuscript.

Place	Date	Hour	Summary of Events and Information	Remarks and references to Appendices
DERNANCOURT (Sheet 62D)	1/2/17		Continue training – still freezing	
	2/2/17		Brigade route march from 11 A.M. – 2pm Through BUIRE – RIBEMONT March past G.O.C. 50th Division – Cold but fine	
	3/2/17		Continue training – Games during afternoon	
	4/2/17		March to ALBERT during the morning for baths. Church parade in afternoon.	
	5/2/17		Continue training	
	6/2/17		Continue training – games during afternoon. CO and Company officers went over area	
	7/2/17		Resting up preparing to move. Inspected by G.O.C. in fields	
MERICOURT-SUR-SOMME (Sheet 62D)	8/2/17		March from DERNANCOURT to MERICOURT-SUR-SOMME via BUIRE – VILLE – CHIPILLY – CERISY – Start at 8am. arrive 12 noon.	
	9/2/17		Foot bathing & cleaning up Company officers go up to the line & remain there. – 5 Officers & 15 OR of 59th Division attached for instruction	

WAR DIARY
or
INTELLIGENCE SUMMARY.
(Erase heading not required.)

Army Form C. 2118

Place	Date	Hour	Summary of Events and Information	Remarks and references to Appendices
BOIS LAPIN (Sheet 62c)	10/9/17		March from MERICOURT-sur-SOMME to BOIS LAPIN – Move off 11 A.M. arrive 12.15 p.m.	
	11/9/17		Cleaning up and preparing to go to the trenches – Church parade in the morning.	
BELLOY (Sheet 62c)	12/9/17		Preparing for the trenches in the morning – leave BOIS LAPIN at 5.15 p.m. Take over trenches from 3rd Battn. 144th French Regiment Quiet relief – complete at 11 p.m. Quiet night. Battn. H.Q. at P.C. BELFORT.	
	13/9/17		Quiet day – very little shelling – a few rifle grenades over T.R. SPECIAL. Quiet night – Trenches in good condition.	
	14/9/17		T.R. ANNAMITES & T.R. ARGONNE shelled during the morning. Started relieving as weather shewn signs of breaking. C Company takes over another company sector on the right from 14th E. YORKS as far as BOIS des ARAS. Relief known as RAVINE. Relief complete 11.30 p.m.	Casualties. 12 noon 14-15 Killed – 1 O.R. wounded – 1 O.R.
	15/9/17		Move H.Q. from P.C. BELFORT to P.C. MARCHEU. Quiet day.	

Army Form C. 2118

WAR DIARY
or
INTELLIGENCE SUMMARY.
(Erase heading not required.)

Instructions regarding War Diaries and Intelligence Summaries are contained in F. S. Regs., Part II and the Staff Manual respectively. Title pages will be prepared in manuscript.

Place	Date	Hour	Summary of Events and Information	Remarks and references to Appendices
BELLOY (Sheet 62c)	16/9/17		ANNAMITES shelled at 9.30 a.m. Hot beating - BOYEA II 815. Shelled between 2.30 & 8 p.m. with gas shells.	Casualties 12 noon 15-16 Wounded - 3 O.R.
	17/9/17		Shew set in - Wet day very little shelling - Rain at night	
	18/9/17		Trenches falling in in many places and very wet. Got line very wet. Practically no shelling.	Casualties 12 noon 17-18 Killed - 1 O.R.
	19/9/17		Trenches getting worse TR. ANNAMITES & TR. COULOIR very bad. Very little shelling. Relieved by 4th N.F. Relief complete at 12 midnight. Battalion moves back to BELLOY arriving in about 2.30 a.m. Quiet relief.	Casualties 12 noon 18-19 Wounded - 1 O.R. missing - 1 O.R.
FAY. (Sheet 62c)	20/9/17		Move just to TRIANGLE COPSE arriving at 11 p.m. Dugouts & trenches very good and filling and cleaning up trenches - 50 men out on working party. Raining	
	21/9/17		Cleaning up and cleaning trenches. Dry & rain most of the day - 150 men out on working party.	
	22/9/17		Cleaning up and cleaning trenches - 60 men out on working party.	
	23/9/17		Repairing trenches & clearing mud - 60 men out on working party.	

WAR DIARY
or
INTELLIGENCE SUMMARY.

(Erase heading not required.)

Army Form C. 21

Place	Date	Hour	Summary of Events and Information	Remarks and references to Appendices
FAY (Sheet 62c)	24/2/17		Wet day - cleaning up camp & improving dugouts. 190 men out on working party, laying overland track.	
	25/2/17		Continue clearing mud & generally cleaning up - 45 men on working party.	
PROYART 26/2/17 (Sheet 62D)			Move from TRIANGLE WOOD to PROYART - leave 2pm - arrive 4pm. Good billets in houses and barns.	
	27/2/17		Cleaning up and refitting.	
	28/2/17		Refitting & cleaning up.	

Vol 19

18/5 NF

CONFIDENTIAL

WAR DIARY.

OF

5TH BN NORTHUMBERLAND FUSILIERS

FROM 1ST MARCH 1917 TO 31ST MARCH 1917

(VOLUME 18)

1-4-17.

Arnold Irwin
Major
Comdg 5th Bn Northd Fus

Army Form C. 2118.

WAR DIARY
or
INTELLIGENCE SUMMARY.
(Erase heading not required.)

Instructions regarding War Diaries and Intelligence Summaries are contained in F. S. Regs., Part II. and the Staff Manual respectively. Title pages will be prepared in manuscript.

Place	Date	Hour	Summary of Events and Information	Remarks and references to Appendices
PROYART	1/3/17		Cleaning up and refilling companies	
	2/3/17		Refilling companies - commence making bombing pit	
	3/3/17		Platoon drill - making rifle range & bombing pit	
	4/3/17		Church parade in afternoon - no parade	
	5/3/17		Easter Sunday - companies commence training of specialists	
	6/3/17		Two companies on rifle range - bombers continue training - remainder of Battalion carry out platoon drill	
	7/3/17		Two companies on rifle range - bombers & signallers under specialist officers - event in evening by NIVETS -	
	8/3/17		Platoon & company drill - looking up	
	9/3/17		Move from PROYART to WARFUSEE - ABANCOURT. Rear billets 9.15am arrive at 11.15am Officers mess in Adrian huts	
WARFUSEE - ABANCOURT	10/3/17		Cleaning up and reorganising and new system of attack	
	11/3/17		Church parade in morning - resting	

WAR DIARY
or
INTELLIGENCE SUMMARY.
(Erase heading not required.)

Army Form C. 2118.

Place	Date	Hour	Summary of Events and Information	Remarks and references to Appendices
WARFUSEE - HEMICOURT	10/3/17		Commence rifle range and building bombing pit	
	13/3/17		Continue rifle range & bombing pit - all Battalion all on work	
	14/3/17		Complete rifle range, &c. & commence training by Platoons	
	15/3/17		One Company on rifle range. The remainder of Battalion continue training - Football in afternoon - inter Platoon matches	
	16/3/17		Training by Platoons	
	17/3/17		Training - Hot rounds - inter Battalion match. Beat 149th M.G.C. & -nil. 2/Lieut TULLATHORNE joins from 5th (R) 8th N.F.	
	18/3/17		Church Parade - Football in afternoon	
	19/3/17		Training by Platoons - Headquarters route march - Football in afternoon.	
	20/3/17		Training - Second round - Inter Battalion football competition. Lose 6th N.F. 1 gaol - 8th N.F. 0	
	21/3/17		Training. 2/Lieut FM HALL joins the Bⁿ from 4th (R) N.F.	

Army Form C. 2118.

WAR DIARY
or
INTELLIGENCE SUMMARY.
(Erase heading not required.)

Place	Date	Hour	Summary of Events and Information	Remarks and references to Appendices
NARFOSEE	22/3/19		Inspection by G.O.C. 50th Division - Route march by Companies	
-AGNICOURT			Shoes & showers all day. 2/Lieut G.H. LEWIS joins Bn from 3rd I.B.D. 2/Lieut G.H. HOBSON from 5th K.S.R. Battalion.	
	23/3/19		Training by Companies in Brigade area. Practising platoon in attack.	
	24/3/19		Two Companies route march. Remainder of Battalion continued training — Two Companies in Brigade area practising attack.	
	25/3/19		Church Parade in morning — Resting.	
	26/3/19		Two Companies route march in morning and practise advance & rearguards. Two Companies practise "Platoon in attack"	
	27/3/19		Companies practise Platoon in attack — Route march by Companies in afternoon.	
	28/3/19		Address to Brigade by G.O.C. II Corps on leaving the Corps. March straight to training area & to fall flong practice. 2/Lieut. O.A. BROWN joins Bn from 4th (R) K.S.R.	

WAR DIARY
or
INTELLIGENCE SUMMARY.
(Erase heading not required.)

Army Form C. 2118.

Instructions regarding War Diaries and Intelligence Summaries are contained in F. S. Regs., Part II. and the Staff Manual respectively. Title pages will be prepared in manuscript.

Place	Date	Hour	Summary of Events and Information	Remarks and references to Appendices
WARFUSEE-ABANCOURT	29/3/18		Route march during morning - rest day. 2/Lt A CLEMENTS (and from 11th R.W.F.)	
CAMON	30/3/18		March from WARFUSEE-ABANCOURT to CAMON (near AMIENS) via WILLERS BRETONNEAUX & LONGEAU. Leave 8.10am. Arrive 1pm. Men billeted in Adrian huts - Officers in private houses.	
BERTANGLES	31/3/18		March from CAMON to BERTANGLES via AMIENS - POULAINVILLE. Leave 9.10 am. arrive 12 noon. Short march - Men billeted in barns etc	

Vol 20

CONFIDENTIAL 149/50

WAR DIARY

OF

5TH BN NORTHUMBERLAND FUSILIERS

FROM 1ST APRIL TO 30TH APRIL 1917.

(VOLUME 19)

1-5-17

[signature] Lieut-Colonel
Comdg 5th Bn North'd Fus.

Army Form C. 2118.

WAR DIARY
or
INTELLIGENCE SUMMARY.
(Erase heading not required.)

Instructions regarding War Diaries and Intelligence Summaries are contained in F. S. Regs., Part II. and the Staff Manual respectively. Title pages will be prepared in manuscript.

Place	Date	Hour	Summary of Events and Information	Remarks and references to Appendices
BERTANGLES Sheet 57.C.	1·4·17		Resting — Church parade in afternoon.	
	2·4·17		March from BERTANGLES to BEAUVAL via VILLERS-BOCAGE — TALMAS — LA-VICOGNE. Bus VIII Corps Commander en route. Fine day. Good billets in barns and Lauders.	
	3·4·17		March from BEAUVAL to FORTEL via DOULLENS — BOUQUEMAISON — MON-LEBLOND — BONNIERES. Commence 8.15 a.m. after 2 p.m. Distance nearly 15 miles — Very cold.	
	4·4·17		March from FORTEL to FRAMECOURT via LIGNY-NUNQ. Showing nearly all morning. Arrive in billets at 12 noon.	
	5·4·17		Resting during the morning — All Companies practice intensive digging and making Bivifoon (?) Shop finals. Rain in afternoon. Church Service in the evening.	
	6·4·17		Training by Companies during the morning. Rain in afternoon. Church service in the evening.	
	7·4·17		March from FRAMECOURT to MONCHEAUX via PETIT-HOUVIN — BUNEVILLE. Move off 11.30 a.m. — arrive 2 p.m.	

WAR DIARY
or
INTELLIGENCE SUMMARY.

(Erase heading not required.)

Army Form C. 2118.

Place	Date	Hour	Summary of Events and Information	Remarks and references to Appendices
Sheet 51.c.	8-4-17		March from MONTHEAUX to GUENCHY-LE-NOBLE via MONTS en TERNOIS - GOUY-en-TERNOIS - MAIZIERES - AMBRINES. Arrive 12.30 p.m. All ranks billeted in Chateau. Drawing stores from Brigade dumps to equip Battalion.	
	9-4-17		Drawing stores to complete - Must be prepared to move at 2 hours notice.	
	10-4-17		Receive orders 12 noon move to HANGUETIN 2 pm via AVESNES-LE-CONTE - HAUTEVILLE	
Sheet 51.B	11-4-17		Standing-to ready to move. Receive Order 4.30 p.m that battalion moves to trenches at TILLOY same night. Brigade marches off on rendezvous at 6/6 m via WARLUS - DAINVILLE - AKRAS - RONVILLE. Relieve 9th K.R.R. (14th Division) in old German line. Relief complete 12.15 a.m.	
	12-4-17		Fatigue parties making dumps all day. Heavy bombardment at night in direction of MONCHY-LE-PREUX from 6pm - 2.30 p.m	
	13-4-17		Officers & N.C.O's reconnoitering roads & trenches. Quiet day. Fatigue parties making dumps.	

WAR DIARY
INTELLIGENCE SUMMARY.
(Erase heading not required.)

Army Form C. 2118.

Place	Date	Hour	Summary of Events and Information	Remarks and references to Appendices
Sheet 51B	14-4-17	5.30 a.m.	Silence (Bombardment on whole front, shave from 106 line to HARP (South)) Received orders and awaiting orders to move.	
		6.45 p.m.	Received orders to occupy NIGER TRENCH (west of HANCOURT)	
		1 p.m.	Relief complete. Patrols sent out to get in touch with supporting company of 29th Division NORTH WEST of HANCOURT	
			Quiet night.	
			Quiet during the morning.	
	15-4-17	3.30 p.m.	Scout out A by as strong patrol to reconnoitre village of GUEMAPPE to held by the enemy. Company advance up communication trench west of HANCOURT	
		4.40 p.m.	MARLIERE. Rifle & M.G. fire heard.	
		4.50	Receive message by visual signal from Lieut SWAN that scouts fired upon by M.G. fire from both flanks.	
		5.5 p.m.	Unable to advance owing to heavy M.G. fire from both flanks & front.	
		5.15 p.m.	Order Company to retire as soon as direct dets [?] on...	

WAR DIARY
or
INTELLIGENCE SUMMARY.
(Erase heading not required.)

Army Form C. 2118.

Place	Date	Hour	Summary of Events and Information	Remarks and references to Appendices
Sheet 51B.	15.11.17	5.30pm	A boy returns and reports village held in force by at least a machine gun, also Machine Guns on both flanks. Heavy bombardment on received front. We stand-to but are not called upon. Comparatively quiet night.	Casualties on 15th wounded - 3 O.R.
	16.11.17		Quiet morning - 100 men out on working party making shelters.	
		5pm	Heavy bombardment on received front. Stand-to.	
		8.10pm	Bombardment continues for an hour, then gradu'ly slackens. Our artillery put up intense barrage.	
		10.15pm	Stand down with exception of	
		10.30pm	Carrying party of 1 Officer & 50 men with grenades forced to front line.	Casualties 16th wounded 2 O.R.
	17.11.17	3 am	Receive orders for two companies to reinforce 6th & 7th N.F. in the BANK.	
		8.30	Orders countermanded. Battalion "Stand to".	
		9a.m	Enemy put two shells into valley N.22a.	
			Learn that consolidation by 6th N.F. on the TOWER has not been	

WAR DIARY
INTELLIGENCE SUMMARY.
(Erase heading not required.)

Army Form C. 2118.

Place	Date	Hour	Summary of Events and Information	Remarks and references to Appendices
Sheet 51B.	15.4.17	Noon	Attack by 9th R.F. unsuccessful, all objects gained	
		4 pm	Relief orders to relieve the 6th & 7th R.F. in TOWER posn to	
		8 pm	Relief commences	
		Mdnight	Relief complete. No casualties	
	16.4.17		Disposition. C & D Coys on front line. 2 platoons A Coy in close support. Remainder of A Coy & B Coy in support in BANK.	
		5:30 am	C Coy capture a German officer, apparently lost, too orderly shot while attempting to escape	
		6:30 am	Another wounded prisoner states that enemy intend to attack at 7 am with new Battalion	
			Quiet morning — very light shelling	
		11:30 am	Receive message from Lt. HEAD that enemy can be seen massing. I form our artillery	
		11:45 am	Artillery of our Brigade have a "shoot" enfilading the enemy trenches. Good shooting and immense amount of damage caused	
		2 pm	Situation quiet — receive word that an enemy relief was in progress. Too open and up by our guns	

WAR DIARY
INTELLIGENCE SUMMARY.

(Erase heading not required.)

Place	Date	Hour	Summary of Events and Information	Remarks and references to Appendices
Sheet 51B	18/4/17	3pm	Heavy bombardment of back area by enemy artillery but no attack	Casualties 18/17 Killed 3 O.R wounded:- 2/Lt HOWARD 5 O.R BRAND
		10pm	Situation prudent doubt. Working parties digging trench to get in touch with 55 "Divn" on the right and also making strong discharge point on left flank connecting COJEUL RIVER. N.9.C.	
			2/Lieuts L.W. HOWARD & H. BRAND wounded	
	19/4/17		Quiet morning	Casualties 19/17 Killed 2 O.R wounded:- 4/Lt MARSHALL 13 O.R
		2pm	Sharp Heavy warfare to village of WANCOURT. N.23.a.3.3	
		5pm	C & D Companies relieved by two companies of H.N.Y. A & B Companies remain in support in BANK. C & D Coys move back to reserve area N.15.d.	
			2/Lieut C.B. MARSHALL wounded.	
	20/4/17		Relief complete 1.30 a.m. Quiet night.	Casualties 20/17 Killed 4 O.R wounded 10 O.R missing 2 O.R
		12 noon	C & D Coys & Bn H.Q move to HARP (about) A & B Coys relieved by 5/D.K.I. move back to HARP South dene Casualties during night relief Artillery active in valley N.15 & N.22.	

WAR DIARY
or
INTELLIGENCE SUMMARY.

Place	Date	Hour	Summary of Events and Information	Remarks and references to Appendices
Sheet 51B	2/4/17	11am	Resting	
			Relieved by 8th R.F. - now back to CAVES at ROCLINCOURT	
		6pm	Move complete	
			Intermittent shelling of town by heavy gun all night	
FIRKA 5	3/4/17		Shelling off and on getting - Boths in the afternoon - heavy	
			shelling of town during the night	
	23/4/17 11.45am		Intense bombardment heard	
			Church Parade in Caves during afternoon. Being St Georges	
			day, 8th were not available toes.	
		2.30pm	Received orders to move and occupy HARP (north)	
		11pm	Move complete	
		11.45pm	Received orders to occupy NIGER TRENCH and some sunken	
			roads of 151st Inf Bgde.	
	24/4/17 3.30am		Move complete - no casualties	
			Resting	
		4pm	Attacked by 15th Division on our left - noticed heavy	
			Quiet night - usual activity	

Army Form C. 2118.

WAR DIARY
or
INTELLIGENCE SUMMARY.

(Erase heading not required.)

Instructions regarding War Diaries and Intelligence Summaries are contained in F. S. Regs., Part II. and the Staff Manual respectively. Title pages will be prepared in manuscript.

Place	Date	Hour	Summary of Events and Information	Remarks and references to Appendices
Sheet 51B	25/11/17	3.15am	Heavy bombardment on 15th Divisional front on our left - Battalion situation normal.	
		4.30am		
		11am	Move from NIGER TRENCH to O.G.1 - arrive 1pm Relieve 9th K.R.R. 14 Div	
			Resting	
	26.11.17		Resting	
		5.30pm	Move to billets in ARRAS - Quiet night.	
	27.11.17		Entrain about 12 noon for MINGOURT - arrive 3.15 pm - All Battalion in billets	
MINGOURT Sheet 57D	28.11.17		Cleaning up & refitting	
	29.11.17		Resting - Church parade in afternoon	

CONFIDENTIAL

WAR DIARY

OF

5th Bn NORTHUMBERLAND FUSILIERS

FROM 1st MAY 1917 TO 31st MAY 1917

(VOLUME 20)

1-6-17

[signature] Lieut-Colonel
Comdg 5th Bn North' Fus

WAR DIARY
INTELLIGENCE SUMMARY.
(Erase heading not required.)

Army Form C. 2118.

Place	Date	Hour	Summary of Events and Information	Remarks and references to Appendices
MONDICOURT. Sheet 57d.	1/5/17		Marched from MONDICOURT to SOUASTRE Via PAS - HENU. Took over Billets hitherto occupied by 86th Brigade. (1st Lancashire Fusiliers).	
SOUASTRE.	2/5/17		March from SOUASTRE to NERGATEL Via MONCHY-au-BOIS - ADINFER - HENDECOURT. Arrived at 12 noon. Batt. went into its former Billets.	
NERGATEL. Sheet 51.B.	3/5/17		Scheme Bombardment on white front at 3.45 a.m. Rested during day. Very hot.	
			Physical Drill.	
SOUASTRE. Sheet 57D.	4/5/17	10.15am 9.30pm	March to SOUASTRE Via HENDECOURT ADINFER MONCHY-au-BOIS, arrived in Billets at 9.45 p.m.	
MONDICOURT.	5/4/17	8am	March from SOUASTRE to MONDICOURT Via HENU - PAS. Arrives in Billets 10.45 a.m. Riding - Church Parade addres by Brigadier 11.15 a.m.	
	6/5/17			
	9/5/17		Company training - Staff ride for officers 1800 under Brigadier.	
	8/5/17		Batt. ammunition checked under Coy. arrangements for efficient clean Coys.	
	9/5/17		Batt. Ammunition Parade under Coy. arrangement. Officers & non-coms.	
	1/5/17		A, B, & D Coys. Brigade relieve reserve & Coy. Batt. ammunition Range.	

WAR DIARY or INTELLIGENCE SUMMARY

Army Form C. 2118.

Place	Date	Hour	Summary of Events and Information	Remarks and references to Appendices
MINDICOURT Sheet 57D	11/5/17		Went ammunition tractor on Rifle Range for Rifles Lewis Guns.	
	12/5/17		Brigade Tactical Exercise reg. orders & B.M's.	
	13/5/17		Gas Hat under General Gas N.C.O. Staff Parade.	
	14/5/17	9am	Conferences at training. 2 hours route march, each day in a different direction.	
			Mounted officers staff ride under Lt.Col. Wyld	
	15/5/17	3pm	Field Strong – 5th & 7th Bn attacked through a wood on to open ground & were not supported with Rifle Bomb Newsonal & Rifle Command were persistent. The tropho taper 2 and an interesting lecture to officers.	
	16/5/17		Brigade Tactical Exercise – Rear Guard Action.	
	14/5/17		Move to SOMASTRE via MS-HEM	
SOMASTRE	19/5/17		SOMASTRE to FAYETTE by truck train – Village a complete wreck – R.E. Sts. resumed. The only place which have escaped was left standing the month of attack were heartily supported by truck General SNOW	

WAR DIARY or INTELLIGENCE SUMMARY

Army Form C. 2118.

(Erase heading not required.)

Place	Date	Hour	Summary of Events and Information	Remarks and references to Appendices
FYETTE	1/5/17		The VII Corps Commander visits Bn HQ during the afternoon. The Bn to remain temporarily attached to the 93rd Division — the whole of the 119th Bde being on patrols.	
	2/5/17		Marched to SENSEE Valley and live ST LEGER. Bn Champdolens in woods - dugouts & "ketty holes". Nothing ready, orders to move forward at 12 hours notice. Orders did not arrive, so Batln spent peaceful night.	
SENSEE VALLEY Sheet 51.B.	3/5/17	9.30 am	Beautiful weather. Some of 23rd Division fought in the afternoon. Wet day. Bn moves into front line trenches astride CROISILLES - ST LEGER rd from 1st Queens & 16th K.R.R. Relief of Queens & R. Queens not completed until 3am or 2.30 am.	Casualties Killed - 1 O.R
	3/5/17	2pm	2/Lieut P.E Cox was wounded slightly during the afternoon.	wounded 2/Lt P.E Cox & 20 OR
		9pm	Patrols from each Coy penetrate as far as the Hun wire during the night. Patrol under 2/Lt SURTEES surprises enemy working party. One German killed & one wounded. The Party documents taken from them shews that they belonged to the 225th Regt.	

WAR DIARY
or
INTELLIGENCE SUMMARY.
(Erase heading not required.)

Army Form C. 2118.

Instructions regarding War Diaries and Intelligence Summaries are contained in F.S. Regs., Part II. and the Staff Manual respectively. Title pages will be prepared in manuscript.

Place	Date	Hour	Summary of Events and Information	Remarks and references to Appendices
CROISILLES Sheet 51.B.	23/5/17	9pm.	Our German arrested by A Coy who caught in hand being right.	
	24/5/17	2pm.	Weather cleared during day. Our Heavy Batteries bombard enemy trenches without our posts. Several slightly shells, H.Q. informed of this, that failed to locate the Battery in front.	Casualties Killed - 3 O.R. wound - 3 O.R.
		5pm.	German pontoon slated on D Coy sector, known as PLUM LANE. Counter attack by C Coy. Barbed light down of our Lewis Gun teams - all killed, re establish and commenced re-building trenching plant. There P.E. Cox met from reserve.	
	25/5/17	7:45am.	Relieved by 6 R.B. in our front line position. Took over the trenches occupied by the 6 R.B. in 2nd line trenches in support. Remainder of the day. Fatigue parties dumping on front trenches during the night.	Casualties Killed - ? wound ? - 3 O.R.
	26/5/17		Remained in support trenches.	
CROISILLES	28/5/17	11:30am.	B.D. Coys. relieved by Worcesters Rgt. Remainder of Bn. vacated their trenches at the same time. Rendezvous at cross roads.	Casualties Killed - 2 O.R. wound - 9 O.R.

WAR DIARY or INTELLIGENCE SUMMARY

Army Form C. 2118

Place	Date	Hour	Summary of Events and Information	Remarks and references to Appendices
MAYENNEVILLE Sheet 51B	1/9/17		On CROISILLES. Bns marches independently to MAYENNEVILLE. Arrived about 2.30 a.m. B⁺ field — Short horse lines.	
MONCHY-au-BOIS Sheet 57.D.	2/9/17	5.45am	Marched to MONCHY-au-BOIS distance 6 miles. Bns bivouac in the open.	
	2/9/17		Raines very hard. after the weather cleared — Route marching took place under Bn Commanders.	
	3/9/17 9am		Signal field day. Buses took up stations on the German frontier and attacks on wire formation. Aircraft took part in the situations & signalling communication was established between them and our big gun.	
	3/9/17	2.30pm	Bandsman took place of all available officers & other ranks.	
	3/9/17	5.15pm	Rest — after Bn evolutions. Reg. of tout Gan officers and in. and, under lt Brigadier.	

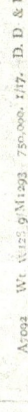

CONFIDENTIAL

WAR DIARY

OF

5ᵀᴴ Bⁿ NORTHUMBERLAND FUSILIERS

FROM 1ˢᵀ JUNE '17 TO 30ᵀᴴ JUNE '17

(VOLUME 21)

1-7-17

[signature] Lieut-Colonel
Comᵈ 5ᵗʰ Bⁿ Northᵈ Fus

WAR DIARY
or
INTELLIGENCE SUMMARY.
(Erase heading not required.)

Army Form C. 2118.

Place	Date	Hour	Summary of Events and Information	Remarks and references to Appendices
MONCHY-au-BOIS. Sheet 51D.N.E.	1/6/17		Company training.	
	2/6/17		A party of 10 officers & 5 N.C.O's visit the SOMME battlefield – 2 inspects	
	3/6/17		enemy's old defences in vicinity of BUTTE-de-WARLINCOURT.	
	4/6/17		Company training.	
	5/6/17		Company training – Battalion is reorganised into 5 Companies each consisting of 2 Platoons – 5th Company – (Z Coy) – contains Officers & Men who will be kept out of the line when the unit goes into action.	
	6/6/17		Battalion inoculated with 2nd dose.	
	7-9/6/17		Companies continue training in delightful weather.	
	10-13/6/17		Battalion & Brigade training – chiefly open warfare tactics & attacked manoevre area in vicinity of ADINFER – DOUCHY-les-AYETTE – AYETTE – BULQUOY & HANNESCAMPS.	
BOYELLES. Sheet 51C	15/6/17		Bn left MONCHY-au-BOIS at 8pm & marched via ADINFER – BOIRY ST RICTRUDE & BOIRY ST MARTIN to Canvas Camps just west of BOYELLES, Arriving at 10.30pm. Brigade is now in Divisional Reserve	

Army Form C. 2118.

WAR DIARY
or
INTELLIGENCE SUMMARY.
(Erase heading not required.)

Instructions regarding War Diaries and Intelligence Summaries are contained in F. S. Regs., Part II. and the Staff Manual respectively. Title pages will be prepared in manuscript.

Place	Date	Hour	Summary of Events and Information	Remarks and references to Appendices
BOYELLES 51B.N.W Sheet	19/6/17 to 21/6/17		Battalion training carried out at BOYELLES – chiefly consisting of route marching & drill. Weather much colder – severe thunderstorm.	
CHERISY	22/6/17		Bn. moves into front line trenches before CHERISY & relieves 8th Bn. K.O.Y.L.I. on Divisional left sector. A, B, & C Coys. in line & D Coy. in local support in MALLARD TRENCH & RAT TRENCH. Quiet relief – no casualties.	
	23/6/17		Quiet morning – As inspected at midnight into CHERISY. Work on digging & clearing saps.	
	24/6/17	2·30 am	151st Brigade on our right attack enemy's front line trenches on their front – Battalion trenches heavily shelled between 2 am & 3 am especially BULLFINCH TRENCH. Intermittent shelling of MALLARD TRENCH during remainder of day.	Casualties 2 OR Wounded J O R
	25/6/17		Intermittent shelling of CURTAIN TRENCH & FOSTER AVENUE during the morning – enemy shelling rather heavy all day. 6th Battalion York'd Lancs'rs relieve us in front line & Bn. moves into Brigade support trenches.	

Wt. W14422/M1160 350,000 12/16 D. D. & L. Forms/C/2118/14.

WAR DIARY
or
INTELLIGENCE SUMMARY.
(Erase heading not required.)

Army Form C. 2118.

Place	Date	Hour	Summary of Events and Information	Remarks and references to Appendices
HENINEL Sheet 51B.NW	28/6/17		Working parties supplied for R.E. work for dugouts — 9" relieved in support by 11th N.F. & moved back to HENIN camp during afternoon. 9" now in Brigade Reserve. Never seen alone during day.	Casualties 28.6.17 Killed - N.C.R wounded - 10.R.
HENIN	29/6/17		Day spent in resting and cleaning up. Inspection by Col. Officer. Vicinity of camp shelled during night but no damage done.	
	30/6/17		Dull weather. Conferences bathing & work at improving camp.	

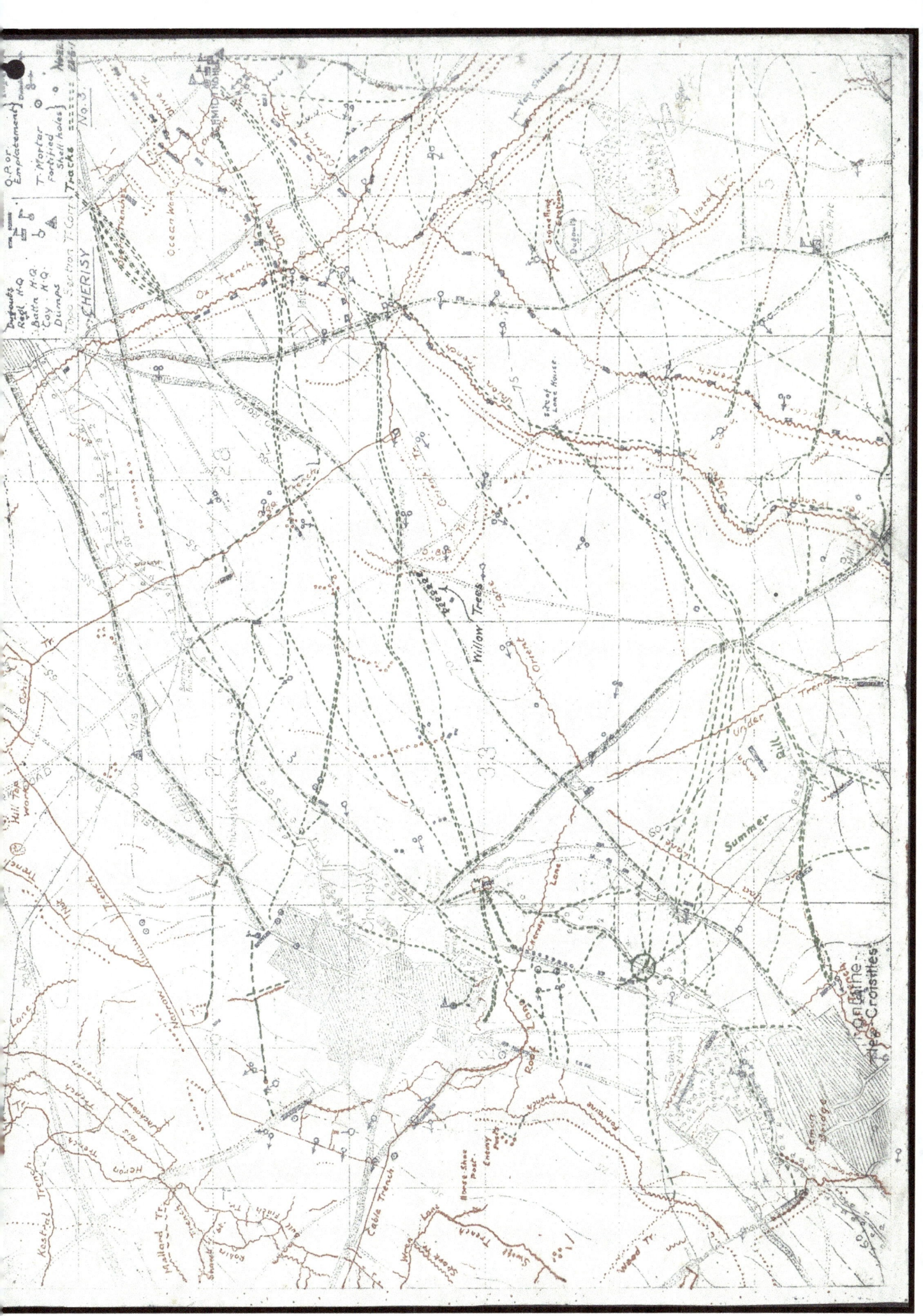

CHERISY

Vol 23

22/5 n 7

CONFIDENTIAL

WAR DIARY

OF

5ᵀᴴ Bⁿ NORTHUMBᴸᴰ FUSILIERS (T.F.)

FROM 1ˢᵀ JULY 1917 TO 31ˢᵀ JULY 1917

(VOLUME 22)

1-8-17

O. P. Phillips, Major
for O.C. 5ᵗʰ Bⁿ Northᵈ Fus

WAR DIARY
or
INTELLIGENCE SUMMARY.
(Erase heading not required.)

Army Form C. 2118

Place	Date	Hour	Summary of Events and Information	Remarks and references to Appendices
HENIN	1-7-17		Resting	
HENINEL	2-7-17		Move into support area. Right Brigade 0.25.b.3.d. Relieve 6th N.F. Quiet night	Casualties wounded - 10 R
	3-7-17		Working parties	Casualties wounded - 5 OR
	4-7-17		Working parties. Night shelling of EGRET TRENCH	
	5-8-17		Relieved by 6th N.F. Take over front line from 4th N.F. from 0.75.5.50.b. 0.26a.5.4. C & D Coys in the line. A Coy in support. B Coy in Reserve. Reg. new trench NORTHUMBERLAND AVENUE.	Casualties killed - 10 R
	6-7-17		More artillery activity than usual in CRATIN Tr. Being front line. Quiet day. Digging on new trench and wiring	
	7-7-17		Artillery active during the morning. Continue wiring	
	8-7-17		Gas released by 21st Division on our right by projectors ahead CHERISY. No retaliation. 6" Howitzers bombard NARROW TRENCH	Casualties wounded - 10 R Casualties wounded - 10 R 2/Lt J.W. McMillen + 3 OR suspected gas poisoning
	9-7-17 1.30am		Quiet day. Relieved by 5/8th K.L. Move back into Divisional Reserve at 1.25 a.	
	10-7-17		Resting	
NEUVILLE VITASSE	11-7-17 7-17		Resting - Cleaning up and general training. Move to trenches right 18/19	Casualties wounded - 10 R
NEWCOURT	19-7-17		Relieve 5/8th Border Regt in Support Area. Left Brigade R 2.4 a 2 N.19.a.	Casualties wounded - 10 R

Army Form C. 2118

WAR DIARY
or
INTELLIGENCE SUMMARY.
(Erase heading not required.)

Instructions regarding War Diaries and Intelligence Summaries are contained in F. S. Regs., Part II. and the Staff Manual respectively. Title pages will be prepared in manuscript.

Place	Date	Hour	Summary of Events and Information	Remarks and references to Appendices
NANCOURT	20/7/17		Working parties to R.E.'s & front line	
	21.7.17		Working parties to R.E.'s & front line - B. Coy in LION Tr shelled between 2-4 pm	Casualties wounded - 1 O.R.
	22.7.17		NANCOURT + MARLIERE shelled heavily all day. Working parties at night	
CHERISY	23.7.17		Relieve 4th M.S. in front line from 0.20.a.6.5 to 0.26.a.5.7. Michaelson A.B.& D.Coys in the line C Coy in Redoubt.	Casualties- Killed - 2 O.R. wounded - 2 O.R.
	24.7.17		Usual shelling of 1615 TRENCH and APE Support during the day. "Fishbacks" active at night. Re-opening APE SUPPORT + Joining up with BISON Tr. Swung front line	
			JACKDAW TRENCH shelled during the morning. Usual "Fishbacks" during the night. Making new trench for garrison joining up APE + BISON trenches.	
	25.7.17		"Fishbacks" active during the morning between 3-4 a.m. Usual intermittent shelling during the day of APE + JACKDAW Tr.	
	26.7.17		Mining & Joining up APE + BISON TRENCHES continued	Casualties wounded- 1 O.R.
	28.7.17	3.45 am	Enemy shelled 5.10 to 14 men attempt to raid No 6 post (A Coy) - driven off by rifle fire - leaving one NCO wounded our lines.	

WAR DIARY
INTELLIGENCE SUMMARY

Army Form C. 2118

Place	Date	Hour	Summary of Events and Information	Remarks and references to Appendices
CHERISY	27.7.17	3.45 am	Identification C Coy 458 I. Regiment (normal). Usual amount of artillery fire. Relieved by 11th N.S. Battalion moved into Brigade reserve NEUVILLE VITASSE. Cleaning up & resting. Companies training & working parties.	
NEUVILLE VITASSE	28-7-17 to 31-7-17		Fighting strength of Bn. on 4/7/17 — 34 Officers & 794 other ranks " " " " 31/7/17 — 36 Officers & 780 other ranks	

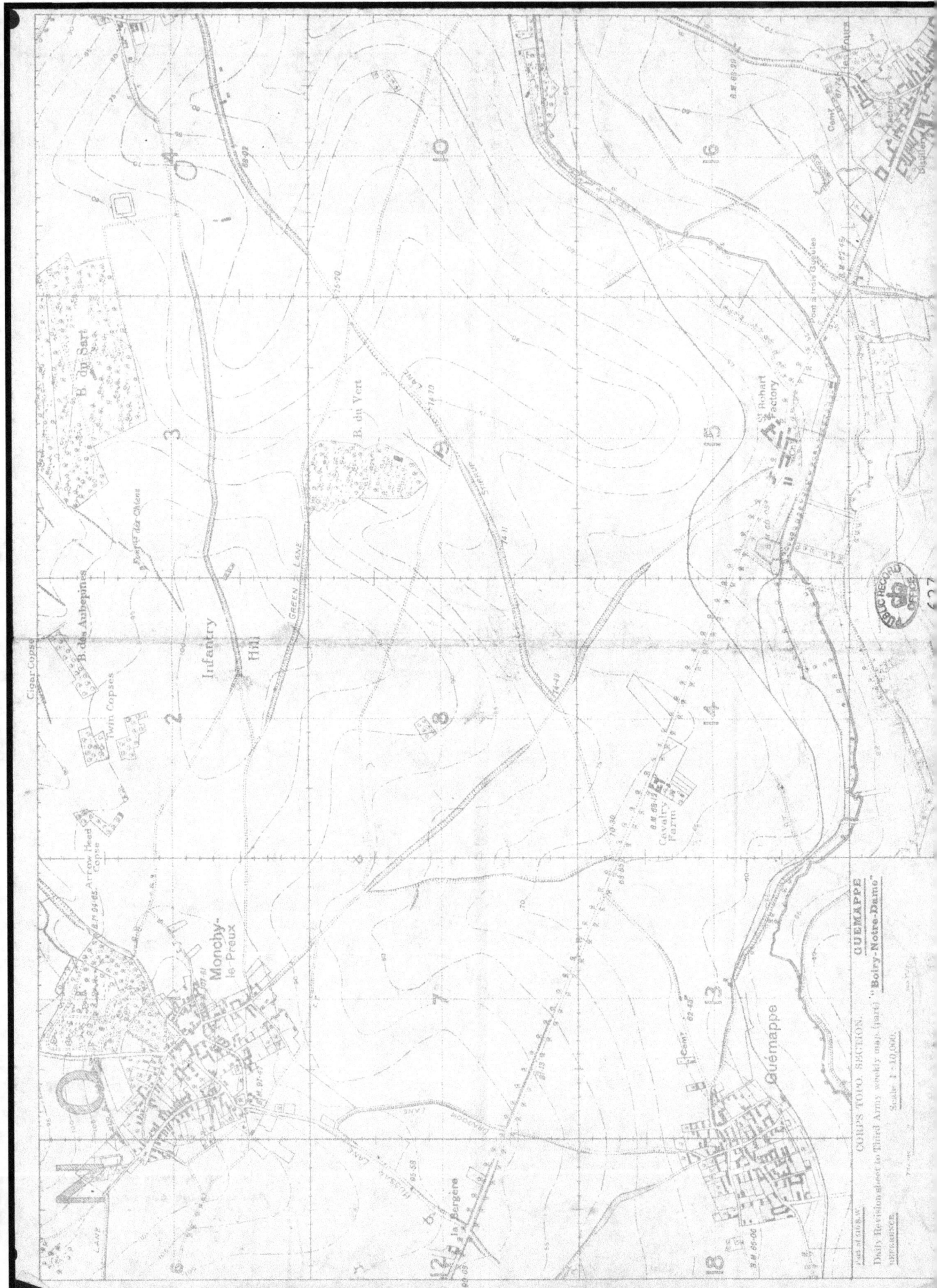

CONFIDENTIAL

WAR DIARY

OF

5TH BN NORTHUMBLD FUSILIERS

FROM 1ST AUG. TO 31ST AUG. 1917

(VOLUME 23)

W.H. Lockhart
Major
Comdg 5th Bn Northumberland Fusiliers

1-9-17.

WAR DIARY
or
INTELLIGENCE SUMMARY.
(Erase heading not required.)

Army Form C. 2118.

Place	Date	Hour	Summary of Events and Information	Remarks and references to Appendices
	1-8-17		Quiet day – Intermittent shelling on whole front – Hostile aerial activity at night.	
	2-8-17		Quiet day. Gas shell bombardment of CATER VALLEY and GUEMAPPE from 0.16 to 0.158. hours. Night otherwise quiet.	
	3-8-17		Gas shell bombardment continues till 8 a.m. Only 3 cases of gas poisoning. Then on front line wearing masks nearly all night. 2/Lieut MERRITT 2.26.O.R. attempted a raid on enemy S.P. at C.26.6.3.8	
	4-8-17	1.45 a.m		Casualties
		2 A.M	Raid – which succeeded after being in NO MAN'S LAND for 2 hours – wounds H.R. reason – lost direction & could not locate enemy trench owing to unsuspected wire being in front of trench.	
			Relieved in front line trenches 0.26.a.2.4 to 0.20.a.1.4 by 4th Bn East Yorks Regt. Moved back to Divisional Reserve in B.25.C.	
	5-8-17		Work generally confined to upkeep of trenches and putting out wire.	
	6-8-17		Cleaning up & refitting. Baths via Company & Battalion training.	
	7-8-17		Whole 151st Infantry Brigade on light duties of Divisional Front 4.1.a.2.6 to 0.26.a.5.4. Battalion moved into support in relief of	M.M.

A6945 Wt. W11442/M1160 350,000 12/16 D. D. & L. Forms/C./2118/14.

WAR DIARY
or
INTELLIGENCE SUMMARY.

(Erase heading not required.)

Army Form C. 2118.

Place	Date	Hour	Summary of Events and Information	Remarks and references to Appendices
	12.8.17		5th Bn. The BORDER REGT. rectifying trenches in O.31.a & O.30.b with one company in trenches in O.25.c.	Casualties 12/8/17 wounded 10.R.
	13.8.17 to 15.8.17		Working parties making dugouts & carrying material to front line. Work carrying support line trenches & making shelters.	Casualties 14/8/17 wounded - 15.R.
	16.8.17		Relieved 4th B:D:Y on right subsector of front line and occupy front line from U.1.a.26 to O.31.8.74. Nothing of importance. General improvement of shelling and Battalion work carried on clearing trenches laying duckboards & trestling.	
	to			
	19.8.17		New C.T. from U.1.a.85.85. to U.1.6.28. bottom amount of missing here mostly in O.31.8.	
	20.8.17		Relieved by 11th N.F. have to Brigade reserve camps HENIN. N.32.a.	Casualties 20/8/17 wounded 1.O.R.
	21.8.17 to 23.8.17		General cleaning up & training.	
	24.8.17		Relieve 11th N.F. in front line sector U.1.a.26.10 to O.31.6.2.17.	
	to		Work done - rectifying trenches - draining and wiring front line in O.31.6. C.T. from U.1.a.85.65. to U.1.6.2.8. Placing new pickets on wire all along the front.	
	25.8.17			Casualties 25/8/17 wounded 3.O.R.

WAR DIARY
or
INTELLIGENCE SUMMARY.

Army Form C. 2118.

(Erase heading not required.)

Place	Date	Hour	Summary of Events and Information	Remarks and references to Appendices
	25-8-17 to 31-8-17		Baths & general cleaning up. Cookery & Lewis Training.	
			Fighting Strength on 1st Aug 1917. 36 Officers & 771 O.R.	
			" " " " 8th " 39 " 775 "	

(CONFIDENTIAL)

WAR DIARY

OF

5ᵀᴴ Bⁿ NORTHUMBERLᴰ FUSILIERS

FROM 1ˢᵀ SEPTʳ TO 30ᵀᴴ SEPTʳ 1917

VOLUME 24

1-10-17

[signature] Lieut-Colonel
Comᵈᵍ 5"B": Northᵈ Fus.

WAR DIARY or INTELLIGENCE SUMMARY

Army Form C. 2118.

Place	Date	Hour	Summary of Events and Information	Remarks and references to Appendices
NEURCATEL	6-9-17		Training under Company arrangements. C Company at Bernetz	
(Sheet 51B.S.W.19-17)			shortly at MENCOURT. 3.50 men at FICHEUX. Relieved By 4th	
NEINCOURT	7-9-17 to 8-9-17		Relieved 5/8" the BORDER REGT in what was left of our trenches in N24 but found very little. Shelling but consisting of supplying unstany saves for	Casualties 2 O.R. wounded 3 O.R.
			reserve trenches. N.E. on front line receiving trenches from C.26.a.4.3"	
GUEMAPPE	9-9-17 to 11-9-17		to 0.20.a.7.5. These trenches in the line was in poor support. Nothing of importance happens although Hostile and Light T.M Active against all the front system. Enemy appears very active against machine gun fire incessant throughout the front line sights. Patrols report at night of 11" Sittenhal that enemy have received but an SPOR LANE D.20.c.9.4.1. Light French mortars and Rifle Grenades contain without result as enemy still holds out in right of 13" Work continued to improving existing trenches & using front line	Casualties 2 O.R killed - 2 wounded 9/2" AP.LETTS 2/Lt casualties 1 O.R wounded 3 O.R

Army Form C. 2118.

WAR DIARY
or
INTELLIGENCE SUMMARY.
(Erase heading not required.)

Instructions regarding War Diaries and Intelligence Summaries are contained in F. S. Regs., Part II. and the Staff Manual respectively. Title pages will be prepared in manuscript.

Place	Date	Hour	Summary of Events and Information	Remarks and references to Appendices
Shed 57 B5.M			2 walking wounded	
	13-9-17		Relieved by 4th N.F. Move into support area N.2.H. for one night	Casualties 13-9-17 wounded – 1 O.R.
			Whole Battalion out on working party carrying ammunition	
			& supplies	
NEUVILLE VITASSE	14-9-17 to 16-9-17		Move back to reserve camp – supply 160 men for working party	
			Resting and supplying working parties by night to front line Battalions	
GUEMAPPE	17-9-17		Relieve 4th N.F. in front line occupying trenches from 0.26.a.4.5.	
			to 0.20.a.7.5. Enemy much more active both with French mortars	Casualties 17-9-17 killed 2 O.R. Seriously 1 O.R.
		to 19-9-17	& Shells & all calibres. Where front line system heavily shelled	wounded 2 O.R.
	20-9-17		during the night of 14th & 18th Both 77mm & 4.2 howitzers. Enemy	
			sniper very active about 0.20.d.9.6. on 18th Battle Patrols	
			& Listening Patrols out but find the enemy on 19th x 20th	Casualties 20-9-17 killed 1 O.R. wounded 5 – 4 O.R.
			Not consists of infantry parties digging & scouting	Hd Qrs Armstrong
			New trench dug from 0.26.a.1.5. to 0.26.a.3.5. joining up	& 6 O.R.
			with 6th B.N.F. on the left & 7th B.N.F. left bn. front	
			covering party across GOTELL VALLEY.	

W.S.

Army Form C. 2118.

WAR DIARY
or
INTELLIGENCE SUMMARY.
(Erase heading not required.)

Instructions regarding War Diaries and Intelligence Summaries are contained in F. S. Regs. Part II. and the Staff Manual respectively. Title pages will be prepared in manuscript.

Place	Date	Hour	Summary of Events and Information	Remarks and references to Appendices
Sheet 51 B. S. W.				
MERCATEL	21.9.17		Relieved by 4th Bn East Yorks Regt & move back to Divisional Reserve	Casualties 21-9-17 wounded – 4 F.S. Spearland
			Northumberland Lines, MERCATEL.	
	22.9.17		Cleaning up and pulling Company during 24" & 25". Two large	
	to		Working parties to HINDENBURG LINE and HENINEL supply working	
	28.9.17		parties daily on tramway in COJEUL VALLEY. Remainder of	
			Battalion out on walking partys daily.	
			Relieve 6th Bn the D.L.I. in support area of Right Sector occupying	
HENINEL	29.9.17		Trenches N.30 & Q.25.c. Working partys for R.E. & front lines	
			supplying stores etc. Not Little activity against trenches	
			HENINEL shelled between 12 Noon – 3 pm. not making fatalities in	
			EGRET LOOP & Infantry shelter.	
	30.9.18			
			Fighting Strength at beginning of month 30 Officers & 775 O. Ranks	
			" " end " 38 " 759 "	
			Reinforcements received during month – 5 Officers & 24 O. Ranks	

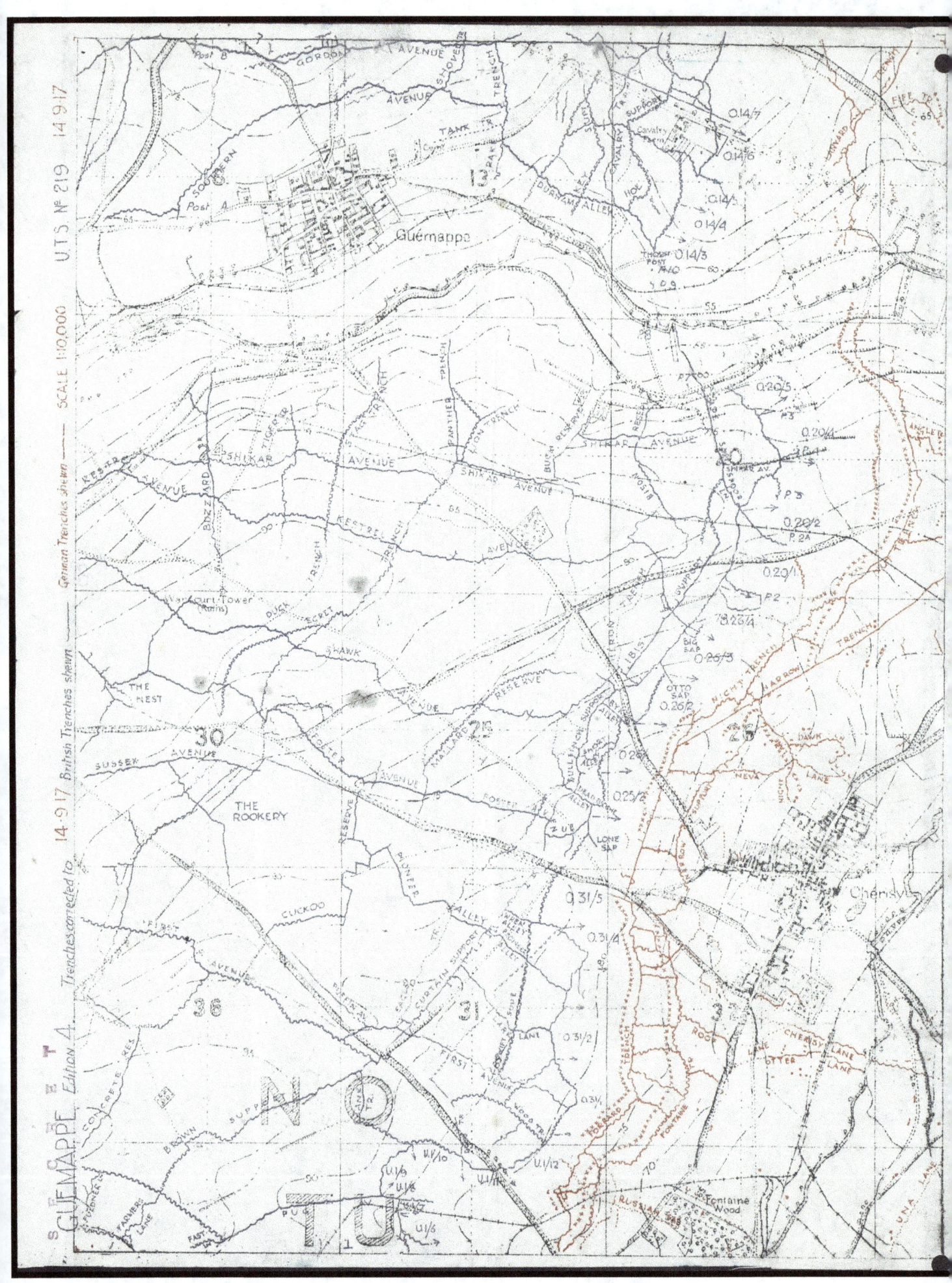

(CONFIDENTIAL)

WAR DIARY

OF

5th Bn NORTHUMBERLAND FUSILIERS

FROM 1st OCTr TO 31st OCTr 1917

VOLUME 25

1st Novr 1917

Lieut Colonel
Comdg 5th Bn Northd Fus.

WAR DIARY or INTELLIGENCE SUMMARY

Army Form C. 2118.

Place	Date	Hour	Summary of Events and Information	Remarks and references to Appendices
CHERISY SHEET 51B)	1-10-17		Battalion in support area THE NEST, & employing working parties to front line. Most parties employing of EGRET T? & making fascines.	
	2-10-17		Very little shelling.	
	3-10-17			
	4-10-17		Relieved by 51st Division, 7th Black Watch & 5/8th Gordon Highlanders. Move back to NORTHUMBERLAND LINES.	
	5-10-17		Travel to OURCELLES-LE-COMTE via BOYELLES - ERVILLERS. Arrive in billets 4 pm.	
BUCELLES LE COMTE	6-10-17		Training by platoons and companies in attack formation. Specialist & recreational training during the afternoon. Brigade rescued practise on the morning of the 11th at 5:45 am — Very successful morning. Inter platoon football competition carried out. Final - No 6 platoon - 1 Goal - BHQ - Nil.	
			Weather very changeable and cold. A Coy & 1 platoon of C boy act as loading party to Mirvaux at MIRAUMONT station from 16th inst.	
	18-10-17		March to MIRAUMONT via ACHIET-LE-GRAND - ACHIET-LE-PETIT and entrain at 12 noon. — Arrive at CASSEL at 10 pm & march to	

Army Form C. 2118.

WAR DIARY
or
INTELLIGENCE SUMMARY.

(Erase heading not required.)

Instructions regarding War Diaries and Intelligence Summaries are contained in F. S. Regs., Part II. and the Staff Manual respectively. Title pages will be prepared in manuscript.

Place	Date	Hour	Summary of Events and Information	Remarks and references to Appendices
ARNEKE	19-10-17		ARNEKE area where Battalion is billeted in farms — Resting	
PROVEN (Sheet XP)	20-10-17		March to PROVEN via LEDRINGHEM — HERZEELE — HAUTEVERQUE, Stop 1½ hours for dinner at HERZEELE. Arrive in PATALA Camp at 4 p.m.	
	21-10-17		Resting & Church Parade.	
	22-10-17		Packing up & preparing for the line	
BOESINGHE (Sheet 28)	23-10-17		Move by train from PROVEN to BOESINGHE & march to SARAGOSSA FARM. Hot day — Battalion in tents. Take out camp from 23rd N.Z.	
SCHAEFBALIE (Sheet 20)	24-10-17		During little blows nothing the morning. Leave Camp at 4 p.m. to take over line V.I.C 95.25 to V.I.C 35.35 from 11th Suffolks. 34th Regt. C Coy on right — D Coy in Centre — B Coy on left — A Coy in support — in neighbourhood of PASCAL FARM. Companies on a platoon frontage one in depth.	
	25-10-17		Very quiet the whole day. Shelling intermittently the whole day on front line system & Gheka roads. Ordinarily traps laid out at Ypres by 2/Lieut YOUNG from TURENNE CROSSING U.I.S 20.H5 to 11DEN HOUSE V.I.C 35.35 Patrols joined up at 11 p.m.	

WAR DIARY or INTELLIGENCE SUMMARY

Army Form C. 2118.

Place	Date	Hour	Summary of Events and Information	Remarks and references to Appendices
SCHAAP-BALIE (Sheet 20)	25/10/17		Rations & hot tea served out after being carried up by 6th & 8th D.L.I.	
	26/10/17	5.40 am	Barrage commenced. Companies go over well – Enemy barrage on roads U.12.b.7.9 to U.18.a.9.1 within 8 minutes of zero hour.	
		7 am	A Coy on V.7.a.5.8 nearly there	
		9.10 am	Report from wounded that all Coys have taken their first objective	
		7 am	Report from wounded to B Coys on left, are on Hill 23 & being heavily fired on by machine guns from direction of wood.	
		9 am	Report that C Coy are held up by machine gun fire from huts V.1.0.10.65	
		11.30 am	One platoon of 6th N.F. move forward and occupy line ADEN HOUSE to TURENNE CROSSING with remains of A Coy.	
		2.15 pm	Lieut LEWIS and remains of C Coy who to TURENNE CROSSING & get in touch with A Coy.	
		2.15 pm	Remains of Battalion back on original line.	
			From wounded the following reports are gathered — B Coy (left Coy) advanced well from assembly point, taking first objective easily, until they reached the road in V.1.c.5.8 which was	

WAR DIARY
or
INTELLIGENCE SUMMARY.

(Erase heading not required.)

Army Form C. 2118.

Place	Date	Hour	Summary of Events and Information	Remarks and references to Appendices
SCHAAP BALIE (Sheet 20)	18-10-17		Joined word between the lines — when the first and second waves reached this and attempted to cut the wire to reach enemy front, situated about 11.c which was full of enemy, they were enfiladed by machine gun fire from N.1.6.9.0. & practically wiped out. The other waves were unable to advance on account of intense M.G. fire. C. Coy & G.N.S. on their right advanced as far as huts on N.8. but were unable to advance further on account of M.G. fire. D Coy having failed first objective advanced under heavy fire. No further adv. can be obtained of the coy.	Casualties 2/Lt. Lapp[?] — 7/8 R Wounded 15 OR
		11pm	Bn. relieved by 4th Bn. Yorkshire Regt. Moves back to ROSE-CROSS Res. Camp.	
BRESINGHE (Sheet 28)	24.6.27.6.30am	Batt. Camp shelled by howitzer. 1 heavy hit causing many casualties	
		2pm	Bn. moves to ROUSSEL FARM, by tram & march route. Resting.	
ELVERDINGHE (Sheet 2)	10/17		Cleaning up & re-organising. Officers & men re-working kits.	

WAR DIARY
or
INTELLIGENCE SUMMARY.
(Erase heading not required.)

Army Form C. 2118.

Place	Date	Hour	Summary of Events and Information	Remarks and references to Appendices
PROVEN (Sheet 19)	31.10.17		Bombing at night quite close to camp by enemy aircraft. Proceeded by march route to SUEZ CAMP via DE WIPPE CAB? – INTERNATIONAL CORNER. Arrived 8p.m. Some bombing in vicinity during night.	
	31.10.17		1 Officer & 50 O.R. on working party at BOESINGHE. Companies resting and reorganizing.	
			Casualties on 26th October were as under:	
			Killed:– 2/Lieut. W.G.VERRILL	
			Wounded:– Capt. E. BISSET, 2/Lieut F. HASWELL, 2/Lieuts R. GRAY, T.M. SCOTT, H.R. PARR, W. CARR, F.K. HILL	
			Missing:– 2/Lieut P. SHAW. 2/Lieuts W.C. NAY, W.W. WILKIN, & Revd P. LOOBY C.F. (R.C. Chaplain)	
			Other Ranks – Killed – 60 Wounded – 149 Missing – 230	
			Total strength of Bn on 1st October – 41 Officers & 763 O.R.	
			" " " " 31st " – 33 Officers & 522 O.R.	
			Reinforcements received during month – 1 Officer & 215 O.R.	

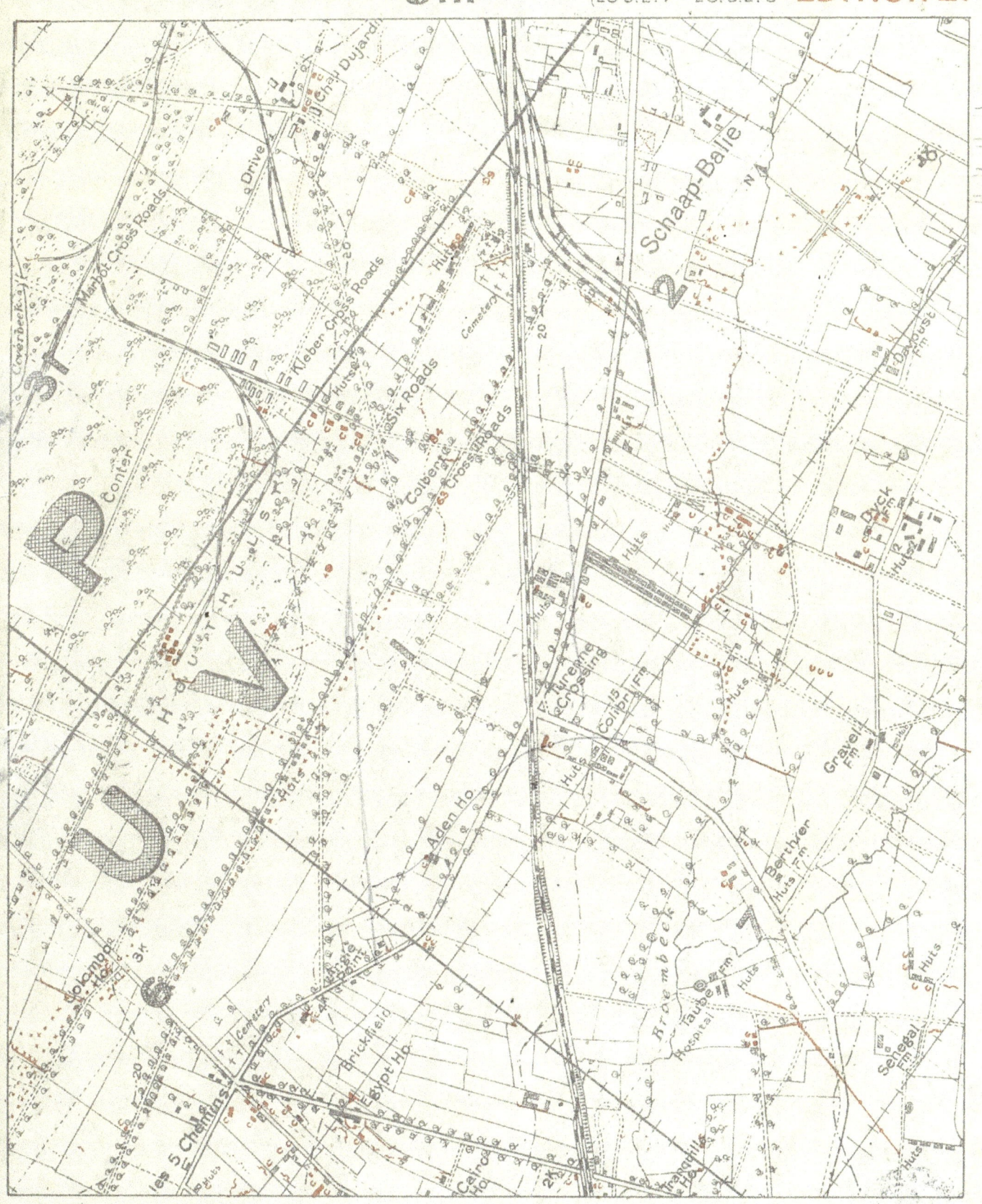

Message Pad.

Your Message must be such as will enable the Addressee to know what the Situation is with You and your Neighbours.

NEGATIVE INFORMATION IS ALSO VALUABLE.

Strike out and alter sentences as necessary.

TO ....

1. Am advancing to..
2. Am putting out (Have put out) protective parties.
3. Am sending out. Have sent out and am keeping out patrols to keep touch with the enemy.
4. Am (Have) consolidating (ed).
5. Our line now runs..
6. I require (give article or articles and number required):—

   Send the above to..
7. Troops on my right are (give situation).

8. Troops on my left are (give situation)

9. My strength now is..
10. Am being shelled from..
11. Am held up by M.G., T.M., rifle, artillery fire from ....
12. Am now ready to..
13. Enemy line runs..
14. Enemy (strength)..at..........
    doing ....
15. Have captured ....
16. Enemy prisoners belong to..
17. Enemy counter-attack forming up at..
18. Other remarks—

Time .... a.m. (p.m.)   Name..
Date..   Rank...
Place...   Platoon............... Company..............
(Map Ref. or mark on back of map).   Battalion....................................

639

CONFIDENTIAL

WAR DIARY

OF

5th Bn NORTHUMBLD FUSILIERS

FROM 1st NOV to 30th NOV 1917

(VOLUME 26)

1st Dec. 1917.

for J.N. Symes Capt
Lieut Colonel
Comdg 5th Bn Northd Fus.

Army Form C. 2118.

WAR DIARY
or
INTELLIGENCE SUMMARY.
(Erase heading not required.)

Instructions regarding War Diaries and Intelligence Summaries are contained in F.S. Regs., Part II. and the Staff Manual respectively. Title pages will be prepared in manuscript.

Place	Date	Hour	Summary of Events and Information	Remarks and references to Appendices
SUEZ CAMP ("PROVEN") XX9.8 Sheet 19	1-11-17 to 10-11-17		Resting and cleaning up. Fatigue parties of 2 officers & 110 O.R. supplied to HM6 Field Co. R.E. at BOESINGHE. Remainder of Battalion employed in upkeep of camp, making trench shelters/roof, and minor alterations.	
A12 c Sheet 28 1-11-17	11-11-17		Move by march route to CARIBOU FARM via INTERNATIONAL CORNER – DeHIPPE CABARET. – resting remainder of day	
	12-11-17		Cleaning up and resting	
	13-11-17		Moved to ELVERDINGHE Station & entrain about 14 noon via BERGUES – CASSEL – ST OMER – HATTEN travel to LeBAS (nude SERQUES) into Billets	
LeBAS R2a Sheet 27A	14-11-17 15-11-17		Cleaning up and resting, making billets comfortable. Re-organising under XVIII Corps scheme and commence training of specialists in Lewis Guns. Rifle grenades etc. Most of time devoted to Platoon Staff. Battalion has use of B Range no 17.26 from 9 a.m. Making chess range on area East of CANAL and Bombay	

Army Form C. 2118.

WAR DIARY
or
INTELLIGENCE SUMMARY.
(Erase heading not required.)

Place	Date	Hour	Summary of Events and Information	Remarks and references to Appendices
Le BAS. R.2a Sh.57A.	21st		Plt. Companies have use of range daily for musketry from 21st.	
	22/11/17 to 30/11/17		Company training. Use of range on L.T.C. Shoots/most of time have devoted to semi-open warfare & companies in attack. Specialist training continued. Use of B range (P.11.D.3 Sheet 44A) on the 29th till 1 p.m. Recreational training every afternoon, boxing, running, wrestling and football. 1st Battalion football match versus 9th D.L.I. lose 2-0. Cross-country run on the 26th inst - whole Battalion out. Came in 3rd place.	
			Strength of Battalion on 1st November last - 31 officers & 499 O.R. " " " 30th " - 33 " 673 " The following decorations have been awarded to the 8th for the action on 20/10/17. <u>MILITARY CROSS.</u> — 2/Lt. G.H. LEWIS. <u>D.C.M.</u> 240357 Sgt J.W. BROWN, 240066 A/c T. McKENZIE <u>MILITARY MEDAL.</u> 241895 Sgt D.E. WRIGHT, 241009 Pte J.WALTON, 240992 A/c/11 L. BURFORD 241870 Pte G.D. WATSON, 242440 " F.HALL.	

(CONFIDENTIAL)

WAR DIARY

OF

5TH BN NORTHUMBLD FUSILIERS

FROM 1ST DEC. 1917 to 30TH DEC. 1917

VOLUME 27

J.C. Leask
Captain
Comn 5th Bn Northd Fus.

Army Form C. 2118.

WAR DIARY
or
INTELLIGENCE SUMMARY.
(Erase heading not required.)

Instructions regarding War Diaries and Intelligence Summaries are contained in F. S. Regs., Part II. and the Staff Manual respectively. Title pages will be prepared in manuscript.

Place	Date	Hour	Summary of Events and Information	Remarks and references to Appendices
LE MARAIS SHEET 7/A	1/9/17 2/9/17		Company training. C.O. goes to hospital. Move from LE MARAIS to TOURNEHEM via SERQUES, MOULLE – NORDAUSQUES. Arrive at 11.30 am.	
TOURNEHEM SHEE 27A	3/9/17 to 9/9/17		Company & platoon training (Vide P.7, P.18) Lt. Col. Alger resumed command.	
	10/9/17		Church parade. Presentation of Ribbons by Brigadier General & memorial march past – Coat shoes. Companies on rifle range. Packing up. Transport moves by road to POPERINGHE	
	11/9/17		March to WATTEN station via NORDAUSQUES – and entrain at 11 a.m. Arrive at BRANDHOEK 2.30 pm & march to ERIE Camp. Receive orders to move forward.	
	12/9/17		Entrain at BRANDHOEK at 7 am and detrain at YPRES – March to St JEAN, Camp POTIJZE. Arrive 9.30 pm. Move off at 2.15 pm and relieve 4th Bn East Yorks in right support area D.16.B (PASCHENDAELE) comparatively quiet day – slight shelling at night	

Army Form C. 2118.

WAR DIARY
or
INTELLIGENCE SUMMARY.
(Erase heading not required.)

Instructions regarding War Diaries and Intelligence Summaries are contained in F. S. Regs., Part II. and the Staff Manual respectively. Title pages will be prepared in manuscript.

Place	Date	Hour	Summary of Events and Information	Remarks and references to Appendices
PASSCHENDAELE SHEET 28	13/10/17		Making shelters habitable and improving existing accommodation. Intermittent shelling during the day — mostly in back areas.	Casualties 13/10/17 wounded 70 R.
	14/10/17		Making & improving shelters. Shelling more lively in area D 16 ? & vicinities during the night.	Casualties 14/10/17 killed - 2 OR wounded - 30 R.
	15/10/17		100 men on working party for 411 Tunnelling Co R.E. 60 men working for R.E. improving shelters. Shelling lively during the afternoon and during the night. Aerial activity normal.	Casualties 15/10/17 wounded - 10 R.
	16/10/17		Comparatively quiet morning. Most improving shelters under R.E. supervision. Relieve 8th Bn R.W.F. in the left sector of divisional front occupying system D still held and strong points as follows. Front line D.6.b.6.2 to D.6.b.8.8. 8 Coy on right, C Coy on left. D Coy in close support in CREST FARM and vicinity D.12.a.3.9. A Coy in reserve occupying HAARLEM, SMITCH D.17.a.?.8. Relief complete 8.30 pm.	
	17/10/17		Lively shelling of PASSCHENDAELE VILLAGE during the day & south of CREST FARM. Nothing of importance happens. Patrols from C Coy states that enemy are not occupying EXERT FARM.	

WAR DIARY or INTELLIGENCE SUMMARY

Army Form C. 2118.

Place	Date	Hour	Summary of Events and Information	Remarks and references to Appendices
PASCHENDAELE SHEET 28	18/10/17		Shelling of ZONNEBEKE ROAD during the day and several activity. B Coy Coy. capture 14 prisoners (including an officer) and 3 machine guns. A party of about 20 of the enemy attempted to approach our post D.6.b.65/25 and were fired on with L.G. & rifles to effect. One man wounded and another M.G. Located in Blockhouse in 1st M.G. Coy. 160th Inf. Regiment. First identification of 15th Division on Corps front.	Casualties 19/10/17 Killed - 10 k wounded - 33 k missing - 1 o k
	19/10/17		CREST FARM. Heavy shells during the early morning. Gas shells during the early morning on D.16.a. No further identification.	
	20/10/17		Quiet day - very misty - very little shelling. Battalion relieved by 6th Bn. K.R.I. Rifles. Relief completed 7 p.m. Moved back to POTIJZE.	
	21/10/17		Three from POTIJZE to BRANDHOEK. Busses which were ordered to not bring up 9 R/2 has to march. Arrive 3 p.m. Cleaning up and resting. Got bathing.	
	22/10/17		Church Parade. Baths at POPERINGHE	

Army Form C. 2118.

WAR DIARY
or
INTELLIGENCE SUMMARY.
(Erase heading not required.)

Place	Date	Hour	Summary of Events and Information	Remarks and references to Appendices
BRANDHOEK (SHEET 28)	24/9/17		Move by bus from BRANDHOEK to POTIJZE and there accommodated in S? JEAN Camp with 7th N.F.	
POTIJZE (SHEET 28)	25/9/17 to 28/9/17		7th Bn. N.F. took over S? JEAN Camp and the entire camp occupied by the (7th) Battalion. Working parties to the 265th Cy R.E. and the 6th Canadian Railway Troops working on Railways to PASCHENDAELE	
	29/9/17		Half of S? JEAN Camp occupied by 6th Bn. Durham Light Infantry	
	1/10/17		Working parties supplied for 5th Army Tramway C? R.E. (350 strong)	

(CONFIDENTIAL)

WAR DIARY

OF

5TH BN NORTHUMBLD FUSILIERS.

FROM 1ST JANY TO 31ST JANY 1918.

VOLUME 28

1/2/18

[signature] Capt for
Lieut-Colonel
Comdg 5th Bn Northd Fus

WAR DIARY
or
INTELLIGENCE SUMMARY.
(Erase heading not required.)

Army Form C. 2118

Place	Date	Hour	Summary of Events and Information	Remarks and references to Appendices
POTIJZE	1-1-18		300 men out on working party making railways under 6th Canadian Railway troops	
	2-1-18		Whole Battalion on working party under Railway troops	
POPERINGHE	3-1-18		Battalion move to POPERINGHE in buses - take over billets and work from 4th King's Own 33rd Division	
	4-1-18 to 17-1-18		Working party consisting of three companies working on types line daily between FROST HOUSE and BRIDGE HOUSE - main route running and returning fell there. Party leave POPERINGHE daily at 8AM by train and arrive back in billets at 5.30pm	
WATOU	17-1-18		B'd HQ and 1 Company move to WATOU area by march route leaving at 1pm. Remainder of battalion detrain at ABEELE station on completion of work and march to billets in farm houses	
	18-1-18	11am	march to ABEELE station and entrain for WIZERNES, via HAZEBROUK - march to LONGUENESS into billets	
LONGUENESS	19-1-18 to		Cleaning up + refitting Baths. Platoon and company training. Have use of 150yds rifle range and 600 yards	

WAR DIARY
or
INTELLIGENCE SUMMARY.

(Erase heading not required.)

Army Form C. 2118.

Place	Date	Hour	Summary of Events and Information	Remarks and references to Appendices
WORMHOUDT			range. Battalion exercises for officers & NCOs & lectures each evening.	
	26-1-18		Xmas thin Christmas dinner on the 24th	
YPRES	27-1-18		March to WIZERNES and entrain at 9 AM - Detrain at ST JEAN march to YPRES and billet in cellars & ruins	
PASSCHENDAELE	28-1-18		Take over left Support area of the PASSCHENDAELE sector from the 4/13" Suffolk Regt (98th Brigade 33rd Division) Quiet relief. Support area shelled with H.E 2 hunts between 10-11 AM and 12-1pm 2nd Wrigley wounded and 3 O.R.	
"	29-1-18		Relieve 1st 13" Middlesex Regt in the left front line sector holding PASSCHENDAELE village. Quiet relief. HAARLEM switch shelled with 900 shells at night between 7-8pm.	
	30-1-18		Artillery fairly active at intervals during the day. Subbing of emplacements	
	31-1-18		Artillery Quiet.	

5th. Batt. NORTHUMBERLAND FUSILIERS.

List of Officers on Strength 31st. January. 1918.

Lieut. Col.	N. I. WRIGHT, D.SO.
Major	ARNOLD IRWIN. (On leave in England.)
Captains	F. N. SYMS.
	J. C. LEASK. (50th. Div. Wing. Depot Battalion.
	J. H. SWAN. M.C.
	G. BRANFOOT.
	H. L. STAFFORD.
	F. W. GRINLING.
	W. EASTEN.
Lieutenants.	A. MORRIS.
	A. J. FIELD.
	C. V. ALDER.
	C. V. MARKS. (on leave in England.)
	F. G. HUTCHISON. (VIII Corps School)
	T. L. ISHMAN.
	J. B. WILSON. M.C.
	J. W. LOUGH. (Fourth Army Infantry School.)
	F. HASWELL.
	R. H. SMITH.
	J. SMITH.
	K. McDONALD.
	G. H. LEWIS. (Sick in Hospital)
	L. W. HOWARD.
2nd. Lieutenants.	C. YOUNG.
	T. A. HERDMAN. (50th. Div. Wing. Depot Battalion.)
	A. E. BROWN. (On leave in England)
	F. BACCUS.
	V. O. HILLYARD.
	R. H. KAY.
	H. WHITE. (On leave in England)
	J. ULLATHORNE. (Sick in Hospital)
	H. GRAY.
	P. GRAHAM. (VIII Corps School.)
	J. A. TAYLOR.
	J. H. YOUNG.
Transport Officer	Lieut. H. T. PAPE. (On leave in England)
Quartermaster.	Lieut. M. McKENZIE.
Medical Officer	Capt. A. R. ORAM. (R.A.M.C. attached)

Total Fighting Strength, 1-1-18.   36 Officers 713 O.R.
"   "   "   31-1-18.   37.   "   826. O.R.

Total reinforcements received during month.   4 Offrs. & 118. O.R.

"   Casualties during month. :-

Killed.	Wounded.	Missing.
1. O.R.	1. Offr. & 3. O.R.	NIL.

Vol. 30

29/527

CONFIDENTIAL

WAR DIARY

OF

5TH BN NORTHLD FUSILIERS

FROM 1ST FEBY TO 28TH FEB 1918

(VOLUME XXIX)

1/3/18

[signature] Lieut-Colonel.
Comdg 5th Bn Northld Fus.

WAR DIARY or INTELLIGENCE SUMMARY

Army Form C. 2118.

Place	Date	Hour	Summary of Events and Information	Remarks and references to Appendices
PASCHENDAELE 1/2/18 (D.M Sht 28NE)	1/2/18		Very quiet day - nearly able to rest PASSCHENDAELE on account of mud. Enemy aircraft active, very little shelling. Relieved in front line by 3rd Bn W.R.I. on relief proceeded to WHITBY CAMP (East of YPRES)	
POTIJZE (Sheet 28)	2/2/18		At WHITBY CAMP. Entrained at SANELLE ROAD SPUR I.3.0.13 for BRANDHOEK at 11.15 a.m. Arrived at BRANDHOEK 12.45 p.m.	
BRANDHOEK (Sheet 28)	3/2/18		ST LAWRENCE CAMP, BRANDHOEK. Cleaning up & foot bathing.	
	4/2/18		Companies at baths. Inspection etc.	
	5/2/18		Two Companies at Morning Baths, POPERINGHE	
YPRES (Sheet 28)	6/2/18		Battalion moves by train to YPRES. Leaves camp at 8 a.m. Improving cellars & billets, cleaning up. Eno dull.	
	7/2/18		Lecturing & foot inspection. Preparing for trenches. Entrained at BARRACK siding. Arrived at BORRY FARM (D.25.6.7.8) Hence via JUDAH TRACK to SEINE D.60.3.5. Relieved 4th N. Zea Support. Relieved 8 a.m. 9 p.m. Very heavy shelling on support area.	Casualties wounded 2 O.R.
SEINE	8/2/18		Sharp H.E. shells. SEINE DUMP shelled. Quiet. Working & carrying parties.	
	9/2/18			Casualties wounded 1 O.R.
	10/2/18		Mostly working & carrying parties on new defence scheme	

WAR DIARY or INTELLIGENCE SUMMARY

Army Form C. 2118.

Place	Date	Hour	Summary of Events and Information	Remarks and references to Appendices
SEINE (D.16.c.3.5.Sh57c)	11/4/18		Heavy shelling between 12 noon & 1.30pm. Recvd orders to relieve 4th N.F. before dawn 12th instant.	
D.23a. Sh28.N.E	12/4/18		Relieved 4th N.F in front line, completed by 6.30am. Rest of the day very quiet.	
	13/4/18		Hot day. Too shot bursts of approximately 30 shells chiefly H.E. & 5.9 reported at 12 km on H.Q. Otherwise quiet day.	
	14/4/18		Exceptionally quiet day.	
	15/4/18		Between 3-5am. very heavy bombardment of front position. A few shot bursts of H.E. 25 or 30.9. Post (Kept by H.Q.) Nothing further to report	
SEINE (D.16.c.3.5 Sh.57c)	16/4/18		Relieved by 6th N.F. in front line - complete by 6.30am. moved back to SEINE. Enemy aircraft active. Heavy Shelling of SEINE DUMP. Relieved by 4th N.F. 9 entrances at BORY FARM. Libraries at SAVILLE ROAD SPUR for WHITBY CAMP. Footbathing 9 foot authority - cleaning up & inspections	Casualties wounded 40x
WHITBY CAMP	17/4/18			

WAR DIARY or INTELLIGENCE SUMMARY

Army Form C. 2118.

Place	Date	Hour	Summary of Events and Information	Remarks and references to Appendices
WHITBY CAMP (Map Sheet 28 19/7/18)	18/7/18		Battle or working parties - Working on Army Battle Zone	
	19/7/18		At Baths in YPRES. Tactical instruction. Boot inspection. Anti-gas instruction.	
	20/7/18		Church Parade. Relieved 6th K.I. at SEINE (D.16.B.9.16). Entrained at SMULLE ROAD SPUR. Detrained at BORRY FARM.	
SEINE (D16.B.9.16 Sh.28 NE)	21/7/18		Rest - Working Parties	
	22/7/18		Relieved by 16 K.R.R.C. (33rd Division). Very quiet day. Entrained at BORRY FARM for MAIDEN CAMP (ST JEAN)	
ST JEAN (I.3.a. 5.0.) Sheet 28 N.E.	23/7/18		Move from MAIDEN CAMP to BOISDINGHEM. Entrained at YPRES - detrained at WIZERNES & marched 13 kilos to billets.	
	24/7/18		Special Parades & cleaning up. Short Parades - re-clothing and re-equipping.	
BOISDINGHEM 24/7/18 (Sheet 2/79 SE)	25/7/18		"A" Range NORTBECOURT. Fired three practices - very windy.	
	27/7/18		Enemy aeroplane found on front of aerodrome. Repetition of new draft.	M.W.a

Army Form C. 2118.

WAR DIARY
or
INTELLIGENCE SUMMARY.

(Erase heading not required.)

Place	Date	Hour	Summary of Events and Information	Remarks and references to Appendices
BUSSINGHEN (Sh. 2/4 S.E)	28/4/18		All officers, W.O's & N.C.O's at demonstration given by Divisional Platoon Red of Bn. — Route march Ref: Killots & moved into camp at aerodrome. Strength of Battalion on 28/4/18. 44 officers & 1055 o.ranks. Reinforcements received during month — 6 officers & 230 o.R. all the officers & 153 of the O.R. being drafts from 16th Bn. Wm Sturt Richard Tucker	

TRENCHES CORRECTED TO 3·2·18.   MESSAGE MAP Nº 8249

149th Brigade.
50th Division.

5th BATTALION

NORTHUMBERLAND FUSILIERS

MARCH 1918

CONFIDENTIAL

WAR DIARY

OF

5TH BN NORTHUMBERLAND FUSILIERS.

FROM 1ST MCH TO 31ST MCH 1918.

(VOLUME 30)

Arnold [signature]
Lieut-Colonel
Comdᵒ 5th Bn Northᵈ Fus

7-4-18

Army Form C. 2118.

WAR DIARY
or
INTELLIGENCE SUMMARY.
(Erase heading not required.)

Instructions regarding War Diaries and Intelligence Summaries are contained in F. S. Regs., Part II. and the Staff Manual respectively. Title pages will be prepared in manuscript.

Place	Date	Hour	Summary of Events and Information	Remarks and references to Appendices
BOISDINGHEM Sheet 24A. S.E.	MARCH 1		Battalion have use of Baths at ACQUIN	
			Coy training	
do	2		284 Officers + other ranks inoculated	
			Remainder training	
do	3		Church Parade	
do	4		Practicing for A.R.A. Competition	
do	5		Battalion on "A" range firing A.R.A. Competition. Very windy + cold.	
do	6		Tactical exercise on the ground without troops	
do	7		Batt. at Baths at ACQUIN	
do	8		Batt. training in counter attack on ground near aerodrome	
			Warning orders to move received at midnight	
do	9		Camp cleaned up ready for handing over to Bn prepared for the road	
		5.30 am	Battn. moved by march route to ST OMER thence by march route to KILLERS AUVERABLES	
		10.5 am	Left ST OMER	
		9.30 pm	Left MOREUIL	W

WAR DIARY or INTELLIGENCE SUMMARY

Army Form C. 2118.

(Erase heading not required.)

Place	Date	Hour	Summary of Events and Information	Remarks and references to Appendices
	MARCH			
BOISDINGHEM Sheet 27A SE.	9	10.15 AM	Arrived VILLERS-au-ERABLES. Fine sunny day, cool in the early morning & evening, good marching weather.	
VILLERS-au-	10		Battn. cleaning up and settling in new area.	
ERABLES Sheet 66E NE	11		Coy. training.	
do	12		Very hot day - Coy training - Foot-bathing & foot dubbing.	
do	13		Route march. Practicing Counter attack.	
do	14	8 AM	Coy. training - Route march practicing advance guard.	
do	15	2 PM	Corps on range - Route march.	
do	16		Platoon Route march - Two Coys. furnished as Battn. for inspection of SBR.	
do	17		Church Parade. Lieut Col. ARNOLD IRWIN assumed command of the Bn.	
do	18		Route March &c	
do	19		Coys. in attack in village Rifle Grenadiers Bombers on Specialist training. Reminders at Gas Drill - Rain during morning - first wet day for nearly a fortnight.	
	20		Rng to march	
			No. 5 Platoon fired Stage "C" of A.R.A. Competition	C-1

A6945 Wt. W14422/M1160 350,000 12/16 D. D. & L. Forms/C./2118/14.

Army Form C. 2118.

WAR DIARY
or
INTELLIGENCE SUMMARY.
(Erase heading not required.)

Instructions regarding War Diaries and Intelligence Summaries are contained in F. S. Regs., Part II. and the Staff Manual respectively. Title pages will be prepared in manuscript.

Place	Date March	Hour	Summary of Events and Information	Remarks and references to Appendices
VILLERS-AUX-ERABLES SHEET 66E NE	21		Received orders to move to forward area. Marched to GUILLAUCOURT station (5 miles) where Bn entrained.	
	22	1am	Detrained at BRIE. Marched to West of GOULAINCOURT where Bn. rested in huts (10 miles) Orders received at 12.45 p.m. for two coys (C+D) to report to front line Battn to dig GREEN LINE	Casualties 22-3-18 Killed: W.J.McGillivray 70.R Wounded: 85.0.R Missing: W.H.T. RICKETTS W.H.J. MARKHAM 350.R
		3pm	Enemy attack broke GREEN LINE. Bn counter attack + held enemy on ridge	
GOULAINCOURT Sheet 62c.S.E	23	2pm	Bn ordered to withdraw and dig in on new line 300/300 x EAST OF MONCHY-LAGACHE.	Casualties 23-3-18 Killed: 2/Lt T. NETTLESHIP 10.R Wounded: 20.O.R Missing: 14.O.R
		10am	Further orders to withdraw + retire on SE of ATHIES.	
		1.30pm	Bn outflanked and retirement to SOMME commenced. H.Q. + 2 Coys A + B Coys becoming crossing river at ST CHRIST at 3pm. detached. Dug in and held line of trenches on West bank of SOMME at ST. CHRIST.	
ST CHRIST Sheet 62c.SE	24	4.15am	Relieved by 2nd. Bn. DEVONS and moved back to MISERY where Bn lay in reserve until 9am. Marched to FOUCAUCOURT along	Casualties 24-3-18 Wounded: 14 O.R missing - 6 O.R

A6945 Wt. W14422/M1160 350,000 12/16 D.D. & L. Forms/C./2118/14.

MESSAGE FORM.

To :—   No.

1. I am at .... { Note :—Either give Map Reference or mark your position by a 'X' on the Map on back. }

2. I have reached limits of my Objective.

3. My Platoon/Company is at............................and is consolidating.

4. My Platoon/Company is at............................and has consolidated.

5. Am held up by wire at........................(Place where you are).

6. Enemy holding strong point........................

7. I am in touch with..................on Right/Left at........

8. I am not in touch with..................on Right./Left.

9. Am shelled from........................

10. Am in need of :—

11. Counter-attack forming at........................

12. Hostile (a) Battery
    (b) Machine Gun   active at........................
    (c) Trench Mortar

13. Reinforcements wanted at........................

14. I estimate my present strength at....................rifles.

15. Add any other useful information here :—

                                    Name........................
                                    Platoon........................
Time.................. m.   Company........................
Date..................1918.   Battalion........................

(A). Carry no maps or papers which may be of value to the Enemy.

(B). Give no information, if captured, except the following, which you are bound to give :—
       Name and Rank.

(C). Collect all captured maps and papers and send them in at once.

WAR DIARY or INTELLIGENCE SUMMARY.

(Erase heading not required.)

Army Form C. 2118.

Place	Date	Hour	Summary of Events and Information	Remarks and references to Appendices
ST CHRIST Sheet 62cSW	MARCH 24	4.45am	ESTREES - VILLERS CARBONNEL ROAD. A + B Coys. reported Bn HQrs area. Rested for about 3 hours.	
		5.45pm	Bn moved off and occupied Precautionary Line EAST of ASSEVILLERS	
ASSEVILLERS Sheet 62cSW	25	10.30pm	Moved from ASSEVILLERS to VILLERS-CARBONELL line - Enemy attacked 66th Div. - Bn counter attacked and occupied trenches SOUTH of BARLEUX. - Held trenches until 9pm when ordered to withdraw to ASSEVILLERS line - Bn concentrated in Sugar Factory + trenches in immediate vacinity - Bn in Bde reserve.	Casualties 25.3.18 Killed - 30 OR wounded - 21 OR missing - 10 OR
	26		Enemy continued attack on ASSEVILLERS LINE. Bn fought rearguard action on SOYECOURT - FOUCAUCOURT line. Reg. Lu on VAUVILLERS - ROSIERES LINE. - Occupied fork line trenches at night. Relieved YORKS + 22nd ENTRENCHING Bn	Casualties 26.3.18 Killed - 6 OR wounded. Capt. I.B.Thistlethwaite 200 OR missing - 12 OR
	27		Heavy attack by enemy. Counter attack by no- Me eventually held at nightfall line ROSIERES in front of CAILLAUCOURT - Bn partly concentrated in HARBONNIERES - WEINCOURT Road.	Casualties 29.3.18 wounded 2nd Lt B. Mason 1 Cy. N. Harris 2nd Lt N.V. Warham 2nd Lt R. Robinson missing 2nd Lt R. Robinson 90 OR

WAR DIARY or INTELLIGENCE SUMMARY

Army Form C. 2118.

(Erase heading not required.)

Place	Date	Hour	Summary of Events and Information	Remarks and references to Appendices
	MARCH			
	28	3 AM	Orders are received to hold GUILLAUCOURT-CAIX line.- Heavy attacks by enemy. Counter attacks by us.- Line broken opposite CAIX.- B⁰ formed fresh rearguard line round HARBONNIERES and fresh rearguard action. B⁰ assembled at MOREUIL and after battle marched to MERVILLE AU BOIS where the night was spent.	Casualties 28·3·18 Killed - 1·O·R. wounded 2nd Lieut. H. THOMPSON Lieut H. WHITE 50·O·R. missing 50·O·R.
MERVILLE AU-BOIS 66 E.S.E	29	10 AM	Left by march route for MOREUIL for Wood S.W. of DEMUIN. B⁰ remained behind Wood during the day & spent night in valley.	Casualties 29·3·18 wounded - 60·O·R. missing - 30·O·R.
	30	11 PM	Shelled out of valley took up position on rear edge of wood. Received orders to reinforce 60th INF. BDE. so an attack was expected.- B⁰ attack materialised before orders could be carried out.- The line fell back about 400x ten wounded. Counter attack regained the original line.- The B⁰ occupied the front line.	Casualties 30·3·18 wounded 2nd Lieut. L.M. HARRIS 60·O·R. missing 3·O·R.
	31	10 PM	Enemy attacked.- Line withdrew thro' HOURGES & DOMART. Rearguard held rally during the night.- B⁰ withdrew	Casualties 31·3·18 wounded 8·O·R. missing 6·O·R.

WAR DIARY
or
INTELLIGENCE SUMMARY.
(Erase heading not required.)

Army Form C. 2118.

Place	Date	Hour	Summary of Events and Information	Remarks and references to Appendices
MERNILLE -	MARCH 31		and dugout 300' N.W. of DOMART on main AMIENS - ROYE Road.	
At BOIS				
Sh 66E. S.E.				

28031 W3125/M2250 1000m 6/17 M.R.Co.,Ltd. (1367) Forms W3091   Army Form W.3091.

Cover for Documents.

Nature of Enclosures.

Notes, or Letters written.

149th Brigade.
50th Division

1/5th BATTALION

NORTHUMBERLAND FUSILIERS

APRIL 1918.

(CONFIDENTIAL)

WAR DIARY

OF

5ᵀᴴ BATTALION NORTHUMBERLAND FUSILIERS

FROM 1ˢᵗ APR. – 30ᵗʰ APR. 1918.

VOLUME 31

1ˢᵗ May 1918.

[signature] Major
Comdg 5ᵗʰ Bⁿ Northᵈ Fus.

Soissons — 22.

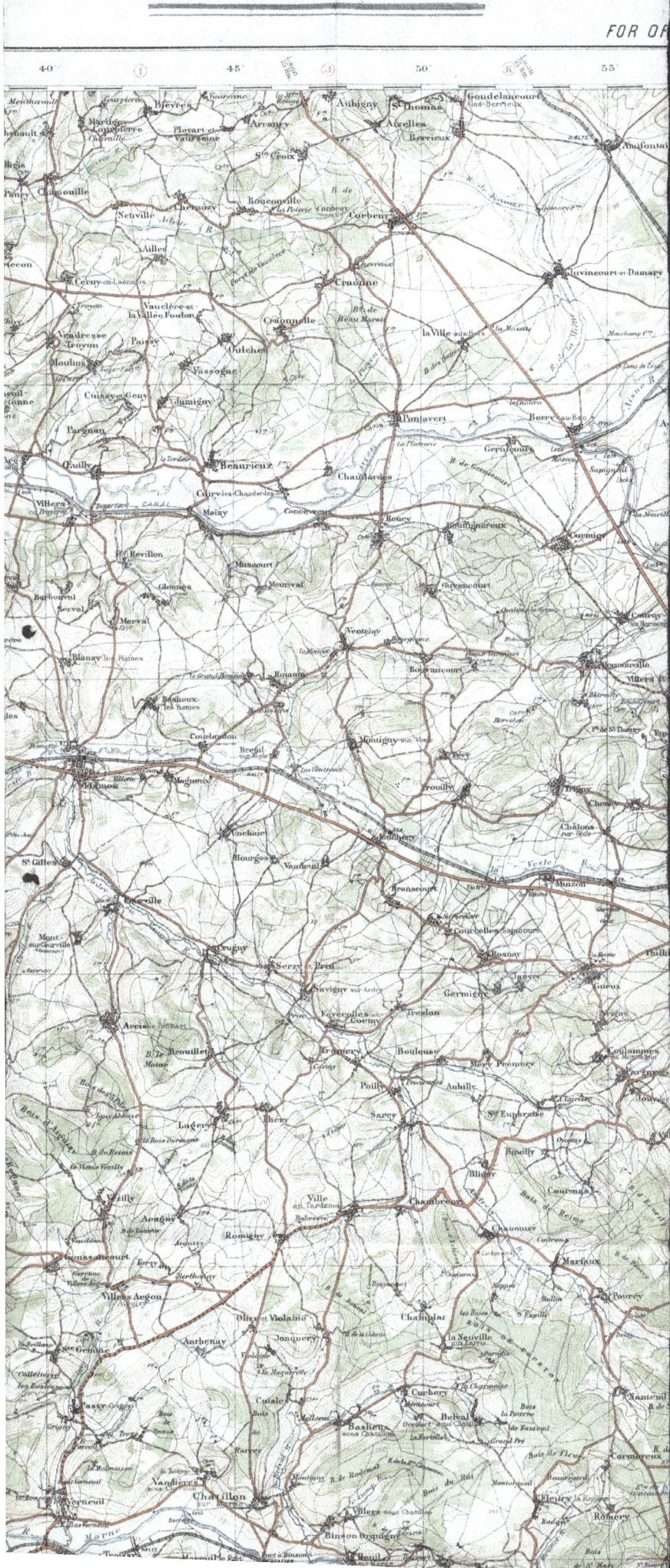

Army Form C. 2118.

WAR DIARY
or
INTELLIGENCE SUMMARY
(Erase heading not required.)

Instructions regarding War Diaries and Intelligence Summaries are contained in F. S. Regs., Part II. and the Staff Manual respectively. Title pages will be prepared in manuscript.

Place	Date	Hour	Summary of Events and Information	Remarks and references to Appendices
DOMART 1-4-18 (Amiens Sh.57)	1-4-18		Battalion dig in on the Crest line S.t WEST of DOMART. Enemy still hold the line across the LUCE. Shelling not so severe as previous night.	Casualties killed – 1 O.R. wounded – 1 O.R.
		8 a.m.	Cavalry attack the crest and retake whole line.	
		11 a.m.	Heavy shelling of DOMART & vicinity by howitzers – Our position heavily	
		4 p.m.	Shelled but situation maintained.	
LONGEAU		6 p.m.	Battalion relieved by 41st Division & march to LONGEAU where we are billeted for the night.	
SALEUX	2-4-18	1 p.m.	March to SALEUX where we entrain for RUE. Strength 8 Officers and 197 O.Ranks on train.	
VIRONCHEUX	3-4-18	7 a.m.	March from RUE to VIRONCHEUX where Battalion is billeted.	
GONNEHEM (Sheet 36.A)	4-4-18	8.45 a.m.	March to LEGISCOURT where we embus to BUSNES Nr St POL – LILLERS. March to GONNEHEM where Battalion is billeted	
	5-4-18 to 7-4-18		Cleaning up and re-organising. Baths etc.	
	8-4-18		Move by march route to LE SART. Heavy bombardment at night. Move into XI Corps	
LE SART (Sheet 36.A)	9-4-18	4.30 am	Heavy bombardment continues. Battalion ordered to Stand-to and be prepared to move at one hours notice.	
		10 am	Battalion proceeds under orders to Concentration point of Brigade	

Army Form C. 2118.

WAR DIARY
or
INTELLIGENCE SUMMARY

(Erase heading not required.)

Instructions regarding War Diaries and Intelligence Summaries are contained in F. S. Regs., Part II. and the Staff Manual respectively. Title pages will be prepared in manuscript.

Place	Date	Hour	Summary of Events and Information	Remarks and references to Appendices
ESTAIRES (Sheet 36A) 36	9.4.18	10 a.m.	CHAPELLE DUVELLE (L.26.a.) MERVILLE being heavily shelled, 2 roads blocked.	Casualties Killed 10 R Wounded 110 R
		1 p.m.	Orders are received that the Battalion will move further forward to TROU BAYARD. — Shelling of ESTAIRES by heavy artillery continues without ceasing	
		4 p.m.	Battalion in Position. Shelling very heavy & sounds of heavy machine gun firing S of ESTAIRES. Position is as follows — 150th Inf Bde are holding the enemy in the line on the River LYS in G.26 - G.27 as far north as SAILLY-Sur-la-LYS. holding PONT LEVIS & SAILLY. Bridge heads respectively. 40th Divn on left & 150th Inf Bde on right. The Battalion is under orders to Counter attack immediately should the enemy cross the river between the points mentioned. Heavy shelling of whole area continues.	
		9.30 p.m.	Take up positions in strong points in vicinity of TROU BAYARD. connects up with 4th N.F. on our right. Quiet move. Shelling not so heavy but enemy seems to have advanced on front of 151st Inf Brigade.	
		11.45 p.m.	Enemy reported to have crossed the LYS at BAS St MUR and driven	

7.15

Army Form C. 2118.

WAR DIARY
or
INTELLIGENCE SUMMARY
(Erase heading not required.)

Place	Date	Hour	Summary of Events and Information	Remarks and references to Appendices
ESTAIRES. (Sheet 36A) " 36	10.4.18	10.4.18. 11am.	back by 40th Division. Two Companies move forward to relieve the 4th B.E. YORKS in the front line from PONT LEVIS exclusive to G.26d.9.8. C. Coy. takes the right flank and B. Coy the left. After this the situation is uncertain, as communication is not able to be maintained with the front line owing to heavy M.G. fire from ESTAIRES. B" H.Q is situated at Fme de BRETAGNE.	
		10.30am	B" Coy in G.26.5. report that the enemy are firing trench mortars against the front line, causing casualties. Unable to get in touch with his flank. Enemy observed across PONT LEVIS moving in N.E. direction towards Fm. QUENNELLE. and also on his flank. D" Coy moves forward to Counter attack but are unable to maintain position they have gained in G.26d.7.7. Later reports from men state that the enemy crossed the bridge on their right and worked round their flank. C" Coy maintained their position and caused heavy casualties to the enemy.	

WAR DIARY
or
INTELLIGENCE SUMMARY.

(Erase heading not required.)

Army Form C. 2118.

Place	Date	Hour	Summary of Events and Information	Remarks and references to Appendices
ESTAIRES 10.4.18 (Sh. 36A) " 36			Part of the men retired, leaving Capt BRANFOOT 2Lt GRAHAM & others still holding the enemy who were encircling them from vicinity of Fm QUENELLE. Nothing further has been heard of these officers and it is thought they died fighting. "B" Coy right flank now being in danger of attack from the rear, they retired in good order under heavy M.G. fire from right suffering heavy casualties. — Capt GRINLING & all his officers not returning. No further news of these officers has been heard.	CASUALTIES 10-4-18. Killed — 19 O.R. Wounded — 83 O.R. Missing — Lieut JALOUGH & 218 O.R.
		3 pm	Enemy reported to have crossed the river LYS. "A" Coy (Capt. STAFFORD) takes up position with remnants of threat at SAILLY Sur-la-LYS.	
		4 pm	Battalion on line Pt de POIVRE — TROU BAYARD, joining up with 4th N.F. in strong points. 150th Inf Bde remnants still hold the line North of TROU BAYARD in the line G.M.C.	
		6 pm	Enemy pressing forward under cover of M.G. fire from Fm. QUENELLE our Lewis Guns & rifles causing heavy enemy casualties in front of TROU BAYARD.	
		8 pm	Enemy still held on line Pt de POIVRE — TROU BAYARD — G.M.C. Remains of Battalion (about 200 men) takes up a line from L.23.c.0.0.	
	11.4.18	4 am		

WAR DIARY
~~INTELLIGENCE SUMMARY.~~

(Erase heading not required.)

Army Form C. 2118.

Place	Date	Hour	Summary of Events and Information	Remarks and references to Appendices
NEUF-BERGUIN 11-4-18 (Sheet 36 M)			(NEUF BERGUIN - ESTAIRES Road) to L.23.d.5.3. holding a series of strong points. - 4th B.N.F. on left - 5th Durham L.I. (151st Inf Bde) on right	CASUALTIES - 11-4-18 Killed - 6 O.R. Wounded - 34 O.R. Missing - Capt F W GRINLING, C+H G BRNEOD?, Lieut R G SMITH, R GRAHAM & 28 O R.
		9.a.m.	The left flank of the 151st Inf. Bde being driven in by heavy attack, our right flank falls back and forms a defensive flank along the road L.236 - L.23.d. after having caused heavy casualties to the enemy	
		11 a.m	After holding up the enemy on this line owing to his working round the right flank, and the hamlets of TROU BAYARD having fallen, the line falls back to L.16.b.	
		1 p.m.	Enemy held on line L.16.d. to L.11.c. Right flank "in the air". In touch with 29th Division on our left. Understand that the Corps Reinforcement Bn should be on our right, but unable to gain touch. Enemy seen advancing towards NEUF-BERGUIN in L.21.b.	
		7 p.m.	Line still held.	
	12-4-18	2.30am	The Battalion withdraws from position owing to the enemy having occupied NEUF-BERGUIN. endangering the right flank of the Brigade. Enemy reported to have occupied road junction L.7.a. 3.7. with machine Guns covering VIEUX - BERGUIN.	

WAR DIARY
or
INTELLIGENCE SUMMARY.

Army Form C. 2118.

Place	Date	Hour	Summary of Events and Information	Remarks and references to Appendices
NEUF BERQUIN (Shee/36A)	12-4-18	1.85 am	Battalion proceeds to take up position from K.12.6.5.3 to L.7.a.3.7 inclusive, marching via L.11.c.4.8 – L.10.c.2.1 – L.3.d.7.7 – L.3.a.3.0 – L.7.a.3.7. Advance and flank guards maintained in case enemy have occupied the position taken up at 6 a.m. Only enemy encountered was M.G. firing from L.7.a.5.0 in direction of VIEUX BERQUIN road causing some difficulty in crossing the road. Owing to 29th Division not maintaining touch with our left flank at L.7.a.3.7, a gap of 1000 yards was left unguarded. Attempts were made to fill this gap with all available men, but the enemy worked round the flank in L.7.b with light machine guns.	CASUALTIES 12-4-18 Killed – N.O.R. Wounded – Lt.Col. A. IRWIN, Capt. R.R. ORAM (R.A.M.C.) Lieut. S. CYRUDER, R. MORRIS, 2/Lt. SHIRLEY ? 25 O.R. missing – Lieut. F.G. HUTCHINSON, 2/Lt. FRENAIER & 28 O.R.
		8 am	Enemy attack in L.7.a and drove our line back to line of road in K.6.d where we maintain touch with the Guards Brigade	
		10.30 am	Guards counter attack and remnants of Battalion move forward in conjunction, occupying old position, but are eventually driven back to same line	
			Heavy Casualties inflicted on enemy by rifle and M.G. fire. About 50 men of Battalion take up position in F.25.c.	
		(noon)	In spite of heavy shelling, line is maintained	

Army Form C. 2118.

WAR DIARY
or
INTELLIGENCE SUMMARY.
(Erase heading not required.)

Place	Date	Hour	Summary of Events and Information	Remarks and references to Appendices
La Couronne (Sh. 36A)	13.4.18	4 p.m.	Line falls back from K.6.d. to K.6.a owing to enemy gaining ground on our left flank. This move carried out by the Guards, who form a line NER HOUCK – K.6.a – LA COURONNE to conform to the line on the left flank as enemy is reported to be close to NERRIS.	CASUALTIES 13-4-18 Wounded - 3 - O.R. missing - 3 - O.R.
		8 p.m.	What remains of the Battalion is withdrawn to E.16.a where the Brigade concentrates ; march to LA MOTTE	
LA MOTTE (Sheet 36A)	14.4.18		Move from LA MOTTE by march route to D.28.C where Battalion is billeted in farms.	
			Work commenced on trenches in J.5.b & J.6.a. – Battalion in Sufflout to 5th Division – Work till 4 p.m & then march back to billets.	
	15-4-18 to 17.4.18		Work continued on trenches daily until 4 p.m. after which time Battalion returns to billets.	
REBECQ (Sheet 36A)	18.4.18		Move by march route via STEENBECQUE – BOESEGHEM – AIRE – MAMETZ to REBECQ. Billets in village.	
	19.4.18 to 25.4.18		Carry on re-organization & Company training. Rifle Range & Baths etc.	
	26.4.18		March to MAMETZ where we embus for PERNES. Entrain at 5 h.m.	

WAR DIARY
INTELLIGENCE SUMMARY

Army Form C. 2118.

Place	Date	Hour	Summary of Events and Information	Remarks and references to Appendices
SOISSONS (Sheet 22)	27-4-18		and proceed to FERE-en-Tardenois, via St-POL - PONTOISE - PANTIN. Arrive Ham and march to COULONGES where Bⁿ is billeted in Camp.	
	28-4-18			
	29-4-18		Company and Platoon training under Company arrangements.	
	30-4-18			
			Strength of Bⁿ 1ˢᵗ APR. 1918. — 31 Officers & 720 O.R. (approx)
" " " 30ᵗʰ " — 37 " " 936 " "	

SUPPLEMENTARY

MOVEMENTS OF PARTY CONSISTING OF DRUMMERS COOKS, MEN FROM LEAVE, CASUALS SENT TO RE-INFORCE THE LINE ON NIGHT OF 11-4-18

Army Form C. 2118.

WAR DIARY
or
INTELLIGENCE SUMMARY.
(Erase heading not required.)

Instructions regarding War Diaries and Intelligence Summaries are contained in F.S. Regs., Part II. and the Staff Manual respectively. Title pages will be prepared in manuscript.

Place	Date	Hour	Summary of Events and Information	Remarks and references to Appendices
MERVILLE (Sheet 36A)	11-4-18	1 PM.	Orders received from Division for all available men to be mustered at once & marched to Div^{nl} H.Q. K.15d as soon as possible.	
		5 pm	A party of 65 men under Capt I.M. TWEEDY reported at 50" Divⁿ H.Q. & received orders to march through MERVILLE & reinforce the line. On reaching road junction at K.29d.0.5 Capt TWEEDY was informed that enemy were at Cross road K.30a.H.O. line running N from there. Party proceeded along road to COLLEGE K.23.6 & thence deployed into line running N&S thro' K.2H.c. held by 150 Bde.	Casualties (Included in Diary for 12.11.18) Killed — 1 Wounded — 1 2/Lt. TH RIGBY & 8.O.R. Missing — 1 F REMMER & 8.O.R.
		8.30 pm	Enemy reported advancing on N & S of MERVILLE. Capt TWEEDY reported to Major KIRKUP 8th Durh. L.I. & was ordered to clear all troops in neighbourhood of COLLEGE back across bridge in K.29a.4.7 & line W. bank of stream.	
		10 pm.	All troops in position on W bank of Stream. 5th N.F. party S. of road in K.29a.4.7 - D.L.I. (composite) - 1 Coy 7th D.L.I. whose R. flank rested at K.29.c.1.9.	
		11 pm	Reported that enemy had crossed bridge at K.29.c.6.2 & D.L.I. had withdrawn. Patrol sent out which reported no-one on right. Capt TWEEDY ordered to take charge of front line & to try & gain touch with entrenched Bⁿ reported to be somewhere at K.34a.	

Jn. Munger

Army Form C. 2118.

WAR DIARY
or
INTELLIGENCE SUMMARY.
(Erase heading not required.)

Instructions regarding War Diaries and Intelligence Summaries are contained in F. S. Regs., Part II. and the Staff Manual respectively. Title pages will be prepared in manuscript.

Place	Date	Hour	Summary of Events and Information	Remarks and references to Appendices
MERVILLE Sheet 36A.	11-11-18		To re-establish line. Some R.E.s of 29th Div.n were withdrawn from N. side of road & later replaced by a draft of about 70 N.F.?	
	12.11.18	5 a.m.	By this time the line was again established with 7th D.L.I. on our right who were now in touch with the Entrenching B.n about K.29.c.1.2.	
		8 a.m.	Patrol driven back across bridge from MERVILLE	
		11 a.m.	Bridge blown up successfully. During next few hours owing to heavy hostile M.G. fire from building on N.W side of MERVILLE, line was compelled to withdraw. A new line was formed under orders from Major KIRKUP from K.21.c.8.0 – K.210.1.5 along line of road to K.22.a.4.4. & north to near about K.16.C.8.3. For the remainder of the day, the withdrawal continued slowly, till a line was reached from K.20.d.1.1 – K.21.a.9.1 – Pt TOURNANT (K.15.d.4.9) where we made touch with the Guards.	
		10 p.m.	Relieved on this line by 5th Division & concentrated at LA-MOTTE	

5 Batt. Northumberland Fusiliers

Nominal Roll of Officers on Strength of Unit 30-4-18

Lieut. Colonel: Arnold Irwin

Major: Ivan M. Tweedy

Captains:
- N. M. North, M.C. — Joined 22-4-18
- H. L. Stafford (Sick in Hospital)
- M. G. Dodds — Joined 22-4-18

Lieutenants:
- W. Easton M.C.
- F. Haswell
- J. F. Stevenson M.C. (R.I. Rifles) — Joined 24-4-18
- J. Smith
- G. W. G. Bowster (R. Dub. Fus) — Joined 19-4-18
- C. Young

2nd Lieutenants:
- B. K. Brown
- R. M. Kay (Sick in Hospital)
- R. H. Quine — Joined 12-4-18
- G. E. D. Burbridge — Joined 24-4-18
- T. M. McMurdo — Joined 25-4-18
- J. MacMechen — Joined 25-4-18
- J. B. Slack — Joined 19-4-18
- L. J. Ross (R.I. Rifles) — Joined 24-4-18
- R. G. Bowie — Joined 25-4-18
- S. Weaterton — Joined 24-4-18
- H. Gray
- J. L. Barry (R. Dub. Fus) — Joined 19-4-18
- E. Phillips — Joined 19-4-18
- J. Bryce (R.I. Rifles) — Joined 24-4-18
- J. H. Ogilvie — Joined 25-4-18
- J. H. Young
- J. E. Corritt — Joined 19-4-18
- R. T. Dennis (R.I. Rifles) — Joined 24-4-18
- W. E. Priestnall — Joined 25-4-18
- F. Baglus
- J. O'Neill (R. Dub. Fus) — Joined 19-4-18

Lewis Officer: Lieut. H. T. Pape

Quartermaster: Capt. M. McKenzie

Officer: Lieut. T. G. Playford (Rank attached)

Major
Commdg 5 Batt. Northumberland Fusiliers

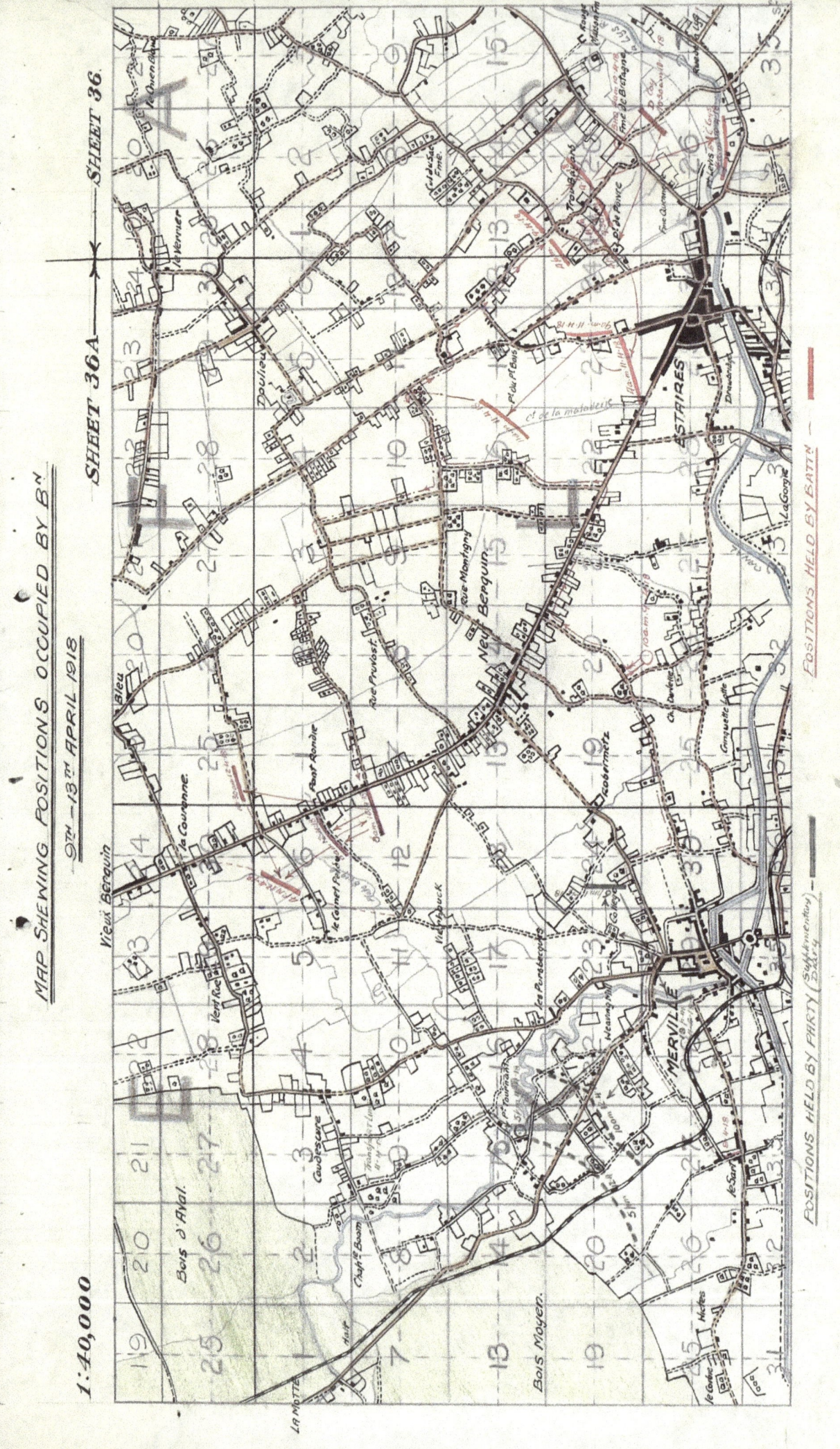

CONFIDENTIAL

WAR DIARY

OF

5th Bn NORTHUMBERLAND FUSILIERS

FROM 1ST MAY TO 31st MAY 1918

VOL 32

[signature]
Major
Comdg 5th Bn North Fus

WAR DIARY or INTELLIGENCE SUMMARY

Army Form C. 2118.

Place	Date	Hour	Summary of Events and Information	Remarks and references to Appendices
COULONGES (Soissons-22)	1-5-18 to 4-5-18		Company and Battalion training. Church Parade. Baths etc.	
	5-5-18		Move by march route to NEURIAL via St GILLES – FISMES – BASLIEUX	
NEURIAL (Soissons-22)	6-5-18		Coy Commanders reconnoitre line. Men resting & cleaning up.	
	7-5-18	9 pm	March to reserve position – CENTRE D'EVREUX via CONCEVREUX. On take over position from 53 R.I. Francaise Battalion in Brigade reserve Gr¹ Regt Brigade keloi. Regiment on right Gr¹ R.I. Francaise - on left 151ᵉ Inf. Bde.	
CENTRE D'EVREUX (N.E. PONTIVERT)	8-5-18 to 12-5-18		Platoon & Company training in the wood – Working Parties at night in forward area. All Officers reconnoitring rest positions and routes to CRAONNE and left of Brigade below.	
	13-5-18		Relief C⁰ⁿ & D⁰ now left out area. Coy HQ and areas as follow:—	Casualties 13-5-18
			HQ – P.C. KLEBER	
			A Coy – in vicinity of VILLE au BOIS	
			B " – CENTRE de QUIMPER	
			C " – CENTRE de MARCEAU	
			D " – TR. LEFEUVRE & T. DARDENELLES	
	14-5-18 to 18-5-18		Working on trenches – improving drainage – supplying working parties to front line – situation very quiet. Practically no shelling and no signs of enemy activity.	

WAR DIARY or INTELLIGENCE SUMMARY

Army Form C. 2118.

Place	Date	Hour	Summary of Events and Information	Remarks and references to Appendices
VILLE-au-BOIS (Soissons-22)	19.5.18 to 24.5.18		Relieve 6th N.F. in front line. Battalion holds the front line. Bn. du MARGRAVE to N d'ECLUME with three companies in front and one in support. This is diluted on 23rd inst. to two companies holding the front line in the form of an outpost scheme with orders to fight to the end. Companies to the rear by forms a line composed of platoon posts on the line Route 44. The red Bn. in Reserve in L. de SULTAN and diversion the Sixth Bay. to cellar Ben. Headqrs. Practically no shelling - situation quiet on whole line. Battalion relieved by H.B.N.F. & moves back to CONCEVREUX into Corps Reserve.	See negs attached Casualties 24/5/18 wounded 2 O.R
CONCEVREUX (Soissons-22)	26.5.18	6.30pm	Shelling and clearing up. Relieve by Brig.Gen. F. RIDDELL, D.S.O. in evening. Message received from Division to adopt secured draft defence scheme. The Battalion being in Corps Reserve does not move.	
		7.30pm	Message received that enemy are expected to attack at 2 a.m. Bombardment expected at 1 a.m.	

WAR DIARY
or
INTELLIGENCE SUMMARY

Army Form C. 2118.

Place	Date	Hour	Summary of Events and Information	Remarks and references to Appendices
	26.5.18	8 p.m.	Bn came into Bivouac Huts but does not move from CONCEVREUX. Our artillery commence counter preparation at 12 midnight.	
	27.5.18	1 a.m.	Enemy bombardment commences. CONCEVREUX shelled with H.V. [high velocity] guns & gas shells.	
		2.20 a.m.	Orders received from Division that we move into Brigade Reserve & move to BEAUREPAIRE.	
		4.40 a.m.	Move to BEAUREPAIRE via CHAUDARDES – Roads heavily shelled.	
N. of CHAUDARDES		5 a.m.	Arrive at BEAUREPAIRE. C.O. reports to Brigade H.Q. Blewn Bivouacs in front of BEAUREPAIRE Wood. Bn are disposed in open ground on S.E. of BEAUREPAIRE WOOD.	
		6.10 a.m.	Message received from Major Sweeny to occupy the intermediate line between BUTTE de l'EDMOND & BOIS des BUTTES. 'C' Coy on left, 'D' Coy on right. Coys move off immediately & run into intense barrage. Message received from 'C' Coy that they are unable to occupy the line owing to M.G. fire and intense barrage. 'A' & 'B' Coys some have intense barrage & have heavy casualties. Bn falls back to CHAUDARDES.	

WAR DIARY
or
INTELLIGENCE SUMMARY.
(Erase heading not required.)

Army Form C. 2118.

Instructions regarding War Diaries and Intelligence Summaries are contained in F. S. Regs., Part II. and the Staff Manual respectively. Title pages will be prepared in manuscript.

Place	Date	Hour	Summary of Events and Information	Remarks and references to Appendices
	27.5.18		Enemy's flanking movement on the left — the enemy having pushed forward to CUIRY & brought heavy M.G. fire on left flank — the line falls back to CANAL BANK	
CONCEVREUX		noon	The line was held until 2.30 p.m. then withdrawn to heights south of CONCEVREUX — The enemy by this time crossed the AISNE at MAIZY & also on the right flank at PONTAVERT.	
VENTELAY		5pm	A party consisting of the remainder of all units in the Brigade take up a line on the heights between NEUFCHÂTEL & ROUCY — VENTELAY Wood and hold this until 11 p.m. when a message is received that the enemy have occupied VENTELAY and are advancing towards ROMAIN.	
LEMONCET FARM 28.5.18		11pm	Early withdrawal to a line 100 yards WEST of LEMONCET FARM facing N.E. the front both right & left in wooded defiles.	Casualties 25/6 wounded 30 k.
		6am	Enemy pushing forward & occupy ROMAIN & wooded heights east of ROMAIN	

WAR DIARY or INTELLIGENCE SUMMARY

Army Form C. 2118.

Place	Date	Hour	Summary of Events and Information	Remarks and references to Appendices
VANDEUIL	28/5/18	6 am	Line withdrawn to SOUTHERN side of VESLE and 2 Coys with 2/5th & 25th Divisions in rearguard action to VANDEUIL. From there sent about noon 29th when a counter and two formed remnants of the Bn fought with 2/9 & 25th Divisions near CRUGNY & SAVIGNY	
BASLIEUX	29/5/18	9 am	Remnants sent formed of all fighting men of the Division and under command of Lieut Col STEAD of 4th L. Yorks Regt. The unit concentrated at CUISLES.	Casualties: wounded 1 OR
	31/5/18		Concentd. Bn, under orders of G.O.C. 9th Inf Bde was ordered to reinforce 2nd Br. D.L.I. & 16th Cheshire Regt. & hold the left. Found N.E. of ROMIGNY. Enemy attacked at ROMIGNY and our line retired west after had flanks had been turned to a line VILLE-en-TARDENOIS (in touch with 5Y Inf Bde.) – N.W. edge of BOIS-de-BONVAL. 10th R.I. (French) in support. Right of 30/31st Brigade.	Casualties: wounded 3 OR
ROMIGNY				

WAR DIARY
or
INTELLIGENCE SUMMARY.

Place	Date	Hour	Summary of Events and Information	Remarks and references to Appendices
B. de BONVAL	31/5/18	8.50 pm	Enemy attacked N°1 of Bois de BONVAL but was repulsed during the night. Battle Patrols reactive active.	Casualties 31/5/18 received 1-O.R.

Casualties 29/5/18 —

Killed:— Pioneer PORROT.T.E. 2/Lt SCHUSTER 2/Lt PHILLIPS.E. T. 10 O.R.

Wounded:— 2/Lieut BONIF.A.S. Lt YOUNG.J.H. Capt PEGG.H.G. (Con shock) + 99 O.R.

Missing:— C/H. NORTH.H.M. Capt DEROS.H.G. Lieut SARGENT.E.V.
2/Lt MITMURDO.J.H. 2/Lt M°MEEKEN.J. 2/Lt WEATHERTON S.
2/Lt MITMURDO.J.H. 2/Lt M°MEEKEN.J. 2/Lt QUINE. R.M.
PRIESTNALL.M.E.
ROSS.L.J. 2/Lt BRYCE J. 2/Lt DENNIS. R.J. (R¹.B¹fus)
              (attach⁴)

374 O.R.

Total Casualties — 19 officers + 483 O.R.

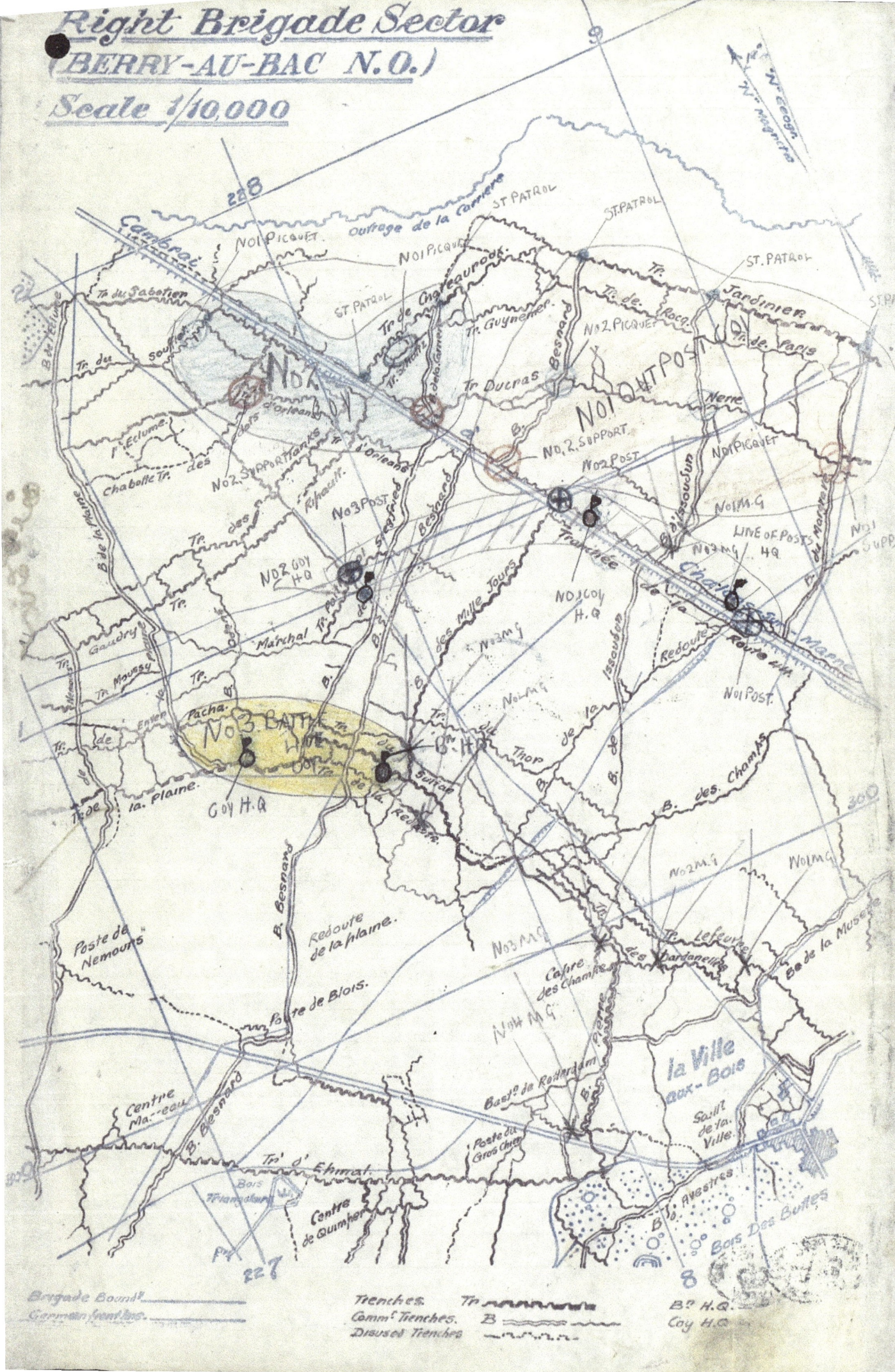

5th.Batt.NORTHUMBERLAND FUSILIERS.

Nominal Roll of Officers on strength of Unit at date - 31-5-18.

Major :-	IVAN.M.TWEEDY.	With Unit.
Captains :-	H.L.STAFFORD.	50° Div' Wing
	F.G.FARINA.	
	B.O.CARTER.	
	J.SMITH.	HH: 92nd Bde.R.A.F.
	F.HASWELL.	
Lieutenants :-	O.YOUNG.	
	E.LISHMAN.	
	J.L.BARRY.	Sick in Hospital.
	G.W.C.BUXTER.	Absent on Leave.
2nd.Lieutenants :-	H.GREY.	
	F.BACCUS.	
	J.O'NEILL.	Sick in Hospital.
	J.H.OGILVIE.	
	H.WHITE.	
	H.R.RAY.	Sick in Hospital.
Adjutant :-	Capt.W.EASTEN. M.C.	
Transport Officer:-	Lieut.H.T.FARE.	
Quartermaster.	Capt.M.McKENZIE.	
Medical Officer :-	Lieut.T.G.PLAYFURD.	

CONFIDENTIAL

WAR DIARY

OF

5th Bn NORTHUMBERLAND FUSILIERS

From 1st June to 30th June 1918

(Vol. 33)

Iain McGrady
Major
Comd 5 Bn North. Fus

WAR DIARY
or
INTELLIGENCE SUMMARY.

(Erase heading not required.)

Army Form C. 2118.

Place	Date	Hour	Summary of Events and Information	Remarks and references to Appendices
CONGY (MARNE)	1-6-18		Commence to form a company out of the remnants of the Battalion. Total numbering about 180 men who are at present serving with 50th Composite Battalion	
VERT-la-GRAVELLE	2-6-18		March to VERT-la-GRAVELLE and bivouced in open field. Commence re-fitting.	
"	3-6-18		Re-fitting and training - Battalion formed into two companies average strength 180. Battalion under command of Major Rott- M.D.F. & forms part of 8th Corps B.n under Brig. Genl. MARSHALL.	
MANTEUIL (SOISSONS) Sh-2R	5/6-18	5pm	Move by buses to MANTEUIL via VERTUS-AVIZE & EUVRES to arrive.	
	6-6-18	2.30am	Heavy barrage on front line	
		9 a.m.	Received news that enemy has taken BLIGNY, BOURCY to reserve position in BOIS-de-CROTON just west of NAPPES	
NAPPES		6pm	Heavy Artillery activity	Casualties 6/18 Killed - 10 R. Wounded 7 O.R.
		10pm	Take over the front line from 8th STAFFS (19th Division) from Mont de BLIGNY inclusive to Capt.	

R. ARDRE

Army Form C. 2118.

WAR DIARY
or
INTELLIGENCE SUMMARY.
(Erase heading not required.)

Instructions regarding War Diaries and Intelligence Summaries are contained in F. S. Regs., Part II. and the Staff Manual respectively. Title pages will be prepared in manuscript.

Place	Date	Hour	Summary of Events and Information	Remarks and references to Appendices
Mont-de-BLIGNY Soissons S.22.1			STAFFORDS Coy. Relief Line S. of Mont-de-BLIGNY. Coy Hqrs. in ruin S.E. of BLIGNY. French have recaptured BLIGNY. Message received that 50th & 8th Corps Bn up on R & L of 19 Staffs. Active shelling on whole line from Henry during the day. Front area shelled heavily but suffered. The village of CHAUMUZY and BOIS d'ECLISSE not occupied recently by supporting troops and enemy patrols sent out nightly encounter no enemy. The valley of the ANDRE and BLIGNY ravaged systematically by field guns. Enemy aeroplanes active every day.	Casualties 7&8 wounded 30 OR Casualties F&G wounded 1 OR Casualties 9 & 10 wounded 2 OR
Mt. de BLIGNY	9.6.18 to 12.6.18			
B. du CURTON	13.6.18		Relieved in front line — move back to reserve in BOIS du CURTON just west of ESPILLY. All men in bivouacs - cleaning & clearing up - Baths etc. Company training during the morning and afternoon. Officers mounting rides & approach etc.	Casualties 13.6.18 Killed 2 OR wounded 6 OR

A7092). Wt. W1859/M1298. 750,000. 1/17. D. D. & L., Ltd. Forms/C2118/14.

Army Form C. 2118.

WAR DIARY
or
INTELLIGENCE SUMMARY.
(Erase heading not required.)

Instructions regarding War Diaries and Intelligence Summaries are contained in F. S. Regs., Part II. and the Staff Manual respectively. Title pages will be prepared in manuscript.

Place	Date	Hour	Summary of Events and Information	Remarks and references to Appendices
GERMAINE (Marsons Sn 22)	15-6-18 to 19-6-18		Relieved by BRESNIA Brigade 20 Division III Corps Italian Army. Moved back into woods WEST of GERMAINE by march route.	Casualties 18-6-18 Killed 1 O.R. Wounded 2 O.R.
BROYES (MARNE)	20-6-18	6 p.m.	Entrain at GERMAINE Halt. Detrain at SEZANNE and march to BROYES.	
	21-6-18 to 22-6-18	11 p.m.	Cleaning up - refitting. Turn in one company under command of Capt. F. HASNELL for new transport Bⁿ.	
	23-6-18		Remainder of Battalion march to LES ESSARTS. No Lorry Transport of Company with transport Battalion under Command of Lieut-Col. FITZHUGH.	
	24-6-18 to 29-6-18		Details at LES ESSARTS carrying out Company training. Details move back to BROYES by march route. Transport Company rejoin the Battalion. Preparing to move.	
	30-6-18			

SUPPLEMENTARY DIARY.

Officers & O.R of 5th Bn Northd Fus with 50th Divn Composite Bn formed. 29-5-18

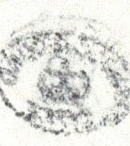

WAR DIARY
or
INTELLIGENCE SUMMARY.

Army Form C. 2118.

Place	Date	Hour	Summary of Events and Information	Remarks and references to Appendices
B. de BONNEIL (SOISSONS)	1/6/18		All organisation of line. At joining British Posts northernmost to Trench line along N.W. Edge of BOIS de BONNEIL & Bn. ordered to conform to that Bn and act under their orders. Enemy attacked from N.W. & our line withdrawn to new position S. of BOUZANCOURT. Bn ordered to concentrate at NAPPES.	Casualties 1678 wounded 20 OR
BOUZANCOURT.				
NAPPES.				
B de COURTON	4/6/18		Quiet night. Bn in Reserve at N.W. corner of Bois de COURTON Order received to move into outpost at S. corner of Bois d'ECLISSE facing N. in touch with 6th Division Composite Bn on left & M.G. Bn (19th Hus.) on right. Quiet night — men suffering.	Casualties 28 OR wounded
NAPPES.	5/6/18 4 pm		Relieved by other Composite Bn. Bn moved into Div. Reserve at NAPPES & came under orders of 5Th Inf. Bde Move complete by 10am 6/6/18. Inspection by G.O.C. & Officers, B.G.C. & Yn. Inf. Brigade.	Casualties 3 OR wounded OR

Place	Date	Hour	Summary of Events and Information	Remarks and references to Appendices
NAPPES	5-6-18 to 7-6-18 8-6-18		A divisional move at NAPPES. Brigr. Genl. MARSHALL'S force which consists of Brigade of Infantry of 52nd Division.	Contents

(CONFIDENTIAL)

WAR DIARY

OF

5TH Bn NORTHUMBLD FUSILIERS

FROM 1st JULY to 31st JULY 1918.

No 34

1/8/18

A. Easten Capt
/o Major
Comg "5"B" Northd Fus.

WAR DIARY
or
INTELLIGENCE SUMMARY.
(Erase heading not required.)

Army Form C. 2118.

Place	Date	Hour	Summary of Events and Information	Remarks and references to Appendices
CONNANTRE (MARNE)	1-7-18		Move by march route from BRAYES to Prisoners of War Camp at St SOPHIE FARM near CONNANTRE.	
	2-7-18		Cleaning up and reorganising.	
	3-7-18		Entrain at FERE-en-Champenoise at 11.30 a.m. Day 8. Detrain at 2.30 a.m.	
OTERNES (HUEBIN)	4-7-18		Detrain at PONT REMY 9 march to OTERNE arriving here at 4 p.m.	
	5-7-18		Training.	
	6-7-18		Refitting to disband.	
	7-7-18		Training. Church Parade. Horse Show at Bde H.Q.	
	8-7-18		Training.	
	9-7-18			
	10-7-18			
	11-7-18			
	12-7-18		Coy training. Preparing to move.	
	13-7-18		Move to HUPPY at 6 p.m. Battalion in billets.	
HUPPY (HUEBIN)			Major H.R. BROWN (Cameron Highlanders) joins & assumes command.	
	14-7-18		Wet day. No parades.	

WAR DIARY
or
INTELLIGENCE SUMMARY.

(Erase heading not required.)

Army Form C. 2118.

Place	Date	Hour	Summary of Events and Information	Remarks and references to Appendices
HUPPY (Abbeville)	14/7/18		Rest day - no parade.	
	15/7/18		The Battalion being reduced to Training Staff Establishment (10 officers & 52 O.R.) All surplus personnel - Lieut H.T. PAPE & 309 O.R. march to PONT REMY & entrain for ETAPLES.	
	16/7/18 17/7/18 18/7/18		Riding Riding - Transport moves by road to MARTIN EGLISE near DIEPPE	
ROUXMESNIL (DIEPPE)	19/7/18		Train (Training Staff) moves by lorry to ROUXMESNIL (5 kilometres E. of DIEPPE).	
	20/7/18 21/7/18 22/7/18 23/7/18		Training Church Parade Training	
	24/7/18 25/7/18 26/7/18 27/7/18		Training - Refresher classes for officers & NCO instructors Church Parade Training	

REPORT OF ADDRESS BY MAJOR GENERAL H.C.JACKSON, D.S.O.
COMMANDING 50TH(NORTHUMBRIAN) DIVISION TO 149TH
INFANTRY BRIGADE ON 11TH JULY 1918.

Brigadier General ROBINSON, Officers, N.C.Os and men of 149th Infantry Brigade. I have had you assembled here this morning to say Good-bye to you all.

I do not refer to the Cadre Battalions but to you men who are going down to the Base and who will be sent to other Units. I want to say how sorry I am to lose you all.

I know how you must feel, especially you men who have served three years or even longer with one Battalion. Your Battalions have become your homes and I sympathise with you in having to leave your friends and associations.

It has been my privilege to command you for over three months, and I have made friends whom I shall be very sorry to lose. It has been your lot to have been in three severe actions during that time, and you have proved to be good soldiers, whom I am sorry to part with. But under present conditions we have no choice in the matter.

When you get to the Base you will be given many opportunities for training. I want you to make the most of such training. Learn to kill Boche. Many of you have killed your Bosche and you know what a serious thing it is to miss your enemy. It means that a Bosche is left alive, who has no right to be so.

Within about a fortnight's time, we will be entering into the Fourth year of the War, and killing Bosche is the only way to end the war. Therefore learn, never to miss your target.

Again I say how sorry I am that you have to be broken up but may good luck go with you where ever you go.

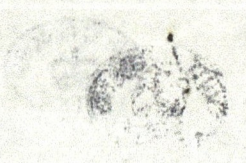

1:10,000   J.I.   Parts of {20.S.W.2 20.S.W.4 / 20.S.E.1 20.S.E.3}   EDITION 2

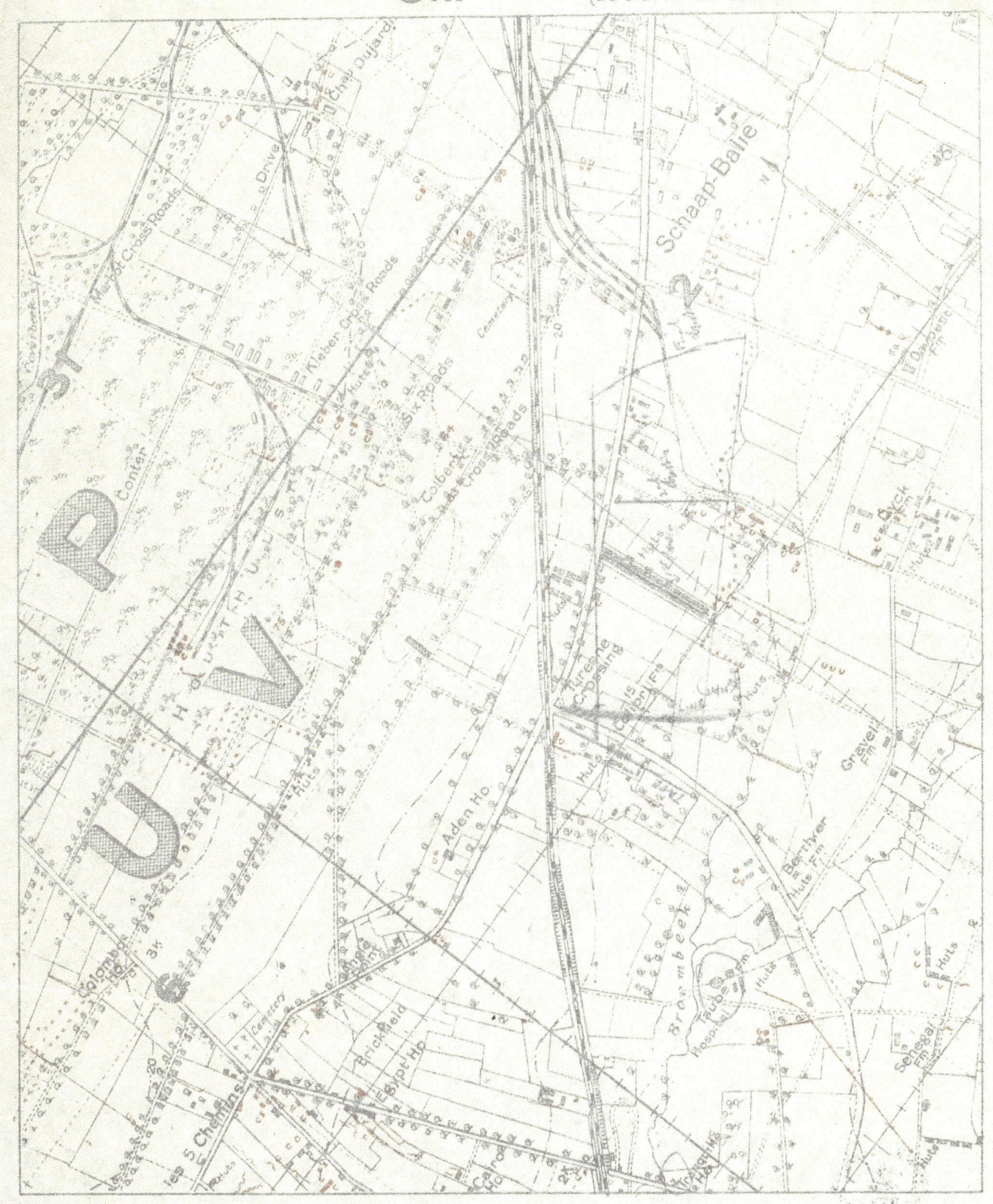

Scale. 1:10,000.

Message Pad.

Your Message must be such as will enable the Addressee to know what the Situation is with You and your Neighbours.

NEGATIVE INFORMATION IS ALSO VALUABLE.

Strike out and alter sentences as necessary.

TO ....

1. Am advancing to...
2. Am putting out (Have put out) protective parties.
3. Am sending out. Have sent out and am keeping out patrols to keep touch with the enemy.
4. Am (Have) consolidating (ed).
5. Our line now runs..
6. I require (give article or articles and number required) :—

   Send the above to..
7. Troops on my right are (give situation).

8. Troops on my left are (give situation)

9. My strength now is..
10. Am being shelled from..
11. Am held up by M.G., T.M., rifle, artillery fire from..
12. Am now ready to...
13. Enemy line runs..
14. Enemy (strength)..at..
    doing..
15. Have captured..
16. Enemy prisoners belong to...
17. Enemy counter-attack forming up at..
18. Other remarks—

Time .... a.m. (p.m.)   Name..
Date ....   Rank..
Place ....   Platoon.................. Company..............
(Map Ref. or mark on back of map).   Battalion...

689

www.ingramcontent.com/pod-product-compliance
Lightning Source LLC
Chambersburg PA
CBHW080832010526
44112CB00015B/2497